CRITICAL DATA STORYTELLING
IN THE COMPOSITION CLASSROOM

Critical Data Storytelling in the Composition Classroom

ANGELA LAFLEN

UTAH STATE UNIVERSITY PRESS
Logan

© 2025 by University Press of Colorado

Published by Utah State University Press
An imprint of University Press of Colorado
1580 North Logan Street, Suite 660
PMB 39883
Denver, Colorado 80203-1942

All rights reserved

 The University Press of Colorado is a proud member of Association of University Presses.

The University Press of Colorado is a cooperative publishing enterprise supported, in part, by Adams State University, Colorado School of Mines, Colorado State University, Fort Lewis College, Metropolitan State University of Denver, University of Alaska Fairbanks, University of Colorado, University of Denver, University of Northern Colorado, University of Wyoming, Utah State University, and Western Colorado University.

ISBN: 978-1-64642-741-3 (hardcover)
ISBN: 978-1-64642-742-0 (paperback)
ISBN: 978-1-64642-743-7 (ebook)
https://doi.org/10.7330/9781646427437

Library of Congress Cataloging-in-Publication Data

NAMES: Laflen, Angela, author.
TITLE: Critical data storytelling in the composition classroom / Angela Laflen.
DESCRIPTION: Logan : Utah State University Press, [2025] | Includes bibliographical references and index.
IDENTIFIERS: LCCN 2025013225 (print) | LCCN 2025013226 (ebook) | ISBN 9781646427413 (hardcover) | ISBN 9781646427420 (paperback) | ISBN 9781646427437 (ebook)
SUBJECTS: LCSH: English language—Rhetoric—Computer-assisted instruction. | English language—Rhetoric—Study and teaching (Higher)—Data processing. | Information visualization—Study and teaching (Higher) | Multimodal user interfaces (Computer systems) | Artificial intelligence—Educational applications.
CLASSIFICATION: LCC PE1404 .L264 2025 (print) | LCC PE1404 (ebook) | DDC 808.0078/5—dc23/eng/20250614
LC record available at https://lccn.loc.gov/2025013225
LC ebook record available at https://lccn.loc.gov/2025013226

Cover art: ©antoniokhr/iStock

Contents

List of Figures vii
List of Tables ix
List of Boxes x
Acknowledgments xi
Introduction 3

1. Charting a Course for Data Storytelling in Multimodal Composition 23
2. Reading Data Stories Rhetorically 49
3. Cultivating Critical Data Communication Skills 77
4. Responding to and Assessing Students' Data Stories 109
5. Using Data as a Tool to Improve Teaching and Learning 144

Conclusion: What Difference Does Data Storytelling Make? 179

Appendix 189
Glossary 199
References 203
Index 219
About the Author 231

Figures

0.1. Infographic "Datafication Powers AI" 10
0.2. Types of data literate citizens 14
1.1. Student activity details report available through Blackboard "Analytics for Learn" 32
1.2. Student response to speculative redesign assignment 46
2.1. Disinformation that circulated on Facebook with a falsified source 53
2.2. Data storytelling composing process 62
2.3. Screen capture from "COVID Cases Since June—Most Cases" 70
2.4. Misleading data visualization shared online by the Georgia Department of Public Health 74
3.1. Guiding principles for critical data storytelling assignments 87
3.2. Questions to guide critical data storytelling assignment planning 91
3.3. Student response to playing with data assignment 99
3.4. Student response to producing small data assignment 102
3.5. Misleading infographic titled "Planned Parenthood Federation of America: Abortions Up ... Life-Saving Procedures Down" 106
3.6. Student response to revising a flawed data story assignment 107
4.1. Student sample of an infographic 110
4.2. Sample infographic composed alongside students 120
4.3. Sample consolidated evaluation criteria 126
4.4. Sample self-assessment form 128
4.5. Sample revised evaluation criteria 130

4.6.	Sample student thumbnail	131
4.7.	Sample student mockup of "graphs"	132
4.8.	Sample excerpt from a student website	133
5.1.	Data inquiry cycle	157
5.2.	Line graph comparing the hours students reported spending on a research project in spring 2019 and fall 2021	166
5.3.	Line graph comparing the hours students reported spending on a research project in spring 2019, fall 2021, and fall 2022	174

Tables

0.1. Adapting Selber's conceptual landscape of a computer multiliteracies program for data literacy   18
1.1. Model of critical data literacy pedagogy for the composition classroom   44
2.1. Strategies for reading digital information sources critically   58
2.2. Critical data literacy pedagogy for rhetorical readers   63
2.3. Critical questions for data stories   64
2.4. Rhetorical chart for data stories   68
3.1. Critical data literacy pedagogy for critical communicators   89
3.2. Road-tested options for critical data storytelling assignments   92
5.1. Example of the complexity of describing constructs   160
5.2. Sources of data for teaching-related data inquiries   163
5.3. Sample student labor log for 1 Week   164
5.4. Example of data before and after cleaning   165
5.5. Excerpt from Excel spreadsheet   165
A.1. Courses included in Phase 1   191
A.2. Courses included in Phase 2   192
A.3. Survey participant characteristics   193
A.4. Interview participants   195

Boxes

4.1. Students' difficulties and recovery strategies in their own words   118
4.2. Recommendations for using instructive assessment in the context of critical data storytelling assignments   136
5.1. Characteristics of a data literate writing instructor   153
5.2. Questions to consider when identifying problems/framing questions   159
5.3. Questions to consider when using data   162
5.4. Results of unpaired t-test   167
5.5. Questions to consider when transforming data into information   169
5.6. Questions to consider when transforming information into decision   172
5.7. Questions to consider when evaluating outcomes   173
5.8. Tips for using data for teaching-related purposes   177

Acknowledgments

When it comes to data storytelling, I have always favored the storytelling part of that practice, and that remains true today even though I have come to appreciate that data provide rich material to tell powerful and compelling stories. Fortunately, I was assisted by a wide range of individuals and organizations to develop the skills and knowledge I needed to work with and prepare students to work with data. I am deeply grateful to everyone who accompanied me on the learning journey that has resulted in the writing of this book.

I wish to thank California State University, Sacramento, for supporting this work with release time to draft the manuscript and with funding that allowed me to attend conferences to share my work in progress and to participate in the Dartmouth Summer Seminar for Writing Research and the Digital Media and Composition Institute (DMAC) at The Ohio State University. I also appreciate the opportunity to participate in several faculty learning communities sponsored by Sacramento State's Center for Teaching and Learning, the College of Arts and Letters, and the Office of Academic Excellence related to data analysis and student success.

I am indebted to Maegan Parker Brooks for encouraging me that this project was worth pursuing, helping me to find and express my voice in the manuscript, and providing valuable feedback throughout the drafting process. This project was also improved by the thoughtful feedback that Brooke Rollins provided on early drafts and Ira Allen, Kate Comer, and Ryan Skinnell provided on later drafts. At Utah State University Press I was fortunate to work with Nate Bauer, Skylar Cooper, and Rachael Levay, who made this book possible. I am grateful to the anonymous reviewers of the manuscript for generously giving of their time to offer attentive and constructive feedback.

Early work on this project was completed at Marist College and motivated by a curricular change to the general education first year writing course. At Marist, I benefited from the friendship of Moira Fitzgibbons, Eileen Curley, Michelle Smith, Kristin Bayer, and Lisa Neilson. This work was also nurtured in the collaborative environment of the Writing Program at Sacramento State that first Angela Clark-Oates and then Hogan Hayes fostered as Writing Program coordinators. I am thankful to both of them, as well as my professional writing colleagues, Sam Dunn and Ruby Mendoza, for creating a collegial space in which I have been encouraged to pursue my research interests. A particular highlight of my time at Sacramento State has been collaborating with Julian Heather to design a writing-intensive course on data literacy.

Most of all, this book would not have been possible without the students who contributed their work to my study and who spent time speaking with me about their experiences in my courses and helped me improve as a teacher over the years. And, finally, the entire journey would have been a lot less joyful without the companionship of Brandon, Benjamin, Elena, and Liana Laflen; thanks for your love and support of my professional work.

CRITICAL DATA STORYTELLING
IN THE COMPOSITION CLASSROOM

Introduction

Critical Data Storytelling in the Composition Classroom argues that *critical data literacy* should be incorporated into multimodal composition pedagogy via the practice of *data storytelling*. *Critical data literacy* refers to the ability to ask and answer real-world questions using large and small data sets through an ethical inquiry process. *Data storytelling* is a methodology for communicating a compelling narrative about data to a specific audience. Data storytelling cuts across multimodal genres, serving as a strategy for working with data based in the recognition that data on their own do not speak; they must be interpreted to have any meaning. As such, data storytelling is fundamentally a rhetorical practice, emphasizing how data are *invented* in a rhetorical sense at every stage—from being collected to cleaned and analyzed to presented to an audience.

Though working with data was traditionally regarded as the province of scientists and mathematicians, today data are ubiquitous because of the explosion of technologies that produce data and programs that make working with data more accessible to members of the public than ever before. As a result, data literacy is becoming a critical literacy skill necessary for people to fully participate as members of democratic society. Although rhetoric and composition scholars have developed multimodal composition pedagogy in recognition that the proliferation of multimodal communication technologies have changed what it means to read and write in the twenty-first century, multimodal composition pedagogy has not adequately accounted for the central role that data play in multimodal genres ranging from infographics to social media posts to white papers. At the undergraduate level, instruction in writing about and with data continues to be restricted primarily to technical and professional writing courses, which reinforces the notion that data literacy is a highly specialized literacy useful primarily to professionals working in or communicating with those in technical fields such as computer science and engineering.

Critical Data Storytelling is premised on the argument that the *datification* of everyday life has transformed contemporary literacy. According to Viktor Mayer-Schönberger and Kenneth Cukier, who coined the term, datafication refers to the process through which human activities are converted to data, which, in turn, allows for predictions about individuals and groups (Mayer-Schönberger and Cukier 2013, 15). Datafication makes more information and more types of information into data that can be analyzed using quantitative methods of analysis. In doing so, it changes the nature of information, by making almost all information a possible source of data, and information environments, by opening them up to study and monitoring through a variety of datafied ways of knowing such as specialized algorithms and data visualization. While the full effects of datafication on individuals and society are not yet completely understood, it is clear that the landscape in which writing, research, and learning take place is changing significantly, with far-reaching implications for all instructors who want to prepare students with the information literacy skills necessary to fully participate as members of society and who are increasingly confronted by data-based arguments about what constitutes good teaching and learning.

This book details a plan of action for including data literacy in multimodal composition pedagogy, supported by research exploring the various opportunities and challenges presented by data literacy: recognizing how data circulate online, evaluating the use of data in multimodal texts, curating corpuses of data, and navigating among various tests, technologies, and visualizations to analyze and present data. Questions taken up in the book include: In what ways can a rhetorical approach to data informed by multimodal composition pedagogy foster students' critical data literacy skills? Also, how can a rhetorical framework for critical data literacy productively contribute to multimodal composition pedagogy and curriculum development?

The genesis of this study was, appropriately enough, in data. When I began including multimodal assignments in my first year writing and professional writing courses by replacing one of my students' research essays with an infographic, I knew I needed to provide lessons and activities related to visual rhetoric, page design, information literacy, and how to use free online programs such as Piktochart and Canva. At that time, I did not anticipate the need to include instruction in data literacy to help students create successful infographics. However, though my students generally liked the assignment, and it helped them improve the organization and development of their arguments, I was troubled by the ways that students' use of data could go wrong and undermine their arguments. Though students were not required to include data in their research infographics (and some did not), the genre of infographics does facilitate the presentation of data, and by including data, students were demonstrating awareness of genre conventions for infographics. Often, though, they just did not have the data literacy skills necessary to work with data. What's more, in reviewing classroom grades and demographic data, I could see that students in particular majors, specifically in STEM-related fields, received higher grades on multimodal projects in which they used data than were students in other majors. I realized that I needed to design and assess multimodal projects carefully so as not to advantage and disadvantage students based on their background working with data and to help all my students be more critical users of data. However, I found no recognition of this gap in the scholarly literature on multimodal composition and few suggestions for including data literacy instruction in multimodal composition.

Consequently, I began exploring how to teach data literacy in the context of multimodal composition, and in 2016 I formally applied for IRB approval to begin collecting the student writing, surveys, and interviews that serve as the backbone for this book.[1] *Critical Data Storytelling* is based on data I collected at two different institutions, one a private, highly selective regional comprehensive university on the east coast and the other a large, regional public university designated an Hispanic-Serving Institution (HSI) and an Asian American and Native American Pacific Islander-Serving Institution (AANAPISI) on the west coast. These data include material from thirteen writing classes of various levels (three first-year writing courses; five upper-level undergraduate professional writing courses; and five upper-level undergraduate digital writing and rhetoric courses). Materials I have collected include introductory biodata surveys, student planning documents, in-progress data stories, revised data stories, and student reflections on working with data and completing critical data storytelling assignments.

---

1. All participants have been given pseudonyms. My procedures for gathering and analyzing artifacts, surveys, and interviews and disseminating the results of this work were approved by the Institutional Review Board (IRB). See the appendix for more information on the participants and my methods.

I have also conducted interviews with fifteen students from across these courses who represent a variety of backgrounds and comfort levels working with data. Through analysis of the data that I have gathered through this work, I have been able to determine that including critical data literacy instruction in multimodal pedagogy can make a significant difference to students' conceptual and practical understanding of how data operate rhetorically in ways that improve their abilities to analyze and compose data stories. I have also gained insight into the process through which students progress in understanding data literacy and have used this information to develop instructional materials and assignments designed to scaffold students' data literacy acquisition in writing courses of various levels. The model for critical data literacy in multimodal composition pedagogy that I present in *Critical Data Storytelling* is the result of these years of exploration.

Why Critical Data Literacy Is Needed Urgently in Multimodal Composition Pedagogy

This work is needed because the significant role data play in multimodal communication has not been sufficiently considered in multimodal composition pedagogy. While composition scholarship is beginning to recognize the value of big data methodologies for researchers and administrators (Licastro and Miller 2021), only sporadic attempts have been made by individual practitioners to develop a consistent pedagogy for rhetorically reading and critically using data in effective and ethical ways in the context of rhetoric and composition instruction (e.g., Beveridge 2015; Beveridge 2017; Danner 2020b; Moxley 2008; Moxley 2013). The prevalence of data in multimodal communication will be a barrier to more widespread inclusion of multimodal composition pedagogy in writing classes and programs without the development of pedagogical strategies to deal with data. As we ask students to read and write multimodal texts, equipping them with a repertoire of rhetorical strategies for working with data will strengthen how they approach and understand multimodal genres and media.

Critical Data Storytelling promises to positively impact composition in at least three important ways. First, it contributes to our ongoing interest in critical literacy, which is a burgeoning area of research and pedagogy. Students—and all members of the public—must contend with a seemingly endless flow of mis- and disinformation circulating in online contexts today. Data often play a role in the spread of mis- and disinformation, injecting confusion into public discourse with serious implications for democratic decision-making processes. When data circulate quickly "through botnet networks that use algorithms to profile users and feed them stories that fit their individual biases" (Miller and Leon 2017, 10), it can be difficult to detect when data have been subject to cherry-picking, misinterpretation, or even outright fabrication. Although detecting and countering mis- and disinformation has always been challenging, increasingly, the fake news that individuals encounter takes the form of data stories that combine data with textual information and iconography to make succinct, persuasive arguments. Mis- and disinformation presented via data stories can be particularly difficult for readers to detect and combat because interpreting these arguments requires unpacking a complex combination of statistical, visual, and textual expressions. Additionally, fake data stories, like fake news stories in general, "often emulate the look and titles of professional news sources," so that "even if a story has been shared a million times on social media, and if it is found on a website that looks and sounds newsy, and if it is repeatedly linked from a popular hashtag, there's no guarantee that it's a credible story" (Laquintano and Vee 2017, 46). The problem of mis- and disinformation is poised to become even greater with the widespread use of generative artificial intelligence (AI). Freely available and largely unregulated generative AI programs make it possible for anyone to generate false information and fake content in vast quantities, including imitating the voices of real people and creating photos and videos, referred to as deepfakes, that are indistinguishable from real ones.

It is in this context that students are being asked to create rhetorically effective texts using information drawn from sources that can be difficult to evaluate using traditional methods. Scholars have produced numerous publications on equipping students with critical literacy skills to help them navigate the sea of mis- and disinformation circulating online. Among the many approaches advocated by scholars, news-as-text pedagogy (Reardon 2021), rhetorical ethics (Duffy 2019), and civic literacy (Leake 2021; Lockhart and Hofmann 2021) have been proposed to help teachers and students cultivate the conscious, thoughtful practices needed today. Across this scholarship, the significance of students' critical data literacy has not received adequate attention. It is crucial to integrate critical data literacy into the teaching of multimodal composition because students who understand how data stories are constructed are more likely to be thoughtful readers and creators of such texts. In addition to frameworks and tools aimed at helping instructors to introduce and students to understand the use of modes, media, and page design principles in multimodal composing, we need frameworks and tools for data literacy instruction as well. *Critical Data Storytelling* moves toward filling this gap by presenting a critical data literacy pedagogy grounded in examination of students' data literacy practices and development.

Second, paying attention to data literacy can add to our understanding of how the rhetorical canons of invention, arrangement, and delivery have changed in the "post-truth" media era. A challenge associated with critically engaging data is the issue of transparency. Data transparency refers to understanding who gathered data and for what purpose; how data were cleaned, analyzed, and visualized; and how data stories circulate through online networks. The lack of transparency around data circulating online means that it can be difficult to determine who gathered data and for what purpose. There have been pushes to make data more transparent and open as a result, so that greater numbers of people can access data and so, for example, consumers can become more aware of how data collected by companies online are using that data. However, I argue the problem is more complex than that. It is not only that data need to be transparent but that people need to understand how data are invented, arranged, and delivered. As the editors of *Literacy and Pedagogy in an Age of Misinformation and Disinformation* contend, "Without critically investigating the mechanisms by which information is shaped, manipulated, and selectively shared or amplified, any critical reading and understanding will be inevitably decontextualized and thus potentially inaccurate" (Lockhart et al. 2021, 4). A focus on data storytelling can help us to understand how data are invented, arranged, and delivered to serve persuasive ends and how readers learn to construct data stories in a range of genres and sources. It can also make visible the role technology plays in mediating reader encounters with multimodal texts as students consider how technology obscures or reveals the intentions behind the text. In this book, I outline a rhetorical approach to critical data literacy for use in writing classes based on making visible to students the choices involved in inventing, arranging, and delivering data. This research can contribute to further investigations into how invention, arrangement, and delivery relate to multimodal composing, and it can aid teachers in helping students learn how to analyze and use data in rhetorically effective and ethical ways in a variety of contexts.

Third, the book provides the foundational knowledge of data literacy necessary to engage generative AI critically. Generative AI refers to the ability of an AI model, such as ChatGPT and DALL-E, to produce new content, ranging from text to images to videos, based on the data it has been trained on. Generative AI has been much in the news since 2022 when text-to-image AI models such as MidJourney, DALL-E, and Imagen were released to the public. These models were quickly followed by OpenAI's ChatGPT, an AI chatbot with natural language processing (NLP) that allows users to have human-like conversations to complete various tasks.

We do not yet have a full understanding of the societal—and pedagogical—implications of generative AI. However, already it is clear that generative AI will impact human behavior and cognition. Within writing studies, much of the emphasis currently is on sketching out what is needed to understand, use, and guide generative AI—frequently grounding this work in earlier scholarship on emerging writing technologies (Graham 2023; Johnson 2023; Stanton 2023). Understandably, given how recently generative AI has been introduced to the public and how quickly it is evolving, there is a considerable focus on identifying the basic functional skills required to use generative AI, such as how to operate AI user interfaces, write effective prompts, and cite information generated by AI (Aguilar 2024; Byrd et al. 2023; Gallagher 2023). The importance of critical data literacy to working with AI has not been fully recognized within writing and rhetoric scholarship so far. Nevertheless, being able to effectively, ethically, and responsibly use AI requires a critical understanding of data because generative AI does not exist without data. As Ben Snaith (2023), a researcher at the Open Data Institute, explains, "Data is foundational to AI models. It provides the information that a machine learning model is trained on and learns from. It is collected, wrangled, curated, aggregated and then used in the model. Data is used to test and benchmark the model's success. And data is inputted for utilisation once the model is operational" (2). Figure 0.1, which was created with the assistance of generative AI, further details the role data play throughout the AI life cycle. Because data are so crucial to the operation of AI, it will not be possible for writing and rhetoric studies to engage AI critically without also engaging data. The framework for critical data literacy pedagogy presented in *Critical Data Storytelling* focuses on helping students and instructors cultivate the foundational knowledge necessary to recognize the ethical dimensions of using generative AI and the strengths and limitations of data generated by AI, understand the level of information a reader needs and how to choose the correct data insight approach, including the use of AI, and evaluate data analysis and visualizations generated by AI.

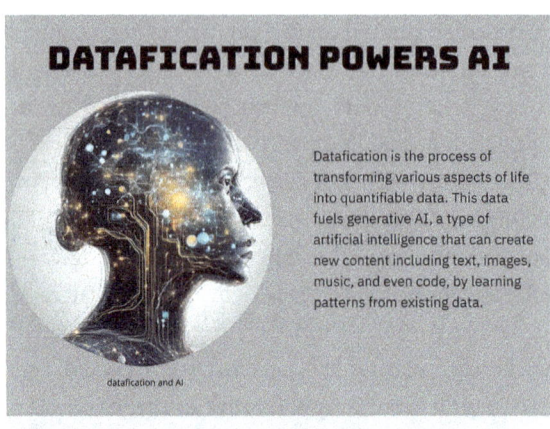

FIGURE 0.1. Infographic "Datafication Powers AI," created in collaboration with AI technologies. Source: Angela Laflen. Note: See the glossary for definitions of the bolded, italicized terms.

The Datafication of Everyday Life

We can appreciate the challenges of reading and composing with data by considering how the concept of data literacy has expanded due to the increasing importance of data in everyday life. Though data stories have always been common in scientific decision-making, technology has resulted in an information explosion that has led to the datafication of everyday life (Mayer-Schönberger and Cukier 2013). Datafication is the result not only of unprecedented amounts of data being generated (Petroc Taylor [2025] reports that the total volume of data worldwide is expected to reach 182 zettabytes in 2025 and 394 zettabytes by 2028) but also of aspects of the world that had not previously been quantified being rendered into data. For example, social media turns connections and likes into data, satellite imagery and remote sensing techniques change location into data, and learning analytics transform student work and interactions into data. Algorithms are put to work mining these data for information to serve a wide range of ends—from refining online marketing to early identification of infectious diseases based on online search patterns. With the advent of generative AI, algorithms are being applied to large language models (LLMs) to create new and original content and data by predicting and generating natural or humanlike language. However, as Safiya Umoja Noble (2018) has discussed, algorithms are never "'neutral' or 'objective' decision-making tools" (2). Instead, "discrimination is also embedded in computer code and, increasingly, in artificial intelligence technologies that we are reliant on, by choice or not" (1), meaning that as datafication transforms formerly unquantified aspects of the world into data, it also expands oppressive social relations.

The process of datafication necessitates new understandings of how information is processed and the environments in which communication takes place. As Mark Frank, Johanna Walker, Judie Attard, and Alan Tygel explain, "By itself data is not information. For data to be useful people must be able to extract information from it. The ability to do this is rapidly becoming a requirement to participate in modern life—as fundamental as the ability to use a telephone or money. Those who do not have this ability are in an important sense disadvantaged" (Frank et al. 2016, 5). Though data literacy used to be largely synonymous with statistical literacy, "the Internet has fundamentally changed the game by potentially allowing anyone with Internet access to access a vast range of data sources" (5). Consequently, "data is now everyone's responsibility" (Dykes 2020, 6). More recently, generative AI has changed the game again by offering new options for extracting meaning out of data and creating data visualizations. Although generative AI promises to make data analysis and visualization more accessible to the public than ever before, James Fisher (2023), chief strategy officer for the software vendor Qlik, explains that data literacy is still required for users "to select and prepare high-quality datasets, recognize and mitigate biases within the data, and help interpret outputs to make data-driven decisions." Rather than making data literacy skills less important, easy access to generative AI tools capable of analyzing and visualizing data increases the need for all members of the public to be able to evaluate how data are used for persuasive purposes and to use data in ethical and effective ways.

Rhetorical Readers and Critical Communicators

The growing importance of data literacy as a critical literacy necessary for all citizens to possess is a central concern of this book. Even if Brent Dykes (2020) is correct that "data is now everyone's responsibility" (6), it is also evident that not everyone has the same needs when it comes to data. Scientists and other technical specialists continue to require a highly developed and sophisticated approach to data, with the thorough understanding of statistics and math that is only cultivated through advanced study of these topics. Most other members of the public do not require this degree of data literacy to read and make use of data to solve their problems. Though the importance of data literacy is widely agreed upon, "there is a lack of consistent and appropriate approaches for helping novices learn to 'speak data'" (D'Ignazio and Bhargava 2016, 84). As a result, efforts to cultivate data literacy more widely across the curriculum and in multimodal composition have been sporadic.

Nevertheless, studies focused on data literacy have found that students and members of the public generally struggle when asked to read and use data even in relatively simple ways. As an example, the Stanford History Education Group (SHEG) (2016) has sounded an alarm about the state of US students' "civic online reasoning," which SHEG defines as "the ability to judge the credibility of information that floods young people's smartphones, tablets, and computers" (3). The results of SHEG's large national study of elementary- through college-level students revealed that "overall, young people's ability to reason about the information on the Internet can be summed up in one word: *bleak*" (4). Based on the exercises used in the study (which are available online at the SHEG website), SHEG clearly considers the ability to read data stories critically an important part of civic online reasoning. For example, one exercise for college-level students presents them with a tweet from MoveOn.org that shares a surprising statistic about NRA members' beliefs about background checks and asks them to explain (1) why this tweet might be a useful source about NRA members' beliefs about background checks and (2) why this tweet might not be a useful source about NRA members' beliefs about background checks. Few students were able to evaluate the usefulness of the tweet: "Only a few students noted that the tweet was based on a poll conducted by a professional polling firm and explained why this would make the tweet a stronger source of information. Similarly, less than a third of students fully explained how the political agendas of MoveOn.org and the Center for American Progress might influence the content of the tweet" (23). The authors of the SHEG study conclude that "when it comes to evaluating information that flows through social media channels, ['digital natives'] are easily duped" (4), and as a result, "we worry that democracy is threatened by the ease at which disinformation about civic issues is allowed to spread and flourish" (5).

Certainly, data stories can be effective vehicles for spreading mis- or disinformation quickly online. Increasingly, fake news creators include misleading or false data displays to imbue their stories with an aura of credibility and increase online engagement. As Randall Chun (2017) explains, the appeal of data stories is their accessibility: "A tweet with an embedded image gets 150 percent more retweets. . . . Sharing an eye-catching data visualization that has an air of credibility (because it's scientific!) is hard to resist, especially with the low-friction tap of a retweet." The appeal of data stories makes them particularly effective at injecting false and misleading information into decision-making and public discourse.

The spectrum of data literacy is wide, with scientists who require advanced mathematical training on one end and members of the public who need to be able to evaluate claims based on data they encounter in daily life on the other. Consequently, appropriate approaches to training "novices to speak data" will also necessarily vary widely depending on the instructional context and goals for the data literacy instruction. The question is, what kind or level of data literacy is appropriate for inclusion in multimodal composition pedagogy?

To help students read data stories critically and use data effectively in their multimodal arguments, I believe that writing instructors primarily need to focus on students' skills as rhetorical readers and critical communicators. In delineating the four types of citizens according to the situations in which they would need to use data shown in figure 0.2, Annika Wolff et al. (2016) have defined readers as those who "need skills to interpret data that is increasingly presented as part of their everyday life," while communicators "make sense of and tell stories about data for others to digest" (18). The other two types of citizens, labeled data scientists and makers, require more advanced training in math and statistics to use data to solve the problems they face. Wolff and

14 : INTRODUCTION

FIGURE 0.2. Types of data literate citizens adapted from Wolff et al. 2016, 18.

colleagues' approach is valuable for suggesting that rather than adopting a one-size-fits-all approach to data literacy, more attention should be paid to the ways different types of people "need to use data intelligently for solving real world problems" (18). Their point is that few people require the level of literacy necessary for a data scientist and that the data literacy skills necessary to function as readers and communicators can be taught across the curriculum separate from advanced statistical training. Indeed, writing teachers are uniquely positioned to help students adapt critical reading skills to data stories and understand how data are invented, arranged, and delivered to advance persuasive arguments.

What the Focus of This Book Does Not Include

It is important that I make it clear what I am not suggesting or advocating for in this book. To begin, I am not suggesting that including critical data literacy in multimodal composition necessarily requires instruction in math or statistics. While it may be appropriate and necessary to focus on math or statistics skills or the use of statistical software in the context of some advanced writing courses or to achieve particular learning outcomes, instructors can often design critical data literacy assignments that foster students' skills as rhetorical readers and critical communicators of data without providing instruction in math or statistics. To this point, work by scholars such as Carol Rutz and Nathan D. Grawe (2009) indicates that students do not have to use advanced math skills or complex technologies to achieve literacy benefits and that student motivation and engagement may be improved when assignments are more accessible. Quantitative reasoning (QR)-across-the-curriculum advocate Lynn Arthur Steen described QR as "sophisticated reasoning with elementary mathematics more than elementary reasoning with sophisticated mathematics" (Steen 2004, 9, quoted in Rutz and Grawe 2009, 1). Building on this idea, Rutz and Grawe argue that students specifically benefit from opportunities to practice using numbers in rhetorically effective ways to provide context, make evidence specific, show change over time, and impart precision in language since "much of their experience with numbers is limited to formal situations that require them to solve problems with correct answers." Similarly, Daniel Anderson (2008) has recommended the use of what he refers to as "low-bridge technologies," or free, consumer-level technologies (42), in multimodal composition instruction. He argues that low-bridge technologies can reduce student "difficulties that can shut down flow, but the challenge of composing with unfamiliar forms opens pathways to creativity and motivation" (44). The model for critical data literacy pedagogy that I present in this book is flexible enough to accommodate a wide range of assignments, from those that rely only on elementary mathematics and low-bridge technologies to those that include more advanced math and/or technologies.

I am also not proposing that we abandon previous approaches to preparing students to conduct research for and in the context of academic argument. The traditional academic research skills that are currently emphasized throughout higher education remain valuable for preparing students to conduct research and write for academic audiences in academic contexts. However, there is evidence that differences between academic literacies and the literacies required to navigate datafied information spaces are growing, especially given the emergence of generative AI. A recent report by researchers at Project Information Literacy (PIL) found evidence of a "large gap between the information literacy skills [students] practice for courses and their grasp of our current information environment" (Head et al. 2020, 11). They describe the information environment that students inhabit as less "a cloister of scholarly knowledge" and more of "an overgrown jungle where every resource must be tested for toxicity, and where students are stalked relentlessly, their data harvested as fodder for unknowable uses" (28). The result is that traditional strategies for evaluating information sources, which grew out of and remain suitable for print-reading practices, are not well-suited to evaluating much of the information students encounter online. PIL researchers also found that "the critical work of understanding the torrent of information flowing through a variety of channels, from social media to commercial search engines, is rarely considered in assignments and classroom discussions" (28). In the absence of critical strategies, students develop a range of informal defensive strategies, which nevertheless leave them feeling "resigned" in the face of datafication (14). AI promises to widen the gulf between traditional academic information literacy skills and those that students need to interact with information in their daily lives and after graduation. My insistence in this book on the importance of attending to students' critical data literacy in multimodal pedagogy is not a call to replace traditional research strategies but a call to supplement and enhance information literacy instruction with the addition of strategies for critically navigating datafied information environments.

Theoretical Foundations

In *Critical Data Storytelling*, I offer a model for critical data literacy pedagogy that can be flexibly adapted for different and changing technological and educational contexts. Specifically, I provide multiple examples and activities to illustrate how the model can be applied rather than recommending a single assignment or syllabus. Focusing on the choices available to data storytellers and the implications of the choices that data storytellers make are central to this approach.

MULTILITERACIES PEDAGOGY

My model for critical data literacy pedagogy is informed by Stuart Selber's (2004) work related to multiliteracies pedagogy. Building on the concept of "multiliteracies" that was articulated in 1996 by the New London Group as a call to develop literacy theory and pedagogy based on linguistic diversity and multimodal forms of communication, Selber described the "conceptual landscape of a computer multiliteracies program" in 2004 as consisting of functional literacy, which positions students as users of technology; critical literacy, which positions students as questioners of technology; and rhetorical literacy, which positions students as producers of technology (25). Selber insisted that instructors not prioritize one type of literacy over another but rather "help students learn to exploit the different subjectivities that have become associated with computer technologies" (25).

Selber designed his framework to accommodate "the continuous and contingent interplay between context and technology" (26), and today this framework remains useful as we chart a course for critical data literacy in multimodal composition pedagogy. In fact, I believe that data literacy in the context of big data is best understood as a different form of digital literacy rather than an entirely distinct literacy (Polizzi 2021). This is not to overlook the fact that computational methods have a far longer history than digitization does as they have been practiced and developed for centuries (Porter [1986] 2020; Poovey 1998) but rather to recognize that the process of datafication operative across society today depends on digitization even though it is not synonymous with it. Mayer-Schönberger and Cukier (2013) explain that "the arrival of computers brought digital measuring and storage devices that made datafying vastly more efficient," although "the act of digitization . . . by itself does not datafy" (83). In addition to digitization, datafication also relies on digitized information being made "indexable and thus searchable" (84). Digital information become data when they can be analyzed for meaning, often through the use of natural language processing and computer algorithms. As a result, working with data in the context of big data involves using computers to collect, organize, analyze, and visualize data. Thus, becoming data literate today, although there is no universally agreed upon definition of what that means, inevitably involves the ability to use computers at some level in the process of asking and answering questions with and about data. For this reason, the conceptual landscape of a computer multiliteracies program that Selber maps out remains relevant to charting the conceptual landscape of data literacy. Although some of the metaphors that Selber used to conceive of computer multiliteracies require tweaking to account for how the concept of data differs from the concept of a computer, as indicated in table 0.1, thinking of data literacy in terms of functional, critical, and rhetorical literacy is useful in delineating the different kinds of data literacies that instructors can emphasize in writing courses to "help students move among them in strategic ways" (Selber 2004, 24).

Instructors attend to students' functional literacy when they ensure students have the basic skills necessary to use data as a resource in ethical and effective ways. Though the basic skills needed will differ depending on context, examples could include being able to identify different types of graphs and the parts of graphs, how to choose among different interpretive levels, and how to use software programs like Excel or Sheets. Instructors foster students' critical literacy by helping students develop a critical consciousness about the role data play in society and strategies for engaging data critically. Asking students to read about or research topics such as online surveillance, data privacy, and generative AI; evaluate sources of information that use data; and identify the affordances and constraints associated with data visualizations or with datafied ways of knowing more generally

TABLE 0.1. Adapting Selber's conceptual landscape of a computer multiliteracies program for data literacy

Category	Metaphor	Subject Position	Objective
Functional Data Literacy	Data as human-made resource	Students as users of data	Effective and ethical use
Critical Data Literacy	Data as cultural artifact	Students as questioners of data	Informed critique
Rhetorical Data Literacy	Data as assemblage	Students as producers of data	Reflective praxis

Source: Adapted from Selber 2004, 24.

are examples of activities that could position students as questioners of data and promote the objective of informed critique. Selber describes rhetorical literacy as "mediat[ing] the binary division between functional and critical literacies to some extent" and suggests that "a curricular implication of this relationship ... is that rhetorical literacy might prove to be a particularly challenging place to start" (Selber 2004, 25). Instructors cultivate students' rhetorical literacy by highlighting how data are invented at every stage of the composition process—from how they are collected to how they are organized, analyzed, and visualized—to serve persuasive aims and by providing opportunities for students to analyze their own rhetorical situation and compose data stories suited to that situation.

CONSTRUCTIVIST PHILOSOPHY

As the metaphors used to describe data indicate, the conceptual framework outlined in table 0.1 reflects a constructivist perspective on data. Constructivist philosophy is associated most with learning theory and has been applied in educational settings for almost fifty years (Honebein 1996). Although interpretations of constructivism vary, I follow Johanna Drucker (2011) and Christian Hennig (2002) by thinking of constructivism broadly as an approach to epistemology. Hennig outlines three principles common to constructivist approaches to philosophy: "There is no observation without observer," "Observations are constructed in social dependence," and "Perception is a means of self-organization, not of representation" (2). When applied to data, constructivist philosophy challenges the idea that data can ever be raw or simply represent the world as it is (Gitelman 2013), which constitutes a more traditional realist view of data. Rob Kitchin and Tracey P. Lauriault (2014) describe the realist view of data: "As the concept of data developed, data largely came to be understood as being pre-analytical and pre-factual, that which exists prior to interpretation and argument; the raw material from which information and knowledge are built." From this point of view, data are taken to be "benign, neutral, objective and non-ideological in essence, reflecting the world as it is subject to technical constraints; they do not hold any inherent meaning and can be taken at face value" (Kitchin and Lauriault 2014). The realist view of data makes humanistic engagement with data difficult if not impossible. As Drucker (2011) explains, "Humanistic inquiry acknowledges the situated, partial, and constitutive character of knowledge production, the recognition that knowledge is constructed, *taken*, not simply given as a natural representation of pre-existing fact" (emphasis in original). Consequently, Drucker argues for "*reconceiv[ing] all data as capta*. Differences in the etymological roots of the terms data and capta make the distinction between constructivist and realist approaches clear. *Capta* is 'taken' actively while *data* is assumed to be a 'given' able to be recorded and observed. From this distinction, a world of differences arises" (emphasis in original).

Drucker's work testifies to the value that humanistic inquiry has to understandings of data—within and outside the humanities. In the humanities, engagement with data makes possible the investigation of new questions and offers new methods for investigating longstanding questions. For example, in *Composition and Big Data*, editors Amanda Licastro and Benjamin Miller (2021) discuss how big data methods provide new ways to approach longstanding questions about writing, such as the extent to which students transfer knowledge of writing gained in one context to another, while raising new questions for researchers to consider, such as how to ensure the ethical treatment of research participants in big data studies. However, in addition to the benefits offered by humanistic inquiries of data to those working in the humanities, Drucker insists that the constructivist approach to data is also valuable to "those that presume an observer-independent reality available to description." These scholars can benefit from "the methods of presenting ambiguity and uncertainty in more nuanced terms." The constructivist approach to data that informs my model for critical data literacy pedagogy is valuable for both facilitating humanistic engagement with data and usefully complicating more realist approaches to data analysis and visualization. In the classroom, this has the effect of making space for contributions from the widest possible range of students, regardless of how their disciplinary background informs their data literacy.

Chapters

Critical Data Storytelling represents my attempt to enact a multiliteracies data literacy pedagogy based on a constructivist perspective on data within multimodal composition pedagogy, focused on cultivating students' abilities as rhetorical readers and critical communicators of data stories. Chapter 1 details a model for implementing critical data literacy pedagogy in multimodal composition that is grounded in rhetoric and composition scholarship and focused on preparing students to act as data storytellers. I begin by discussing the exigence for this model in more detail by considering how datafication changes information and knowledge-making practices, using the example of learning management systems in higher education to illustrate how the process of datafication works and the possibilities for and limitations of datafied ways of knowing. I focus on learning management systems because they exemplify how the information environments in which students compose texts and interact with course materials, instructors, and other students are being shaped by computational and algorithmic modes of thinking that neither (most) students nor (most) instructors fully understand or are prepared to engage critically. Next, I review recent scholarship that indicates that despite the widespread transformation of information and information environments, writing instruction—and higher education generally—continues to be characterized by a static approach to information that does not account for or prepare students to engage critically datafied ways of knowing. I outline my model for critical data storytelling pedagogy and explore the connections between literacy and storytelling. I argue that the position of data storyteller is an agentive role that can encourage students to ask and answer genuine questions with and about data. In the current context in which students often feel powerless to resist datafication and datafied ways of knowing, claiming the right to tell one's own stories about and with data is a critical way to respond. At the end of the chapter, I describe a speculative design assignment I have included in first-year composition to encourage my students to engage critically the learning analytics dashboard of our course's LMS site.

In chapter 2, I focus on the first part of the model of critical data storytelling pedagogy, which prepares students to act as rhetorical readers of data stories. I define rhetorically reading data stories as being able to recognize when data stories use data ethically to support arguments and which data stories might help a reader answer their own questions or solve specific problems.

I begin by considering the challenges of reading data stories in the current post-truth era, the stakes of which were clearly exemplified by the spread of mis- and disinformation during what scholars have termed the "misinfodemic" that accompanied the viral spread of COVID-19. Next, I review recent scholarship on reading digital information sources critically and discuss how the range of strategies that scholars advocate using to read digital texts are useful but insufficient for reading data stories due to the unique challenges associated with reading and evaluating data stories. I present my model for a rhetorical approach to reading data stories, which addresses the unique difficulties associated with reading data stories by focusing students' attention on the context surrounding data stories to increase their comprehension. To demonstrate the efficacy of my model for a rhetorical approach to reading data stories, I offer a case study of two data stories to show how it can be used to read data stories critically.

Chapter 3 considers the second half of the model of critical data storytelling pedagogy, which focuses on preparing students to communicate about and with data. I begin by discussing the context for what is often referred to as a data literacy crisis, one precipitated by the rapid and widespread transformation of information in the big data era. Next, I compare approaches to cultivating data literacy, which vary considerably despite generally embracing the concept of data storytelling as a way to make data actionable. I also discuss how the emphasis on critical data storytelling in rhetoric and composition scholarship makes this approach particularly suitable for use in a wide range of writing courses. I present a variety of pedagogical resources I have developed to assist in the process of designing critical data storytelling assignments for different levels of writing classes and students. To represent the range of possibilities for critical data storytelling assignments, at the end of the chapter I share three critical data storytelling assignments and include a sample student response for each assignment.

Chapter 4 focuses on an instructive approach to responding to and assessing students' data stories aimed at preparing students to both evaluate and compose data stories simultaneously. The chapter opens by defining instructive assessment and contextualizing it within multimodal pedagogy. I report results from my research of students' development of data literacies that indicate the extent to which critical data storytelling assignments require students to engage in a process of trial and error and risk failure as they acquire the new skills necessary to complete these assignments. I discuss specific instructive assessment strategies I use to help students understand criteria for evaluating data stories and how to assess their own and others' work, and I share one example of a data storytelling assignment from a first-year writing class to demonstrate how these strategies can support students in the data literacy learning process. The chapter closes by considering how instructive assessment can be used with different grading schemes and by offering recommendations for using instructive assessment with critical data storytelling assignments.

While the first four chapters of *Critical Data Storytelling* focus on preparing students to navigate the changes that big data has brought to information environments and ways of knowing and emphasize the value of a critical perspective to examine and respond to these changes, in chapter 5 I explore how rhetoric and composition teachers can use data for teaching purposes. The chapter begins by considering calls from within the field of rhetoric and composition for instructors to cultivate data literacy and the kind of data literacy described as being necessary for rhetoric and composition teachers. I also examine some of the concerns that surround data use, in particular, the use of data to monitor students and teachers. Next, I discuss how the concept of data literacy for teachers (DLFT) can be adapted by college instructors. Then I share resources that instructors can use to cultivate their own data literacy and design data inquiries, and I present an extended example of a classroom data inquiry. The chapter closes with recommendations for using data in teaching contexts.

1
Charting a Course for Data Storytelling in Multimodal Composition

Several years ago, the private, regional comprehensive college in New York, where I was teaching at the time, revised the general education curriculum to encourage more focus on quantitative reasoning. I took this as an opportunity to build a focus on data literacy into my first-year, general education writing course, the goal of which was to prepare students for academic research writing. When I asked the students in this course to describe how they interact with data in their academic or personal lives, most of them immediately began describing the most recent math course they had completed. A few of them indicated they used data in jobs as retail store managers or bookkeepers. Quite a few said that data were not part of their regular life in any way and that they did not expect them to be in the future. However, when I then asked them how many of them had at least one social media account, almost all of them raised their hands. Moreover, when I asked them what the last date was that they made an online purchase—through Amazon or another retailer—most of them had a very recent example—some even from earlier in the same day. They began to see where I was going with this line of questions.

When I asked again how the students interacted with data in their academic or personal lives, the nature of the examples changed. In the context of their online activities, they recognized numerous ways they regularly interacted with data: tracking the numbers of likes that their social media posts received, comparing prices and ratings when making consumer decisions, navigating corporate privacy and data use policies. As the discussion proceeded, students also began to name ways that they were aware that their data were being collected and used to track them online. Many of them recounted the familiar if unsettling experience of casually searching for a product on Google and then finding themselves inundated with ads for that product for days. They recognized that their news feed filtered the information they received based on previous searches they had conducted and articles they had clicked on to read. The students were aware that the search results they received to a Google query would differ from their classmates' results because of their history of prior searches.

It became clear during this discussion that in one way or another data were driving the majority of students' interactions online and were causing increasing offline effects as well—even when students did not intend for this to happen or were not aware that it was happening. How did they feel about the fact that the digital trails they left behind them online were being used as data to then determine the interactions they had? Some of them were indifferent, and some of them were resentful, but all of them were resigned, seeing the collection of their data as the price they paid to use the Internet. They reported using few concrete strategies to resist the collection and use of their data. The most commonly mentioned strategy—which came up specifically in reference to avoiding a news "filter bubble"—was to check what CNN, MSNBC, and Fox were reporting on a particular issue to make sure they were not only getting one side of a story.

I have since found that the resignation expressed by the first-year students in this class is common to college students when they discuss data. It is rarely news to them that their data are being collected; most of them understand well that they are the product that companies like Google sell to advertisers through the digital trails they leave behind as they conduct activities on the Internet. They also recognize that social media likes and numbers of followers, like consumer ratings and reviews, can be manipulated in a variety of ways and that fixation on these numbers is not productive or healthy. Yet they are almost inevitably drawn to do so.

The director of Project Information Literacy (PIL), Alison Head, and her coauthors suggest that it is not surprising that students did not initially think of their online activities when asked in a first-year writing class about how they interact with data. When Head and her colleagues talked with students during focus groups about their interactions with algorithms during focus group interviews, they learned that most students do not see the relevance of the information literacies required to complete academic assignments to their life outside college (Head et al. 2020, 23). As Head, Fister, and MacMillan explain in a recent report titled "Information Literacy in the Age of Algorithms," "Because most students believed that they knew more than their teachers about algorithmic technologies, they saw no value in addressing them in the college classroom" (23). A surprising number of the thirty-seven instructors that Head et al. interviewed as part of the study also shared this general conclusion. Although many of them confirmed that they did not understand algorithmic technologies themselves, they nevertheless felt confident that a general focus on critical thinking in the classroom would suffice to prepare students to navigate any information environment (23).

Since Google began to make a profit based on mining data from the digital trails left by users in the early 2000s, the entire information landscape in which our students—and ourselves—work and learn has changed, yet formal instruction in information literacy still primarily emphasizes traditional, print-based information paradigms (Head et al. 2020, 28; Norgaard and Sinkinson 2016, 20). This has implications for students' abilities to recognize mis- and disinformation as discussed in chapter 2, and it also has implications for students' abilities to use data critically. Computer science scholar Lev Manovich (2012) notes a growing "data analysis divide" between those with the skills needed to work with and use data and those without the necessary skills (461). To help close this gap and ensure that datafied knowledge production is understood and used appropriately, pedagogical strategies are urgently needed to help students and many instructors understand and respond to the process of datafication—including in the writing courses in which information literacy skills are often introduced and cultivated.

This chapter presents a critical data literacy pedagogy grounded in rhetoric and composition scholarship and focused on preparing students to act as critical data storytellers. I begin by considering how datafication changes information and knowledge-making practices, using the example of learning management systems (LMSs) in higher education to illustrate how the process of datafication works and the possibilities for and limitations of datafied ways of knowing. I focus on LMSs because they illustrate how the information environments in which students compose texts and interact with course materials, instructors, and other students are being shaped by computational and algorithmic modes of thinking that neither (most) students nor (most) instructors fully understand or are prepared to engage critically.

Next, I review recent scholarship that indicates that despite the widespread transformation of information and information environments, writing instruction—and higher education generally—continues to be characterized by a static approach to information that does not account for or prepare students to critically engage datafied ways of knowing. I outline the parameters of critical data literacy pedagogy, emphasizing the connections between literacy and storytelling. I argue that the position of data storyteller is an agentive role that can encourage students to ask and answer genuine questions with and about data. In the current context in which students often feel powerless to resist datafication and datafied ways of knowing, claiming the right to tell one's own stories about and with data is a critical way to respond. At the end of the chapter, I describe a speculative design assignment I have included in first-year composition to encourage my students to engage critically the learning analytics dashboard of our course's LMS site.

Datafication and the Changing Information Landscape

In the twenty-first century, information environments and knowledge-making practices have changed dramatically due to a relentless process of datafication. Datafication refers to the process through which human activities are converted to data, which, in turn, allows for predictions about individuals and groups (Mayer-Schönberger and Cukier 2013, 15). Although computational methods have existed for centuries, the process of datafication achieved greater importance in the twenty-first century due to the widespread digitization of information. In higher education, LMSs have played a key role in expanding both digitization and datafication. LMSs such as Canvas, Blackboard Learn, and D2L Brightspace are now widely incorporated into higher education—as well as in K–12 education—providing tools to digitize many course activities including assessment, document sharing, attendance, and discussion. As these activities become digital, LMSs collect massive amounts of information about student users and their interactions using the LMS, including not only all of the work that a student submits through the LMS but also information about what pages and files students access on the LMS, how long students spend logged on to the LMS, how long students take completing assignments or interacting with pages or files, students' assessment scores and peer and instructor feedback, and even students' locations while accessing the LMS. However, the information collected by the LMS does not become data until it is made available in a format that makes data analysis possible. To facilitate data analysis,

LMS systems now commonly include both data extraction tools that make it easy for human users to analyze the information collected by the LMS as well as artificial intelligence (AI) analysis tools that use machine learning algorithms to analyze learner data and behavior, often for the purpose of creating personalized learning paths or providing individualized feedback and support (Brown et al. 2015; Firat 2023, 4; Macfadyen and Dawson 2010, 590). As a result, most of the student information collected by the LMS can become data that can be analyzed.

The same forces of datafication operative in higher education are also working widely across society. Mayer-Schönberger and Cukier (2013) argue that "we are in the midst of a great infrastructure project" that will "bring about fundamental changes to society" (96). New media author José van Dijck (2014) has explained that "with the advent of Web 2.0 and its proliferating social network sites, many aspects of social life were coded that had never been quantified before—friendships, interests, casual conversations, information searches, expressions of tastes, emotional responses, and so on" (198). Consequently, "over the past decade, datafication has grown to become an accepted new paradigm for understanding sociality and social behavior" (198). These new understandings of sociality and social behavior are fueled not only by the quantity of data available for analysis, but, more specifically, by what are often referred to as datafied ways of knowing. Specialized algorithms, statistical models, natural language processing (NLP), computer vision algorithms, and data visualizations all represent datafied ways of knowing and constitute an emergent form of knowledge production.

Early in the twenty-first century, some predicted that datafied knowledge production would usher in an era of perfect information and bring an end to the scientific method. For example, in an article for *Wired*, Chris Anderson (2008) famously imagined "a world where massive amounts of data and applied mathematics replace every other tool that might be brought to bear" and that "with enough data, the numbers speak for themselves." However, in the years since, it has become clear that data cannot speak for themselves and that making sense of the massive amounts of data generated by datafication requires the use of specialized algorithms and statistical models to identify patterns in large data sets. In the case of unstructured data such as text or images, which constitute up to 90 percent of the data collected online (Harbert 2021), the use of NLP or computer vision algorithms are also needed to analyze the data for meaning. Additionally, data visualization techniques are often employed to help users understand and interpret data.

Recently, developments in AI technology ignited hope that AI might automate data analysis and visualization, which would represent another form of data speaking for themselves (Colenso 2024; Farmer 2024; Rasheed et al. 2024). Nevertheless, while generative AI tools can automate some repetitive tasks involved in working with data such as suggesting code to extract, clean, and analyze data, these tools have also been found to require significant human oversight to perform data analysis and visualization (Aizenberg and Van Den Hoven 2020; Dwivedi and Mahanty 2024; Nouri et al. 2024) because AI-generated content can have logical flaws, biased views, and factual errors from its training data. Additionally, these models quickly fall behind real-world changes because updating them requires a lot of computing power, time, and money and they cannot critically evaluate the accuracy or relevance of their sources. As a result, generative AI will not fully automate data analysis or visualization any time soon, and likely it will always be necessary for human users to oversee the management of the massive amounts of data produced by datafication.

To provide effective oversight, human users need to understand what datafied knowledge makes it possible to see and what it renders invisible. Datafied ways of knowing represent "a set of techniques, operations and logics at work in emergent attempts to see, know and govern social affairs in new ways" (Bonde Thylstrup et al. 2019, 4). However, these ways of knowing are constrained by their own "contingencies, limitations and complexities" just as are all forms of knowledge production (Bonde Thylstrup et al. 2019, 1). Awareness of both the strengths *and* the limitations of datafied knowledge production is necessary to use data wisely, especially in ways that might reshape society.

In the context of higher education, learning analytics constitute a datafied way of producing knowledge using data collected by LMSs and made available for analysis by LMS data extraction tools. Learning analytics are understood as "the measurement, collection, analysis and reporting of data about learners and their contexts, for purposes of understanding and optimising learning and the environments in which it occurs" (Long and Siemens 2011, 33). Learning analytics draw on data about and produced by students to build predictive models that are then used to estimate the probability of student success in a course, identify points at which instructional interventions might increase the likelihood of student success in a course, and support retrospective analysis of instructional materials, instructional interventions, and teaching effectiveness (Palmquist 2019, 2). Sources of data for learning analytics include students' performance in a specific course as well as admissions, enrollment, and academic history data (Jones 2019).

Learning analytics make use of statistical techniques and model not only to better understand students' learning processes and identify how to improve student performance and outcomes but also to project specific educational outcomes such as graduation rates. Proponents for learning analytics, such as education researchers Adedayo Quadri and Nurbiha Shukor, contend that "this type of data will provide a solid foundation for establishing target courses, developing new programmes, making beneficial academic decisions, and bringing about a number of changes to higher education institutions" (Quadri and Shukor 2021, 11). Certainly, the widespread use of learning analytics changes the experience of higher education, as both instructors and students are pushed to monitor student performance based on activities that can be quantified—whether or not these activities are strongly connected to the subject matter of a given course or representative of student learning generally.

Datafied ways of knowing (i.e., specialized algorithms, NLP, data visualization, etc.) are based on computational and algorithmic modes of thinking. Although specialists in computer science and engineering debate the precise meanings and dimensions of these terms, Mayer-Schönberger and Cukier (2013) explain that fundamental to computational and algorithmic modes of thinking is "seeing the world as information, as oceans of data that can be explored at ever greater breadth and depth" (97). As a result, these ways of knowing offer "a perspective on reality that we did not have before. It is a mental outlook that may penetrate all areas of life" (97). Although Mayer-Schönberger and Cukier suggest that computational and algorithmic thinking should be regarded as offering one perspective on reality, increasingly these modes of thinking occupy a privileged place in society because datafied ways of knowing are incorporated into automated decision-making processes. For example, automated decision-making is already being used to decide who gets admitted into college, hired for a job, and offered a mortgage. In the case of LMSs, automated decision-making is sometimes used to categorize students as at risk of failing a course or dropping out of school based on a statistical model or computer algorithm that is not understood or subject to review by either instructors or students and that cannot consider relevant information outside the model that might inform any individual student's context. For example, digital media researchers Marcus Carter and Ben Egliston focus on how the Blackboard LMS relies on data collected about students' clicks and page views to "identify motivation and persistence to learn, and help 'identify and overcome barriers to student success' while also 'optimizing student outcomes.' Students with irregular and infrequent page views may—based on historical data of previous years—be categorised as 'at risk', creating a new view about members of a student cohort" (Carter and Egliston 2023, 487–488). These patterns can have more to do with a student's family or professional responsibilities or their lack of access to technology than with their motivation or persistence. Carter and Egliston point out that "Categorising this student at risk is based on an often unacknowledged political claim about what 'good learning' might look like, and the design of learning analytics systems that omit such realities are a similarly political claim about what 'good educators' should know and consider in their teaching" (488).

Nevertheless, although the datafied way of knowing a student constitutes only one perspective on that student—and on "good learning" more generally—this perspective is seemingly accorded special status when automatic warning notifications, which may also be archived as part of the student's educational record, are triggered that the student is at risk. And being labeled "at risk" carries a stigma that can affect how an instructor interacts with the student and discourage the student from continuing with the class. Anna Lauren Hoffman (2018) refers to the type of harm done by data systems as the result of implicit and explicit choices in data and engineering as "data violence"; this violence does not have to be intentional to have negative material impacts on individuals and groups. Too often, the datafied way of knowing something or someone becomes the primary or only way of knowing. At the least, this oversimplifies the complex realities of humans and human interactions; more seriously, research has found that bias and error have been encoded into automated decision-making systems that are frequently "opaque, unquestioned, and unaccountable" (O'Neill 2017, 12).

Data visualization further contributes to the special status accorded to datafied knowledge production. Data visualization is itself a datafied way of knowing; it is "both a manifestation of and force for datafication" (Nærland and Engebretsen 2023, 640). Essentially, data visualization is a way to access and make sense of data, and the increasing pace of datafication has led to a growing importance of visualization methods (Kennedy and Hill 2018). Data visualization, like computational methods more generally, has existed for centuries, but it achieved greater importance in the twenty-first century as powerful computing techniques have been applied to ever-growing amounts of data (Womack 2014, 12). Moreover, although data visualization is a way of translating datafied information into visual form, it also obscures the translation process, meaning that data visualizations rarely acknowledge how data were translated (Agostinho 2019, 2). As a result, "data visualization largely reinscribes the figure of the omniscient, autonomous subject placed in an observer-independent relation to knowledge" (Agostinho 2019, 2), and data visualization often presents datafied knowledge production as knowledge itself (Drucker 2011).

When it comes to LMSs, the data visualizations used to deliver LMS-based learning analytics to instructors and students can reify the assumptions about good learning built into the model that is used to analyze LMS data. These visualizations are usually available through learning analytics dashboards (LADs), which "allow users to view and explore information within a personalized display that 'aggregate(s) different indicators about learner(s), learning process(es) and/or learning context(s) into one or multiple visualizations'" (Brown 2020, 386). As an example, the Blackboard LMS offers several dashboards as part of what it refers to as "Analytics for Learning," that present the results of LMS-based analytics that instructors and in some cases students can access. Figure 1.1 shows one of the scatterplots that Blackboard provides as an example in materials designed to introduce instructors to the Student Activity Details Report. The Student Activity Details Report is available to both instructors and students in Blackboard Learn courses and provides a graphical representation of a "student's hours in course per week" compared to other students in the course. Each week begins on Monday, and the current week's information is updated every twenty-four hours in the early morning. The selected student's activity displays in purple, and the average course activity is in gray. Users can select a dot to see exact dates and hours in course for a student or the course average. Activity per week is defined as the hours in a course accumulated by a student per week. Hours in course are counted from the time students select something within the course to when students select something outside the course. If a student is logged out from their course session for inactivity, only the time before their last action within the course is counted.

This visualization implicitly makes an argument that the hours spent in course per week represent course activity and explicitly makes an argument about a particular student's weekly activity in a course compared to their classmates. The sample scatterplot depicted in figure 1.1 shows that Lucas White is somewhat inconsistent in his course activity compared to his classmates.

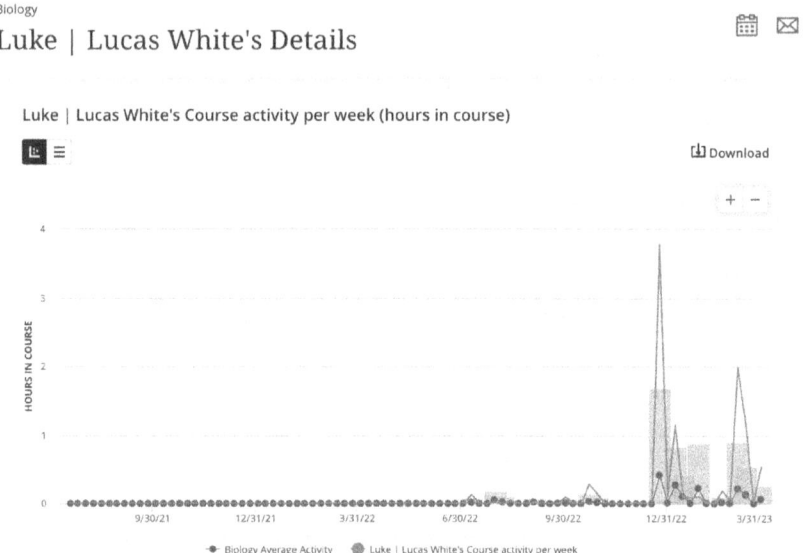

FIGURE 1.1. Student Activity Details Report available through Blackboard "Analytics for Learn" from Blackboard Help Center. Screenshot of scatter plot. Student Activity Details for Courses. 2022, https://help.blackboard.com/Learn/Instructor/Ultra/Performance/Course_Reports/Course_Activity_Related_to_Grades/View_Individual_Student_Course_Activity_Data.

While there are weeks during which his "hours in course" exceed those of his classmates, there are other weeks during which he spends no hours in the course or noticeably fewer than his classmates. By visualizing "hours in course," the scatterplot places special emphasis on how many hours a student has spent in the course and implies that hours in course per week is representative of student activity. Simultaneously, the scatterplot does not visualize the nature of this activity by indicating exactly what Lucas or his classmates are doing during their hours in course, what they are doing during the weeks they are not spending much time in the course (perhaps they complete work outside the LMS that week?), or whether they are really engaged or learning during the hours they spend in course. Although this information is missing largely because the LMS cannot collect this information and therefore it is unavailable for analysis and visualization, the absence of visualizations on these issues nevertheless implies that they are not important or at least not as important as the number of hours spent in the course. Although I have discussed only one of the many visualizations available through Blackboard's Analytics for Leaning, this example illustrates how data visualization renders particular student behaviors in a course LMS highly visible and others, which may arguably be more important in any given course context, invisible.

The fact that data visualizations cannot be all-encompassing and are necessarily contingent and limited is not, in and of itself, a problem. As Ben Williamson, Sian Bayne, and Suellen Shay point out, despite their limitations, LADs can serve a useful supplemental role by illuminating student actions that instructors usually cannot observe in the classroom. However, the narrow view of the classroom that they can represent risks "pedagogic reductionism" by drawing attention "to features such as 'engagement' and 'risk of drop-out' which can be easily quantified and visualized through the activities of students on digital platforms" (Williamson et al. 2020, 358). As institutions of higher education place increasing importance on datafied ways of knowing to make decisions about what constitutes good learning, and good teaching, Williamson, Bayne, and Shay warn that there are risks that pedagogy will be reshaped to ensure that it registers on the platforms used to generate data and that students quantitatively classified as at risk will think of themselves and be treated by teachers differently (358). When the limited perspective provided by data visualization and other datafied ways of knowing is mistaken for knowledge itself, these incomplete and contingent forms of knowledge can assume greater social importance than they should properly have and can even shape the thinking and behavior of individuals and groups as they work to make themselves "algorithmically recognizable" (Gillespie 2014, 184).

The process of datafication is not only making more information and more types of information into data available for analysis but also transforming human behaviors and thinking as people "shift their worldviews to accommodate the underlying logics and implicit presumptions of the algorithms they use regularly" and "to internalize [algorithmic] norms and priorities" (Gillespie 2014, 187). Students and instructors thus confront an information environment in which information is increasingly subject to data analysis, datafied ways of knowing are accorded special privilege, and thought and behavior conforms to computational and algorithmic logics.

The process of datafication—and with it the transformation of human behaviors and cognition—is also poised to expand as AI becomes more pervasive throughout society. Datafication is required to provide the data necessary to both train AI models and enable them to perform their tasks. For these reasons, digital information environments such as LMSs that already rely on the digitization and datafication of information have provided ideal environments for the earliest applications of generative AI. However, similar modifications of other—even physical—environments are now on the horizon to facilitate future developments in AI. As an example, Andrea Lavazza and Mirko Farino explain how physical roads will have to be engineered to be suitable for self-driving cars, which come with "specific requirements due to AI technology that allows the vehicle to move without a human driver," including being able to move in "an environment that allows it to have all the feedback necessary for the efficient execution of its task, which is to move from point A to point B with maximum safety and comfort of the passengers and all who may be in its path" (Lavazza and Farino 2023, 844). Just a few of the infrastructure changes that will be required to support self-driving cars are the installation of roadside sensors on lanes, curbs, and sidewalks to allow the vehicles to see dangerous or unexpected situations ahead of time, machine-readable code embedded in signs and transmitted or broadcast, and machine-readable radar-reflective road markings (Odukha 2023). These kinds of changes are needed to provide the data necessary for AI to perform the task of driving, and until they are made to the physical road system, self-driving cars will "have a narrow range of available destinations and thus condition the mobility of those who want to rely on them" (Lavazza and Farino 2023, 844). Because generative AI is not in fact intelligent at all but only a type of machine-learning model designed to produce new content based on the data it has been trained on, in any context in which AI is implemented (from LMSs and wearable health devices to self-driving cars, autonomous drones, and beyond), human reality has to change to become more amenable to AI rather than the other way around (Floridi 2015).

Yet because the pace of datafication has generally "outstripped the pace of reflection," as information studies and digital design professor Annette N. Markham (2019) explains, few people are aware of how powerful the process of datafication and computational and algorithmic modes of thinking have become or how greatly they have shaped human reality (754). In fact, according to Markham, most people today have "impoverished knowledge about how our data is gathered and used (by, e.g., companies who design platforms using incomprehensible algorithms) or how computational processes impact what we see (e.g., advertising), what we don't see (e.g., numerous companies buying or selling our data), and how decisions are made on our behalf (e.g., news feeds or music recommendations)" (754). Considering the widespread changes that datafication has brought to information and knowledge-making practices, students need to be provided with opportunities to cultivate the information literacy skills necessary to understand and respond to the process of datafication.

The Persistence of a Static Approach to Information in Writing Instruction

Despite widespread recognition that datafication has transformed information environments and knowledge-making practices, these changes have not so far been widely incorporated into information literacy or writing instruction. Instead, higher education generally continues to employ a "static approach to information, which fails to acknowledge how the world has changed in the 20 years since Google began capturing and exploiting individuals' digital trails" (Head et al. 2020, 28). This static approach does not take into account the social and economic conditions that shape and influence the design of current information systems, and it is evident in the persistence of highly structured college writing assignments—across the university—that limit students to the use of traditional scholarly sources and, as a result, do not provide opportunities for them to "address the significant social and ethical questions raised about the workings of influential information systems on the public sphere" (10–11). Failing to adapt writing assignments and course instruction to prepare students to navigate the complexity of today's information landscape has widespread implications for students, including limiting their ability to evaluate the credibility of online sources of information and formulate questions of their own.

In rhetoric and composition, many scholars have theorized multimodal approaches to engage an expanded notion of literacy beyond the alphabetic-only that consider how information systems and knowledge-making practices have evolved in the twenty-first century. For example, the Council of Writing Program Administrators' (CWPA) 2014 revision of the WPA Outcomes Statement for First-Year Composition recognizes the need to expand the concept of writing to include multimodal texts:

> In this Statement "composing" refers broadly to complex writing processes that are increasingly reliant on the use of digital technologies. Writers also attend to elements of design, incorporating images and graphical elements into texts intended for screens as well as printed pages. Writers' composing activities have always been shaped by the technologies available to them, and digital technologies are changing writers' relationships to their texts

and audiences in evolving ways. ("WPA Outcomes Statement for First-Year Composition [3.0]" 2014)

More recently, the Modern Language Association (MLA) and Conference on College Composition and Communication (CCCC) Joint Task Force on Writing and AI recognized the need to address AI in writing and literature instruction since, as the writers argue, "Critical AI literacy is now part of digital literacy, and students and teachers should be made aware of bias and inaccuracy in model outputs and the particular vulnerability of students who may not yet have sufficient expertise to critically evaluate language model outputs, including seeing them as sentient" (Byrd et al. 2023, 11).

The rhetorical approach to multimodality that emerges in rhetoric and composition scholarship stands in contrast to the static approach to information because it recognizes that "writing and technology are not monolithic, determined, or static entities but exist as a nexus of complex and nonlinear historical developments, social and economic situation(s), and political and institutional apparatuses," as the authors of "On Multimodality: A Manifesto" explain (Wysocki et al. 2019, 19). It also provides a critical lens through which students can "engage in not only the technical (how-to) aspects of works with digital communication and composition media and technologies but also in critical analysis of that media" (19). In this way, multimodal composition pedagogy has the potential to serve as a useful pedagogical response to changing information and information environments.

However, though "the theoretical conversations around multimodal composing are already quite sophisticated in some respects" (Khadka and Lee 2019a, 3), recent work by composition scholars Chen Chen (2021) and Santosh Khadka and J. C. Lee (2019a) indicate that multimodality has not been fully integrated even into composition instruction, let alone across the university. Print-based assignments with strict source requirements remain common in rhetoric and composition courses (Chen 2021, 72), and multimodality is incorporated into writing programs and classrooms only sporadically and in widely varying ways (Chen 2021, 75; Khadka and Lee 2019b, 4). Instructors' perceptions of multimodal writing also differ significantly. In her 2021 "snapshot" of the current state of the field with regard to the implementation of multimodality in composition, Chen found that "while some instructors already assume the importance of multimodal composition and have moved beyond tool-oriented concerns to a more in-depth and critical understanding of the tools used, others still believe that multimodal writing is displacing important traditional writing practices" (76).

The persistence of tool-oriented concerns is evident in many of the resources aimed at helping students to create citations and multimodal texts. Rolf Norgaard and Caroline Sinkinson observe, for instance, that "what matters most to many disciplinary faculty are that the citations are in the correct shape, not that the process of acquiring and evaluating information has given students insight into the discursive and cognitive features of a discipline" (Norgaard and Sinkinson 2016, 20). As another example, technical communication textbooks, which have long provided one or more chapters to help students compose data visualizations, generally focus only on formal understandings of visualizations. In her survey of twelve technical communication textbooks, Joanna Wolfe (2009) explored how they discussed data visualization and presenting data and results, concluding that the textbooks showed a "general disregard for numbers and data. Numbers are key elements in engineering discourse, but our textbooks do little to teach students how to construct arguments that rely on numbers as evidence" (364). Instead, the books focused on the formal features of data visualizations and how to use tools such as Microsoft Excel to create graphs and charts. A more recent survey of technical writing textbooks indicates that Wolfe's findings remain relevant over a decade later (Joswiak and Duncan 2020, 32). This formalistic, tools-based approach to composing multimodal texts does not provide the kind of critical perspective on information that would help students "think about how information is created and encountered on different online platforms" (Head et al. 2020, 22). Nor does the emphasis on "important traditional writing practices" (Chen 2021, 78), which Norgaard and Sinkinson explain refer primarily to style, organization, and citations (20). They point out that the continuing emphasis on these skills in writing instruction reflects "the still widely entrenched 'current-traditional' paradigm of writing instruction [that] limits our ability to enact a more robust approach to [information literacy]" (20). In other words, despite the widespread availability and even acceptance of multimodal approaches that focus on helping students compose within and analyze digital environments, the static approach to information continues to characterize writing instruction.

Although the static approach to information can be beneficial for helping students learn to write scholarly texts, the dominance of this approach to information has led to a "worrisome disconnect between the critical information practices learned in college and the information skills students need in their daily lives and after graduation" (Head et al. 2020, 9–10). This disconnect became increasingly difficult to ignore with the release of generative AI to the public in 2022. Many were astonished with the speed with which programs like ChatGPT could produce correctly written content and how smoothly it could converse with users. Almost immediately traditional approaches to teaching writing and information literacy in college interpreted this technology as a threat. For example, within one month of the release of ChatGPT, Stephen Marche (2022) published an article in *The Atlantic* declaring "The College Essay is Dead," a sentiment that was subsequently repeated in other newspapers and magazines. Many working within the field of rhetoric and composition echoed these concerns as well, expressing what Courtney Stanton (2023) describes as a "steady mix of fear and fervor . . . a sense that we are on the brink of a revolution and that its full consequences, still frightfully unknown, will be profound" (184). These fears resulted almost immediately in calls to ban AI in writing instruction—if not in higher education more generally (J. Taylor 2024; Mearian 2023), and companies such as TurnItIn raced to release AI-detection tools that instructors could use to police their students' use of AI (Knox 2023).

Efforts to ban and police AI, in addition to being doomed to fail, represent, as S. Scott Graham (2023) has explained, a "problematic commitment to a limited and linear process-based model of writing" (162). Rather than attempt to further shore up static approaches to teaching writing and traditional approaches to information literacy by banning the use of AI, we need to draw more widely on approaches to teaching writing that help students navigate datafied information environments such as AI. This is particularly urgent given how generative AI exacerbates the problem of mis- and disinformation by making it easier and faster to churn out fake information—including text and images—than ever before, certainly faster than humans are capable of fact-checking and debunking it (Verma 2023). The new reality of datafication and AI requires cultivation of critical data literacy practices that are not currently widely fostered in higher education and that position students more as active producers of information rather than as passive consumers.

After all, students are not sitting idly by waiting for instructors to provide formal instruction to help them learn how to navigate changed information environments. In the absence of such instruction, scholars have found that students develop informal understandings, or folk theories, about how computer systems and algorithms work through "abductive reasoning," which refers to understandings formed through observation and synthesis of their daily experiences (Devito et al. 2018; Eslami et al. 2015). Head and colleagues identified several strategies that students in their study used defensively to try to control what data was collected about them and how it was used. The most common strategies were running ad blockers and regularly clearing browsers of cookies. Some students reported avoiding Google products and using alternatives like DuckDuckGo as a search tool or Firefox as a browser. Others ran virtual private networks (VPNs) to shield their identity or created multiple accounts on platforms like YouTube, Google, and Instagram to avoid having all their online activities linked to one identity. However, the defensive strategies that students employed did not help them to feel like empowered information users. Instead, Head and colleagues conclude that "their concerns were often accompanied by a sense of impotence, and for some, nihilistic dread" (27). Without the critical tools needed to channel their concerns into activism, the students adopted a "reflexive skepticism" (22) toward information and expressed "profound ambivalence . . . about algorithm-driven platforms that collect data about their personal lives" (14). As Head and colleagues' research indicates, students are generally aware of the problems associated with datafication, which are experienced daily, and are eager to learn more effective strategies for navigating information systems. Some of them are more aware of available defensive strategies due to technical knowledge they bring with them, but as a group they require much more critical knowledge. As writing and rhetoric instructors work to develop pedagogical strategies for helping students navigate big data and AI, it is particularly important to bridge from students' existing knowledge and practices to the more critical data literacy that can help them learn to act—and not merely react—with regard to data.

Critical Data Storytelling in the Writing Classroom

I argue that to counter the powerlessness students feel to resist datafication and datafied ways of knowing, instructors should help them cultivate the skills of rhetorical readers and critical communicators, roles in which students exercise agency over data. In making this claim, I build on an emerging body of scholarship from rhetoric and composition teacher/scholars that considers ways to incorporate big data into composition instruction (e.g., Bay and Atherton 2021; Beveridge 2017; Danner 2020b; Fanning 2020; Hoag and Emmelhainz 2021; Laflen 2020; Laflen 2021; Pigg et al. 2018; Sorapure 2006; Sorapure 2010; Wolfe 2015). This work recognizes, as Aaron Beveridge (2017) explains, that "as multimodal writing continues to shift and expand in the era of Big Data, writing studies must confront the new challenges and possibilities emerging from data mining, data visualization, and data-driven arguments."

When scholars of rhetoric and composition discuss including data literacy instruction in writing courses, they generally do so by framing this work in terms of cultivating students' abilities to use and question and produce big data as a technology. All of them recognize, as Beveridge (2017) puts it, that "data-driven arguments and their accompanying visualizations are now a prevalent form of multimodal writing." The growing importance of data means that in addition to learning how to read multimodal texts that include data, students also need to learn how to produce their own multimodal texts with and about data. What this requires in practice is learning to use, question, and produce data visualizations since visualizations are the key to "organizing, exploring, analyzing, and creatively deriving meaning from the deluge of information that we face in our everyday lives" (Sorapure 2010, 59).

Although data visualization has not so far been incorporated in writing and rhetoric courses as widely as other types of multimodal communication such as video, audio, and gaming, the relevance of visualizations to composition instruction becomes clearer when data visualizations are conceived of as stories. Consequently, rhetoric and composition scholars frequently discuss data visualization as storytelling when arguing that big data should be included in writing and rhetoric courses. For example, Wolfe (2015) contends that the value of a "storytelling orientation" to data visualization is that it "gives us a framework for comparing the various rhetorical choices writers make in presenting their data" (349), and Fanning (2020) explains that thinking of data visualization in terms of narrative helped her "to recognize the place data visualization has in the composition classroom."

Data analysts and statisticians also regularly describe data visualization as a form of storytelling (Abelson 1995; Few 2007; Gershon and Page 2001; McCandless 2012; Segel and Heer 2010). Notably, statistician and artist Edward Tufte, whose four books on data visualization helped to define the field, emphasized the narrative qualities of data visualization when he described Charles Joseph Minard's graphic of Napoleon's invasion of Russia as "a rich, coherent story with its multivariate data" (Tufte 1983, 40) and by including a chapter titled "Narrative of Space and Time" in his book *Envisioning Information* (Tufte 1990). Since then, it has become common for guides to creating data visualizations to embrace the idea of storytelling (Duarte 2013; Duarte 2019; Knaflic 2015). More recently, data analysts have also begun to suggest that the complexity of data storytelling makes it quite difficult for generative AI to automate and that human oversight of data storytelling will always be necessary even as some aspects of data analysis and visualization become automated (Aizenberg and Van Den Hoven 2020; Dwivedi and Mahanty 2024; Nouri et al. 2024). Data analysis advisor Gane Kesari (2024) is among those who contend that generative AI is unable to produce data stories that automatically and conversationally answer nuanced questions about data. To provide guidance to professionals seeking to understand how to incorporate AI into data communication, Kesari created a matrix that matches data communication strategies to specific needs for information. He explains that while AI is able to answer simple exploratory and explanatory questions, such as "What was last month's sale performance?" or "What is the top driver of customer churn?," the technology is not well-suited for answering what-if questions about data, which is a strength of interactive data dashboards, or strategic planning questions that require the kind of sophisticated presentation of data in context that data stories can provide. Consequently, in the age of AI, the concept of data storytelling seems to be more relevant than ever before as the term is coming to be associated with the dimensions of data analysis and visualization that cannot be performed by generative AI.

However, while there is widespread agreement about the value of data storytelling, it is less clear exactly what "story" means when used in reference to data communication. This ambiguity is evident in the popular resources designed to help writers compose data stories. Almost all these resources equate storytelling with particular narrative structures, although they do not agree on which structure is best suited for use with data stories. As a result, some resources recommend the use of Aristotle's three-act framework, while others find value in Joseph Campbell's *Hero's Journey*, and still others adapt Freytag's Pyramid (Andrews 2019; Duarte 2019, 64; Dykes 2020, 163; Knaflic 2015, 117). In these works, story is synonymous with a specific arrangement of content, with little attention paid to how the data included in data stories are invented in the first place, how writers' choices about arrangement are impacted by their audience and purpose for the text, or how the stories are delivered. As a result, this formalist approach to data storytelling unnecessarily constrains the agentive role of storyteller, limiting writers' choice-making to placing content within predetermined story structures or templates.

In contrast, storytelling is used in rhetoric and composition scholarship to refer to a methodology for communicating a compelling narrative about data to a specific audience. This means that structure is just one component of the methodology rather than a defining attribute of "story," and storytelling involves choosing among all the available resources within a communicative context based on the writer's intentions for the text rather than inserting content into a particular story structure. The role of data storyteller as described in rhetoric and composition scholarship is also fundamentally critical in nature, meaning that critical data storytellers recognize the rhetorical dimensions of data stories and data more generally. In this approach to data storytelling, both reading and composing data stories require active engagement as readers participate in creating the meaning of data stories through their analytical and interpretive work, and writers craft data stories by choosing among available options for inventing, arranging, and delivering these texts. Since data stories are produced and circulate within complex information networks, learning to read and compose these texts provides numerous opportunities to consider how datafied knowledge production represents "the output of social processes" rather than "objective facts" (Tygel and Kirsch 2016, 117). In other words, students can gain greater awareness of the process of datafication by learning more about and practicing data storytelling.

Critical data storytelling extends the "long history of efforts to raise consciousness of citizens about how they are part of larger ideological systems of power and control" to datafied information environments (Markham 2020, 229–230). As Sorapure (2010) explains, one of the primary incentives for including data visualization in writing courses "is to develop students' awareness of the limitations and biases of the software they use in our courses and elsewhere. We can encourage students to see software not as a neutral tool but rather as an object of analysis" (60). Inherent in this approach is that learning to act as a data storyteller will help students to engage data critically in other contexts, whether academic, personal, or professional and enhance their skills as readers of data stories as well. "As students find and analyze data and design their own visualizations," writes Sorapure, "they can develop more effective strategies for reading the charts, graphs, and other data displays that they encounter in the news, online, and elsewhere" (68). Hoag and Emmelhainz (2021) contend that "attuning students to the promise/peril of big data, machine analysis, cultural critique, and more, reflects a commitment to prepare students for continuing education beyond the university" (32). In talking with my own students about their experiences with data after they have completed my class, I have been encouraged that many of them are able to imagine agentive roles for themselves in their engagements with data following completion of a critical data storytelling assignment.

Critical Data Literacy Pedagogy

Students' ability to imagine agentive roles for themselves as members of a big data society is significant considering the widespread "impotence" that more generally characterizes students' engagement with data (Head et al. 27). Critical data storytellers not only understand how to use data ethically to make persuasive arguments or explore topics but also how to question the assumptions underlying datafied information environments and ways of knowing and can act on the analysis of contexts and audiences to design and compose data stories. In the writing classroom, this means that instructors who wish to prepare students to navigate datafied information and information environments need to focus on students' functional, critical, and rhetorical data literacies. To assist in these efforts, the model of critical data literacy pedagogy shown in table 1.1 reflects a multiliteracies approach to data storytelling and is designed to help students cultivate the data literacy skills of a rhetorical reader and critical communicator. This model reflects rhetoric and composition scholarship on including data in writing courses as well as my own research on students' development of data literacy. It connects specific characteristics of rhetorical readers and critical communicators to classroom strategies and instructional goals.

Critical data literacy pedagogy can be implemented and adapted in a variety of ways to prepare students for the information environments in which they live and work, which I discuss in greater detail in chapters 2 and 3. Although cultivating critical data literacy is an ongoing process and no single course or assignment can ensure that students master rhetorical reading and critical communication, the model aims to provide direction for data literacy instruction in multimodal pedagogy by identifying characteristics, strategies, and goals associated with developing the functional, critical, and rhetorical literacies necessary to use data ethically and to ask and answer questions with and about data. To demonstrate how I have applied critical data literacy pedagogy myself, in the following section I detail one critical data storytelling assignment I have used to foster my students' multimodal composing and data literacy skills.

Speculative Design Assignment: Reimagining the Canvas Gradebook Interface

I included this assignment in a technical writing course that I taught in 2024 to encourage my students to engage critically with the interfaces with which they

TABLE 1.1. Model of Critical Data Literacy Pedagogy for the Composition Classroom

	Characteristic	Classroom Strategies	Goals
Rhetorical Readers	Familiar with the data-driven inquiry process	· Introduce the data-driven inquiry process · Practice lateral reading and discussion of sample data stories	1. Help students recognize data stories as resulting from a composition process that is familiar to them 2. Help students move beyond any cognitive shortcuts they may have adopted for data stories
	Understand available strategies for representing data	· Introduce basic vocabulary for identifying and discussing data visualizations · Discuss how writers represented data in sample data visualizations · Examine how writers used data visualizations to support their persuasive arguments	1. Provide a starting point for discussing the choices that a writer made in constructing a data story 2. Begin to recognize common data visualization types and the patterns in data they make visible
	Construct the rhetorical context for a data story	· Model taking bearings of data stories through lateral reading · Practice constructing the rhetorical context for a data story	1. Equip students with critical reading strategies they can use to read and analyze data stories 2. Utilize the networked capabilities of the Internet to aid in reading data stories
Critical Communicators	Understand how to use data ethically to make persuasive arguments or explore topics	· Introduce technical skills required to use data at an appropriate level · Introduce ethical practices for collecting, analyzing, and/or visualizing data · Practice using data to make an argument or explore a topic	1. Foster students' digital literacies 2. Help students recognize the ethical dimensions of working with data 3. Recognize how data serve useful exploratory and explanatory purposes
	Question the assumptions underlying datafied information environments and ways of knowing	· Introduce characteristics of and assumptions underlying datafied ways of knowing and information · Discuss relevant tactics and strategies for navigating datafied information environments and ways of knowing · Examine the affordances and constraints of data in sample data texts	1. Recognize how datafied information and ways of knowing differ from other forms of knowledge and the strengths and limits associated with datafied knowledge production 2. Begin to identify effective strategies for using, critiquing, or resisting datafied information environments and ways of knowing

continued on next page

TABLE 1.1. —continued

	Characteristic	Classroom Strategies	Goals
Critical Communicators	Act on the analysis of contexts and audiences to design and compose data stories	· Model analyzing the rhetorical situations of data stories · Practice designing and composing a data story appropriate to its rhetorical context	1. Develop facility in using data to respond to a variety of situations and contexts 2. Understand and use a variety of technologies to address a range of audiences 3. Match the capacities of different data sources and visualizations to varying rhetorical situations

Source: Angela Laflen.

interacted for class. This assignment asked students to reimagine one of the interfaces we had used throughout the semester, including our course Canvas site. I used a speculative design assignment to call students' attention to how technical communication practices and students' educational experiences are shaped by and framed within the interfaces of digital programs and tools.

Speculative design is a method of critical analysis and inquiry that focuses on "creating imaginative projections of alternate presents and possible futures using design representations and objects" (DiSalvo 2012). Designers have long used speculative design to reflect on "contemporary conditions and express possible implications of current trends in science and technology" (DiSalvo). In the context of the dominant approaches to data visualization, the critical practice of speculative design offers a way to imagine other ways of visualizing data, including ways that "embody qualitative expressions" (Drucker 2011).

To familiarize my students with speculative design, I shared with them Bethany Monea's (2020) "Screen Reading: A Gallery of (Re)Imagined Interfaces" published in *Kairos*. Monea presents six reimagined digital interfaces "intended to disrupt expectations and provoke reflection. They are designed not for interaction but for imagination." As one example, Monea reimagines the Google Maps interface with a "topsy-turvy" orientation that encourages readers to question how they typically read maps and why maps are normally oriented the way they are. As another example, Monea presents a reimagined Craigslist interface that prompts readers with pop-up questions as they move their cursors across the page such as "What is your body doing right now?" and "How is your posture?," highlighting not only the physical

Part 2: Speculative Interface Design

Canvas Gradebook	Grades for Student X			
Assignment Title	Due Date	Submission Details	Score Received	Instructor Feedback
Assignment #1	Jan 28th, 2024	submitted	10 out of 10	Great work!
Assignment #2	Feb 4th, 2024	submitted	8 out of 10	Good effort! Let's have a chat on Monday to fig [...]
Assignment #3	Feb 11th, 2024	submitted	9 out of 10	Keep it up!

Click "here" to send message to instructor.

Excerpt from Student Reflection

I chose to redesign Canvas's gradebook page to enhance accessibility for users who have never worked with computers before. My inspiration came from observing older students in an ESL class I intern for. I noticed that although they have the webpage translated to their first language, they still have difficulty accessing features of the gradebook, such as instructor comments. My redesigned interface prioritizes simplicity and clarity, employing visual cues, such as distinct categories and color-oriented metaphors, to guide users through the gradebook. Essentially, it should be as straightforward as possible to the point that the user wouldn't need to have any prior experience with this sort of interface to be able to access all of its features. As Monea does in her "Gallery of (Re)Imagined Interfaces", and specifically her collection of interfaces titled "Welcome Home", I wanted my Canvas redesign to evoke a sense of belonging. This is why I opted for an interface similar to what a paper-based gradebook would look like. I chose to limit the use of color and other more bold design elements to mimic this format.

FIGURE 1.2. Student response to speculative redesign assignment. Source: Sokolov 2024.

effects of spending time on activities mediated by interfaces but also that the machines with which we interact regularly do not notice signs of our bodily discomfort caused by interactions with them.

For my students' speculative designs, I encouraged them to be imaginative by creating the design in any way they wished, drawing by hand or using the program of their choice. They did not have to create a working interface or visualization, but only the design. After students created their speculative designs, they wrote a reflection in which they discussed the assignment and the design process.

The Canvas Gradebook turned out to be the most popular interface for students to reimagine in their speculative designs. The Canvas Gradebook organizes and visualizes grade data for students, and it is one of the tools with which they interact most throughout the semester. Students can use the Gradebook not only to see their grades on specific assignments but also to access instructor feedback and track any late or missing assignments. The students who chose to reimagine the Gradebook for their assignment often recounted that they found the tool overly complicated to use and the presentation of grade data and feedback unclear.

The assignment yielded interesting results. For example, one student, inspired by Monea's reimagining of various home screens, redesigned the Canvas Gradebook interface to be more accessible to users with limited computer skills or who were English language learners (see figure 1.2). In analyzing the Canvas Gradebook interface, this student observed that the tool was valuable for "tracking progress and managing deadlines, allowing for a structured and proactive approach to learning" but that the interface itself could be made more accessible and usable.

Although the students' speculative designs were completed quickly for this informal assignment, the assignment still provided opportunities for me to implement critical data literacy pedagogy in my course. Specifically, this assignment fostered students' functional, critical, and rhetorical data literacies as they:

- Learned basic vocabulary for identifying and discussing interfaces and data visualizations
- Discussed the rhetorical context for interfaces and data visualizations
- Learned characteristics of and assumptions underlying interfaces
- Discussed relevant tactics and strategies for navigating interfaces
- Created a speculative design for an interface and/or data visualization

Additionally, students practiced multimodal composing and thought more about how interfaces mediate technical communication and educational data and experiences.

This example illustrates how even low-stakes, informal assignments can be useful for fostering critical data literacy in our writing courses. Instructors need not radically reinvent writing instruction to include critical data literacy in their course. Whether an instructor is working with a class on critical reading strategies, navigating the course LMS, choosing and using research sources, or other skills, there are already numerous times during a semester when it would be appropriate to incorporate classroom strategies intended to help students rhetorically read and critically communicate data stories.

Conclusion

The students in our writing and rhetoric courses are immersed in datafied information environments that are reshaping cognition and behavior in ways we do not entirely understand even though we can perceive their effects. The information literacy skills required to navigate environments in which most information is rendered into data and the analysis of which is guided by algorithmic and computational processes necessarily differ from those required to complete traditional academic research assignments relying primarily on the use of peer-reviewed scholarship. Sociologists Helen Kennedy and Rosemary Lucy Hill describe how "pervasive data and related quantitative rationalities create new pressures on ordinary citizens who wish to participate in civic, social and cultural life as it becomes more data driven, for example to have the skills to comprehend large datasets and how they are operationalized" (Kennedy and Hill 2018, 831). In this context, data visualization has emerged as the primary means through which "ordinary citizens" gain access to data because of its alleged capacity to make data transparent and accessible (Few 2007; Zambrano and Engelhardt 2008). For this reason, the "entanglement of the numeric and the visual is at the heart of most people's engagements with data" (Kennedy and Hill 2018, 831).

Although data visualization, commonly conceived of as data storytelling, has not yet been widely incorporated into multimodal composition pedagogy, a growing body of scholarship explores the possibility of fostering students' critical data literacy in writing classes. I believe that critical data storytelling assignments are particularly well-suited for use across a spectrum of writing classrooms as they provide a conceptual framework for approaching datafied knowledge production, particularly data visualizations, as forms of narrative and an agentive role for students to act as critical data storytellers. Including these types of assignments in writing courses allows instructors to cultivate students' critical data literacy along with multimodal composing skills.

The speculative design assignment described in this chapter represents one example of the type of critical data storytelling assignment that provides an opportunity for students to critically and rhetorically examine data visualizations and digital interfaces, but there are many other, perhaps limitless, ways to engage data in the writing classroom. While this open-ended flexibility is a strength of critical data storytelling assignments since they can be crafted for use with many kinds of students and to meet any number of learning outcomes, it can also be a barrier to the widespread use of these assignments since instructors rarely have time to wade through all the alternatives and test out different approaches. Chapters 2 and 3 include additional examples of road-tested assignments I have used in my own courses to foster critical data literacy along with resources to assist with designing and adapting critical data storytelling assignments for use in writing courses.

2
Reading Data Stories Rhetorically

Jordan and Ahri were both successful English majors who were preparing to graduate. They enrolled in a digital writing course because they were excited by the possibilities for telling stories and making arguments in multimodal genres. Jordan, an avid reader of comics and graphic novels, was eager to learn more about how multimodal texts are composed, while Ahri maintained a blog that she wanted to improve through a better understanding of design. Both Jordan and Ahri recognized that data were common in the multimodal texts they encountered in daily life, most often via social media. However, when it came to how they felt about working with data and how they understood the data they encountered in multimodal texts, Jordan and Ahri represented opposite backgrounds and approaches. Jordan described themself as "uncomfortable" working with data generally, while Ahri rated herself as "comfortable." Jordan avoided college-level math courses to the greatest extent possible; Ahri chose to take statistics as a college course and used data regularly for her position in an accounts payable office. While Jordan tended to take data at face value, Ahri was inherently skeptical of arguments based on data. In recounting their most common approach to reading texts that included data, Jordan observed: "I take data for granted, and I haven't really thought about cherry-picking either. I just normally see things and take them as they are." In contrast, Ahri preferred to work with raw data because she worried about how often data were manipulated in unethical ways. As she recalled, "If it's like raw data that's in a list that we have to organize and kind of see patterns, I feel a little more comfortable with that, but if it's reading a whole report and trying to understand the language of it, that's where I'm like 'okay I cannot wrap my head around this.'" In a reflective assignment for class, she explained further that her mistrust of data stories stemmed from the fact that "misinformation is so prevalent in America and on social media."

Jordan and Ahri illustrate what the two most common responses to data stories look like in the classroom—and among members of the public more generally. The first response is to unquestionably accept data when it is presented in seemingly authoritative ways. The second response is to unquestionably reject data as too potentially manipulated to accept as evidence. Readers often choose between these responses based on the extent to which the data presented support their existing beliefs and opinions. In Jordan's and Ahri's cases, their typical responses also correlated with their own comfort levels working with data and the knowledge each of them had about data. Jordan, who generally did not like information to be presented as data and had not studied statistics, tended to just accept data stories at face value, while Ahri, who better understood how to work with data from statistics courses and professional work, was inherently skeptical of data stories as potential manipulations. However, though both responses to data are common, neither represents a critical strategy for engaging data stories. Rather, they are both cognitive shortcuts that people use to avoid engaging and analyzing data stories critically. The prevalence of these strategies points to the difficulty of reading data stories and the need for critical reading strategies suited specifically to data stories.

This chapter presents a rhetorical approach to reading data stories. I define rhetorically reading data stories as being able to recognize when data stories use data ethically to support arguments and which data stories might help a reader answer their own questions or solve specific problems. I begin by considering the challenges of reading data stories in the current post-truth era, the stakes of which were exemplified clearly by the spread of mis- and disinformation during what scholars have termed the "misinfodemic" that accompanied the viral spread of COVID-19. Next, I review recent scholarship on reading digital information sources critically and discuss how the range of strategies that scholars advocate using to read digital texts are useful but insufficient for reading data stories due to the unique challenges associated with reading and evaluating data stories. I present my model for a rhetorical approach to reading data stories, which addresses the unique difficulties associated with reading data stories by focusing students' attention on the context surrounding data stories to increase their comprehension. This model helps to move readers beyond simple acceptance or rejection of data stories and encourages students to slow down enough to engage critically and analyze the use of data in these texts.

In doing so, the rhetorical approach to reading data stories promotes the kind of "slow thinking" that scholars such as Thomas P. Miller and Adele Leon (2017) and Lester L. Faigley (2006) suggest is key to "focused deliberative effort" on the part of students—and readers in general (Miller and Leon 2017, 14). What Miller and Leon refer to as the "click-and-go literacies" (11) of networked information ecosystems, through which data stories most commonly circulate, do not provide space for such deliberation and, instead, foster cognitive shortcuts that lead to the type of shallow engagement with data stories that prompts readers to either unthinkingly accept or reject data stories. To demonstrate the efficacy of my rhetorical approach to reading data stories, I offer a case study of two data stories to show how the model can be used to help students read data stories critically. By analyzing a chart focused on county-level COVID-19 data shared by a state department of public health early in the pandemic, alongside an interactive chart correlating state-level COVID-19 data with political partisanship created by a web developer and shared on his personal website, I demonstrate the importance of reading both texts rhetorically. Although students might dismiss the personal website in lieu of a state agency website, neither source is what it initially seems to be and either one could be valuable to students in particular contexts. Including data stories in rhetoric and composition courses and taking time to help students learn how the data stories these texts invent are designed to persuade audiences and circulate through online networks is one step in bridging "the expanding gap between the literacies we teach and the ones our students enact" (Miller and Leon 2017, 11–12). Moreover, because "lines between true and false, real and fake, rumor and threat, are hopelessly blurred," as professor of rhetoric and composition Bruce McComiskey (2017) observes, it is essential to share strategies with students that they can use to read the data stories they encounter in their daily lives.

The Stakes of Reading Data Stories

The stakes of being able to read data stories critically are evident in considering the role that data played in spreading mis- and disinformation during the "COVID-19 misinfodemic" (Chou et al. 2021, 9; Kington et al. 2021). As COVID-19 spread around the globe, the amount of information being shared increased exponentially due to social media. With more than four billion people using social media regularly, it became the primary source of information and communication during the COVID-19 pandemic, regardless of the credibility of the information (Dixon 2022). Indeed, a significant proportion of the information circulating online about COVID-19 was mis- or disinformation; that is, information based on myth, rumors, pseudoscience, or altered facts. During the pandemic, mis- and disinformation spread more quickly than the virus itself. As an example, a 2020 poll by the Pew Research Center found that 47 percent of Americans had been exposed to news that COVID-19 was not real (Pew Research Center 2020). The misinfodemic caused tangible harm, exacerbating the effects of the pandemic. A joint statement by WHO, UN, UNICEF, UNDP, UNESCO, UNAIDS, ITU, UN Global Pulse, and IFRC (2021) outlined some of these effects: "The consequences of mis- and disinformation can be harmful to people's physical and mental health; increase stigmatization; threaten precious health gains; and lead to poor observance of public health measures, thus reducing their effectiveness and endangering countries' ability to stop the pandemic."

A considerable amount of the information that circulated through social media about the pandemic focused on sharing data. Although many of these data stories were intended to communicate factual public health information and recommendations, data stories also played a leading role in the misinfodemic. Figure 2.1 shows posts that circulated widely online during the misinfodemic even though they are patently fake. The creator(s) falsely attributed the stories to a well-known source, UNICEF, to give an air of authority to the completely fabricated recommendations the posts share about how to avoid COVID-19.

The role that data played in spreading mis- and disinformation during the misinfodemic underscores the importance of data-reading skills in what has been termed the current "post-truth era." The *Oxford English Dictionary* defines "post-truth" as "relating to or denoting circumstances in which objective facts are less influential in shaping public opinion than appeals to emotion and personal belief" (*Oxford English Dictionary* 2023). In philosopher A. C.

Reading Data Stories Rhetorically : 53

FIGURE 2.1. Disinformation that circulated on Facebook with a falsified source from UNICEF USA. "Don't fall for misinformation. Don't spread misinformation. There's a lot of bad info going around social media about #coronavirus." 2020. Facebook, March 14, 2020. https://www.facebook.com/UNICEF-USA/photos/a.10150427150690797/10158074044355797/.

Grayling's words, "The whole post-truth phenomenon is about, 'My opinion is worth more than the facts.' It's about how I feel about things" (Coughlin 2017, 4). A post-truth approach to using data is evident when distorted or fabricated data are used to support an opinion irrespective of whether the data really do support that opinion or even whether supporting data exist at all. In this context, what data actually say or can ethically be interpreted to mean are less important than supporting an opinion. Although the roots of post-truth culture are debated and certainly precede and are not unique to the present moment, what is unique today is the abundance of technologies that provide outlets for people to share opinions as easily as facts with a wide audience. As rhetoric and composition scholar Ellen C. Carillo (2018) explains, post-truth culture thrives in a society that "has as many outlets for people to share those opinions as there are outlets to disseminate facts" (4). During the COVID-19 misinfodemic, public health researchers found that a number of common myths about the virus spread everywhere in the world due to social media regardless of where the myth originated (Otto 2021).

New Approaches for Evaluating Information Sources

In light of the prevalence of mis- and disinformation circulating online, equipping readers with strategies to analyze data stories like those in figure 2.1 has become an urgent task. Annika Wolff and colleagues (2016) have recently explained that being able to read data stories is foundational to being data literate, and they define readers as those "who can apply their knowledge of a data-driven inquiry process, in which the data is a reflection of real-world phenomena, and can use this knowledge to critically assess data-related arguments" (18). As this definition indicates, the ability to discern when data are misused—when they do not reflect "real-world phenomena"—is essential to being a reader of data stories. As such, cultivating skills in reading data stories can help students recognize when data stories spread mis- and disinformation.

Although equipping readers with strategies to analyze data stories is clearly necessary, less clear is how rhetoric and composition instructors ought to translate this need into specific pedagogical strategies. Data stories vary widely, and although they are often created and disseminated in the context of traditional scholarly publications by authors with scholarly credentials in peer-reviewed journals or scientific reports, members of the public—and our students—are more likely to encounter data stories circulating online. These data stories more closely resemble what medical rhetoric specialist Sarah Ann Singer (2019) has termed "wildcard sources" rather than scholarly sources. Singer explains that wildcard sources would generally be labeled "bad" according to traditional source-evaluation criteria because their authors may not have traditional scholarly credentials, they may draw on a wide range of evidence to support their claims, they may not "be easily validated by their domain name," they may be sponsored by corporations or others with a stake in the topic under consideration, and "they may use superlative statements to bolster their authority or claims" (155). Wildcard sources run the gamut from "factually erroneous" to "accessible, valuable, and trustworthy," but Singer insists that rhetoric and composition instructors must prepare students to work with them rather than just dismiss them as "bad" sources because "students will encounter increasing numbers and variations of wildcard sources as they engage in undergraduate research" (155).

Traditional strategies for evaluating information sources grow out of print-reading practices and are not well-suited to evaluating wildcard sources beyond labeling them "bad." Numerous heuristics are available to help students and researchers evaluate sources, and source evaluation checklists remain among the most popular tools used for identifying credible information sources. Rhetoric and composition scholar Jacob W. Craig (2017) analyzed one such checklist, by Columbia University's Millstein Undergraduate Library, to consider its suitability for use with digital information sources. This checklist directs students to consider factors such as authorship, publishers, accuracy, and objectivity; timeliness; footnotes and bibliographies; and sponsorship. This checklist, and others like it, "aim to compare unknown sources to traditional scholarly sources, in which features such as authorship and citation information are always clearly evident" (Singer 2019, 156). Singer points out that such checklists oversimplify the extent to which source credibility is rhetorical: "Source checklists imply that sources are either 'good' or 'bad,' which is simply inaccurate. Instead, sources may be considered 'good' or bad' within specific contexts" (157). She points out that many potentially valuable sources do not meet all of the criteria on these checklists, and, I would add, many fake or deceptive information sources mislead students into thinking they are credible simply by mimicking the content of credible sources. Indeed, much of the concern about generative AI in classroom contexts is that chatbots like ChatGPT, Claude, and others not only commonly produce fabricated citations but that these fake citations look convincingly like real citations (Weise and Metz 2023).

Although traditional strategies for evaluating information sources remain useful for evaluating the credibility of data stories, they are not fully sufficient for reading or evaluating data stories today, and new approaches to evaluating data stories are needed that account for the unique difficulties readers face as they read data stories that are more wildcard than scholarly source. It is important to develop new approaches to evaluating data stories since there are at least three distinct challenges to helping students improve their abilities to read data stories. First, the process through which data stories are invented and composed is unfamiliar to most readers despite being central to functioning as a reader of data stories. Data stories are subject to a lengthy composition process, and as data scientist Randall Chun (2017) explains, the "long trail that leads from the raw data to the final visualization" means that there are "many opportunities along the way to introduce bogus information, making the accuracy of graphs more difficult to assess." As a result, technical and professional communication scholars Aaron Beveridge and Joanna Wolfe insist that more awareness of how quantitative arguments are invented is necessary to avoid either of the extremes represented by Jordan and Ahri's responses to data stories; that is, treating data as "'extrinsic' or 'inartistic' proof" (Wolfe 2010, 439) or as "impenetrable and unquestionable forms of evidence" (Beveridge 2015). As we help students learn to read data stories, instructors can cultivate students' knowledge of the data-driven inquiry process that produces data stories by pointing them toward a variety of sources to discover what can be learned about how data were collected, cleaned, analyzed, and presented in a story. Students can also be directed to sources to help them name the types of data visualizations included in a story, identify the types of information those visualizations are good at communicating and tips for reading that type of visualization, and see what other sources say about the topics of those visualizations.

A second difficulty associated with reading data stories stems from the challenge of "reading symbolically represented numbers" (Franconeri et al. 2021, 113). Data stories rely on a wide variety of charts that represent numbers symbolically, and previous research has found that readers asked to evaluate arguments presented with and without charts find information presented in charts more persuasive than information presented in text. The persuasive power of charts is particularly pronounced when the visualization seems to confirm a bias that the reader already has (Pandey et al. 2014). Recent research focused on how people read data visualizations sheds light on both the benefits of presenting data in charts as well as the specific challenges of reading charts. A team of psychology researchers led by Steven L. Franconeri found that "visualizations allow powerful processing of an entire two-dimensional rectangle of information at once, in stark contrast to the limitation of reading handfuls of symbolic numbers per second" (112–113). However, they also point out that "reading symbolically represented numbers takes time. As you seek patterns within each set, or make comparisons among the four sets, progressively processing more pairs of values becomes increasingly difficult" (113). This difficulty stems from the limitations of working memory, which quickly becomes exhausted by "symbolic processing of numbers" (113). A study by data analytics experts found that the difficulty of reading charts predictably led readers to adopt one of the cognitive shortcuts commonly used by readers confronted with graphs: either uncritically accepting or rejecting the chart based on whether the information presented seemed to confirm or contradict existing beliefs (Pandey et al. 2014). Franconeri and his coauthors argue that the difficulties associated with reading charts warrant taking special care to support readers' comprehension, especially for readers with limited experience reading graphs (150).

A third difficulty associated with reading data stories—particularly the wildcard data stories circulating online—involves the way these texts most commonly reach the public. Today, as Miller and Leon (2017) have explained, information "circulates through botnet networks that use algorithms to profile users and feed them stories that fit their individual biases" (10). The result is, as rhetoric and composition scholars Timothy Laquintano and Annette Vee explain, that mis- and disinformation circulates through networks as human and nonhuman actors facilitate the spread of data stories with "the veneer of credibility, aided by confirmation biases and easy mechanisms for sharing, and then magnified by popularity algorithms" (Laquintano and Vee 2017, 46). Fake data stories, like fake news stories in general, "often emulate the look and titles of professional news sources," so that "even if a story has been shared a million times on social media, and if it is found on a website that looks and sounds newsy, and if it is repeatedly linked from a popular hashtag, there's no guarantee that it's a credible story" (46). In the context of online information ecosystems, it is not enough to migrate criteria for evaluating print sources to networked information. In this environment, distinctions between primary and secondary sources and between sources subject or not subject to peer review remain useful but are not sufficient for helping students assess the credibility of networked information.

Rhetoric and composition scholars have begun to map out approaches focused on preparing readers to evaluate digital information sources that are potentially useful for helping students learn to read data stories. Craig (2017), adapting an idea originally developed by rhetoric and composition scholar Ben McCorkle, has recently distinguished between "strategies of immediacy" and "strategies of hypermediacy" in efforts to promote digital literacy (30). Strategies of immediacy involve emphasizing similarities between old and new technologies, while strategies of hypermediacy involve emphasizing what new technologies can do differently and perhaps better. Table 2.1 charts a range of strategies for reading digital sources of information critically, culminating in my own rhetorical approach to reading data stories.

Composition scholars who advocate for strategies of immediacy insist on the continuing relevance of traditional reading practices, as Janine Morris (2015) does, for example, when she suggests that there is no need to develop specific digital reading practices. According to Morris, since reading practices are always "situational and goal based," scholars should avoid drawing a firm line between print and digital (129) because making too much of the distinction among tools "ignores the incredible overlap between the reading

TABLE 2.1. Strategies for reading digital information sources critically

Type of Strategy	Traditional Print-Based Reading Strategies	Strategies of Immediacy	Strategies of Hypermediacy	Strategies for Rhetorically Reading Data Stories
Description	Heuristics that compare unfamiliar sources against the characteristics of scholarly sources	Adapt print-based strategies for digital texts and environments	Capitalize on the affordances of digital texts and environments	Examine data stories in the context of their rhetorical situations
Examples of Pedagogical Strategies	Lists of criteria for evaluating sources; evaluation checklists	Mindful reading; slow reading; genre awareness	Networked literacy; contextualization; rhetorical chart	Taking bearings; lateral reading; rhetorical chart for data stories
Sources for More Information	Modern Language Association 2018	Carillo 2018; Miller 2016; Rodrigue 2017	Cohn 2021; Craig 2017; Overstreet 2021; Singer 2019	Laflen 2020; Wineberg and McGrew 2019; Wolff et al. 2016

Source: Angela Laflen.

strategies we use to read both print and digital texts" (126). Consequently, strategies of immediacy focus on adapting print-based reading strategies for digital environments, including critical reading strategies such as annotation and modeling (Carillo 2018), the practice of slow reading (Miller 2016, 156–157), and instruction in genre awareness so students can recognize the formal features of texts and how those features shape reading (Rodrigue 2017). These and other strategies of immediacy provide instructors with concrete ways to adapt print-based reading strategies to digital texts and environments.

Although strategies of immediacy have proven beneficial in helping students read some multimodal texts, data stories can be incredibly difficult to read critically using traditional print-based strategies or strategies of immediacy because these strategies focus on helping readers extract meaning from target texts themselves—whether by comparing the text to a set of criteria that generally characterize credible texts, reading the text slowly or mindfully, or examining the genre characteristics of the text. When data stories present data in ways that are unfamiliar to the reader or appear credible despite intentionally or accidentally spreading mis- and disinformation, readers struggle to decipher the texts themselves for meaning.

Sam Wineburg and Sarah McGrew (2019), researchers with the Stanford History Education Group (SHEG), provide a detailed picture of this struggle in their study comparing the reading practices of different types of digital readers, including professional fact-checkers, historians, and college students. Though the study was not focused specifically on reading data stories but rather reading digital texts more generally, one of the three texts included in the study was a data story. Participants were given eight minutes to evaluate the credibility of a data story titled "Denmark's Dollar Forty-One Menu" posted to the website minimumwage.com. This article relied on statistics to argue that if the US followed the example of Denmark and raised wages, higher food prices and diminished job opportunities would result, and it also included a link to an interactive map where users could click on different states and compare minimum wage rates and unemployment statistics. Wineburg and McGrew explain that the article was included in the study to test if the different groups of readers could identify the organization that had created the website on which the article was posted and, if so, how long it took them to identify the parent organization. Wineburg and McGrew found that the students and historians in the study most often attempted to read the sample data story "vertically, staying within a website to evaluate its reliability," and they relied on a reading strategy that Wineburg and McGrew identify as "fluttering" (23) or "aimlessly moving across the screen, 'touching or not touching pieces of information . . . unconscious to its value and without a plan'" (23–24). The students in the study were particularly drawn to the interactive data visualization included in the article and spent considerable time fluttering over it even though this strategy did not help them to understand the visualization or evaluate the credibility of the article generally. Wineburg and McGrew conclude that reliance on the types of vertical reading strategies that characterize strategies of immediacy led participants to "[fall] victim to easily manipulated features of websites, such as official-looking logos and domain names" (1).

While Wineburg and McGrew illustrate the difficulties that participants had reading the data story using strategies of immediacy, they also highlight the value of strategies of hypermediacy for reading the data story. Writing studies scholar Matthew Overstreet (2021) characterizes strategies of hypermediacy as making use of "the internet's networked properties to accomplish reading goals" (365). The most promising reading strategy identified by Wineburg and McGrew is what they refer to as taking bearings through lateral reading (30), a strategy of hypermediacy in which readers draw on diverse Internet sources to quickly construct a rhetorical context for a data story they need to read. Wineburg and McGrew found that the fact-checkers in the study spent virtually no time fluttering over the data presented in the data story like the students and historians did but instead quickly took bearings by practicing lateral reading. As an example, one of the fact-checkers spent only six seconds on the article before clicking on the page's "About" tab, where she quickly identified the parent organization as the Employment Policies Institute (EPI) (19). She then used keyboard shortcuts to navigate to EPI's home page in a new tab but spent only three seconds on the home page before clicking the "About Us" link on the home page. After noting that the "About Us" page was not helpful, she opened another new tab and Googled "Employment Policies Institute." From there, the fact-checker clicked on the fourth search result, a SourceWatch entry on EPI, which she scrolled until she found a link to a *New York Times* article, which she clicked. She later clicked on a *National Public Radio* story about EPI, used the command-F function on her computer to search for EPI and corroborate the claims made by SourceWatch. Only then did the fact-checker return to the original article and read it more closely for its argument about the minimum wage, having concluded that "it's a very legitimate looking website but clearly, this is also advancing an agenda" (22).

Importantly, none of the participants in Wineburg and McGrew's study, including the fact-checkers, had expert knowledge of data to draw on in reading the data story, so the difference among the groups is attributable to the different reading strategies they employed. As writing and rhetoric instructors work to develop pedagogical strategies for helping students read and evaluate data stories, we can learn a lot from the reading strategies employed by expert readers like the fact-checkers in Wineburg and McGrew's study. I believe that it is particularly important for writing and rhetoric instructors to adapt strategies of hypermediacy to help students learn to read data stories rhetorically. Reading data stories rhetorically requires readers to "apply their knowledge of a data-driven inquiry process . . . to critically assess data-related arguments" (Wolff et al. 2016, 18). While some of the students in our writing and rhetoric courses bring knowledge of a data-driven inquiry process to our classes, many others do not. Fortunately, strategies of hypermediacy can be adapted to help all our students practice rhetorically reading data stories by constructing rhetorical contexts for these texts that enable students to read data stories whether they already possess knowledge of the data-driven inquiry process or not.

A Rhetorical Approach to Reading Data Stories

Writing studies scholars Christina Haas and Linda Flower (1988) first identified expert readers as rhetorical readers in their study of how readers construct meaning during the reading process. Comparing the reading practices of expert readers with student readers, Hass and Flower discovered that expert readers constructed richer schemas, or "complex networks, like dense roadmaps, made up of many nodes of information," that contain representations of text, prior texts, and context than student readers did and that these schemas helped the expert readers understand texts more deeply (168). Wineburg and McGrew's (2019) study confirms that expert readers of data stories are also rhetorical readers. Reading a data story rhetorically does not require a reader to first master statistics or data science but rather to know how to construct the rhetorical context for a data story. This context then serves as a rich schema the reader can draw on to evaluate and engage the text. In *Skim, Dive, and Surface: Teaching Digital Reading*, Janae Cohn (2021) refers to this practice as "contextualization," and she explains that although "engaging in contextualization can take some additional time and labor on the part of readers, especially since they may even need to return to engaging in contextualization multiple times over the course of a reading to remind themselves of their purposes and contexts for reading," the practice "becomes faster with time, and doing so and discovering even more about the information they are reading shapes the reading process even more centrally" (203). As Cohn's discussion of contextualization indicates, though constructing the rhetorical situation for a text is not always easy, it is a skill that writing and rhetoric instructors can, and often already do, incorporate into the classroom, though often without a specific focus on data stories.

Although we cannot expect our students to become expert rhetorical readers of data stories during a single assignment or semester, we can help them cultivate the skills of rhetorical readers regardless of the knowledge they bring with them to class or how long we have for addressing the topic during the semester. Table 2.2 presents my model for a rhetorical approach to reading data stories. This model addresses the unique difficulties associated with reading data stories, including the unfamiliar inquiry process through which data stories are invented and composed, the challenge of reading symbolically represented numbers, and the circulation of data stories through online networks. Included in the model are recommendations for how instructors and students can work together to examine the way data stories are constructed and the strategies they use to persuade readers. Altogether, the different aspects of the model support the development of students as rhetorical readers who understand how data stories are constructed and reach audiences.

RHETORICAL READERS ARE FAMILIAR WITH THE DATA-DRIVEN INQUIRY PROCESS

My model for a rhetorical approach to reading data stories begins by formally introducing students to the data-driven inquiry process through which data stories are invented and composed. The data literacy landscape, as shown in figure 2.2, is a rich space for rhetorical action as writers construct meaning throughout a sometimes-lengthy inquiry process. Although most members of the public only see the data stories that result from this process, the composition process itself includes the familiar stages of pre-writing, drafting, and revising with which students are likely to be familiar. Introducing students to the data-driven inquiry process and focusing on the production of data stories does not require writing instructors to teach math and statistics skills but rather to consider how writers choose to use data in support of persuasive arguments. Indeed, Wolff and colleagues (2016) argue that "knowledge of the

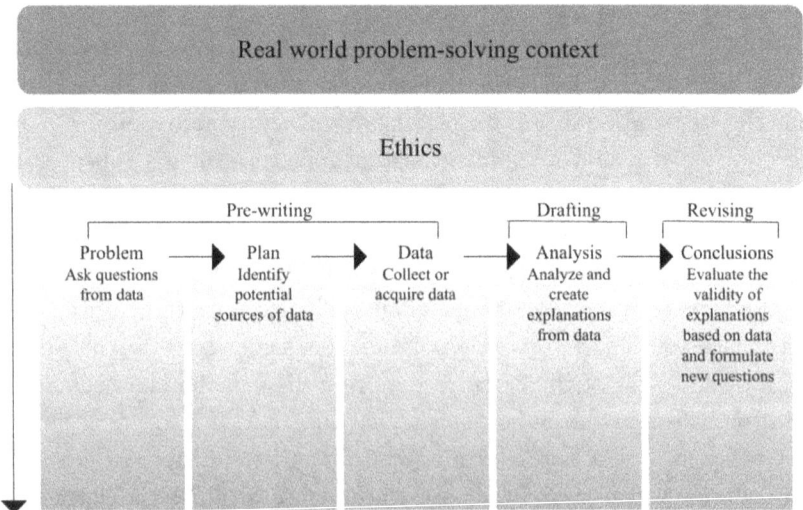

FIGURE 2.2. Data storytelling composing process adapted from Wolff et al. 2016, 15.

TABLE 2.2. Critical data literacy pedagogy for rhetorical readers

Characteristic	Classroom Strategies	Goals
Familiar with the data-driven inquiry process	· Introduce the data-driven inquiry process · Practice lateral reading and discussion of sample data stories	1. Help students recognize data stories as resulting from a composition process that is familiar to them 2. Help students move beyond any cognitive shortcuts they may have adopted for data stories
Understand available strategies for representing data	· Introduce basic vocabulary for identifying and discussing data visualizations · Discuss how writers represented data in sample data visualizations · Examine how writers used data visualizations to support their persuasive arguments	1. Provide a starting point for discussing the choices that a writer made in constructing a data story 2. Begin to recognize common data visualization types and the patterns in data they make visible
Construct the rhetorical context for a data story	· Model taking bearings of data stories through lateral reading · Practice constructing the rhetorical context for a data story	1. Equip students with critical reading strategies they can use to read and analyze data stories 2. Utilize the networked capabilities of the Internet to aid in reading data stories

Source: Angela Laflen.

overall inquiry process and the activities it entails is a pre-requisite to applying" statistical knowledge (15).

In my classes, I ask small groups of students to examine a variety of data stories that I provide to them and to answer the questions shown in table 2.3 about each of the examples. Students practice lateral reading during this activity by first attempting to answer the questions based on information available within a data story itself and then by turning to external sources to fact-check the information provided in the data story and to answer questions for which no information was provided in the data story.

As a whole class, we discuss their answers, and students begin to think more rhetorically and critically about data stories. They quickly recognize that all the data stories have shaped data to tell a particular story but that some of the data stories use data in ways that are unethical and noncredible, such as fabricating a data source or presenting data in a way that skews them. They

TABLE 2.3. Critical questions for data stories

1	Data Source	Who conducted the study that this data story is based on and why?
2	Data Alteration	How were the data manipulated from their raw form into the visualization that we see? Are details about the data alteration provided?
3	Data Analysis	What terms are central to the writer's argument (quantitative and otherwise)? How does the writer define the terms? Who would disagree with the way the terms have been defined, and why? Would the writer's argument change if the definition of the term(s) changed; if so, how?
4	Data Presentation	Who is the audience for this data story and what are they supposed to do with this information? How do the data, images, and design elements work together to draw the audience into feeling a particular way about the topic of the data story?
5	Data Presentation	What story does this data story tell? What organizational pattern(s) did the writer use to tell that story? How would using a different organizational pattern change the argument?

Source: Angela Laflen.

also often observe that the same qualities that characterize credible, ethical academic scholarship also characterize credible data stories, including clear attribution and citation, context for the evidence included, and details about how data were gathered and altered.

My primary goal for introducing the data-driven inquiry process is to help students recognize data stories as resulting from a composition process that is familiar to them even though it involves data and even if they have never composed a data story themselves. Helping students to recognize that data stories are constructed through a long process of pre-writing, drafting, and revising demystifies the process through which these texts are composed and opens them up to analysis and critique just like any other text. A second goal is to help students move beyond any cognitive shortcuts they may have adopted for data stories so they can engage these texts more deeply and critically.

RHETORICAL READERS UNDERSTAND AVAILABLE STRATEGIES FOR REPRESENTING DATA

The rhetorical approach to reading data stories emphasizes helping students understand the available strategies for representing data. Unpacking symbolic representations of numbers—often in the form of data visualizations—is one of the most difficult parts of reading data stories. Nevertheless, symbolically represented numbers warrant special consideration when reading data stories because the patterns in data that they make visible to readers usually serve as evidence to support whatever persuasive argument the data story is making. Although writers use data visualizations to help readers see patterns in data for themselves, those visualizations are carefully designed to make the particular patterns visible that writers want to emphasize and that support their argument. In doing so, data visualizations also, by necessity, suppress or render invisible other possible patterns that might exist in a set of data. For this reason, examining the presentation of data is essential to rhetorically reading a data story.

Examining the presentation of data requires the reader to consider how writers choose among available strategies for representing data to design their data visualizations and how these choices are defined by the contexts in which writers operate. While writers always have a range of options available for representing data, their choices are constrained by the rhetorical context in which they are writing. In fact, even what counts as credible data will vary depending on context, as well as what steps writers can permissibly take to "clean" data for analysis and present it visually. As a result, there is no one set of guidelines that writers can follow to create a data story that all readers will accept as unquestionably persuasive. Consequently, Patrick Danner (2020a) contends that "scholars should understand 'storytelling' as a process of coordinating persuasive or actionable goals with the limits of what data can say within the bounds of a writer's given circumstances" (175). This means that within every data set "there are multiple statistically supportable stories shaped by a range of forces and activity. The chosen story is a result of situated realities for the writers and the very human choices they made in response to those realities" (175). Writing and rhetoric instructors can help students discuss the choices that writers made in representing data in their story by introducing students to basic vocabulary related to different types of data visualizations and strategies for labeling and annotating data visualizations. Understanding some of the options available to writers gives students a starting point for reading and analyzing data stories.

My primary goal for introducing basic data visualization vocabulary and strategies to students is to give them a starting point for discussing the choices that a writer made in constructing a data story. A secondary goal is to help them begin to recognize common data visualization types and the patterns in data they make visible. To support these goals, I also choose short and simple data stories to work with in class while students are learning how to identify data visualizations and recognize the patterns they make visible. Since many students are still developing their "working memory capacity" for reading data visualizations (Franconeri et al. 2021, 150), I have found that it is beneficial for them to work with shorter and simpler texts.

RHETORICAL READERS CONSTRUCT THE RHETORICAL CONTEXT FOR A DATA STORY

Finally, my model for a rhetorical approach to reading data stories encourages students to construct the rhetorical context for a data story in order to develop the kind of rich schema that will help them understand the text more deeply. Given the circulation of data stories online and the prevalence of mis- and disinformation mimicking the attributes of credible texts, it is essential that students learn to look outside a target text for information to construct an accurate picture of the text's author, purpose, audience, exigence, and composition process. Singer (2019) contends that "one of the most important contributions of rhetoric and writing teachers . . . is that we are equipped to help students understand the context surrounding information" (158). In the case of data stories, the context surrounding the text is what Wolff and colleagues (2016) have referred to as the "real-world problem-solving context" in which writers create data stories (15). Considering the rhetorical context for data stories and the choices that writers make in composing these stories is key to constructing a rich schema for the text that allows students to read them deeply for meaning and to evaluate whether a particular data story might serve as a useful source for them.

In writing and rhetoric classes, instructors can model and provide opportunities for students to practice taking bearings through lateral reading to help students construct the rhetorical situation for data stories. Of particular importance is helping students recognize when they need to turn to external sources of information and what sources are worth consulting for credible information. It does little good to take bearings, after all, if a reader only consults untrustworthy sources. For this reason, it is important to encourage students to consult diverse sources of information, including wildcard sources that instructors often steer students away from but which, nevertheless, can provide valuable insight into the context for a data story.

In my courses, I use the rhetorical chart for data stories shown in table 2.4 to guide students to take bearings by looking beyond the data story they want to read to see what can be learned about it. The rhetorical chart extends the critical questions for data stories in table 2.3 that I use to introduce the data-driven inquiry process to students, adding additional elements of the rhetorical situation for them to consider and asking them to document the sources they consulted.

As they take bearings on a data story, I encourage students to look for answers to the questions on the rhetorical chart within the target text itself, on pages or texts published alongside the target text (such as on an "About" page of a website), and available from external sources found through web searching. I model lateral reading in class by showing students how to open up multiple browser windows alongside a data story and performing a Google search of different terms and phrases related to the data story. In class we discuss how to recognize useful sources of information that provide context for the data story they need to read, encouraging them to look beyond the first few search results and sometimes even beyond the first page of search results for helpful information.

My primary goal for helping students learn how to construct the rhetorical situation for a data story is to equip students with concrete critical reading strategies they can use when confronted with data stories in their personal, academic, and professional lives. A secondary goal is to help them develop their digital literacy skills so they can utilize the networked capabilities of the Internet efficiently and effectively to aid in their reading of data stories.

Rhetorically Reading Data Stories

In what follows, I show how the rhetorical approach can be used to read and evaluate data stories. I analyze two data stories that circulated widely online and helped shape public discourse during the COVID-19 pandemic: an interactive chart called "COVID Cases Since June 2020" that was published on the website Dan's COVID Charts and a chart called "Top 5 Counties with the Greatest Number of Confirmed COVID-19 Cases" that was posted to the Georgia Department of Health website in May 2020.

"COVID CASES SINCE JUNE 2020"

"COVID Cases Since June" is an example of a style called "bar chart races," which is an interactive, animated bar chart. This bar chart race tracks COVID-19 cases by state and partisanship beginning June 1, 2020. It was updated regularly until April 30, 2022. "COVID Cases Since June" went viral on Twitter in October 2020, with one Twitter post featuring the chart having

TABLE 2.4. Rhetorical chart for data stories

Questions to Guide Rhetorical Reading	Student's Response	Source(s) Consulted
ROLE Who created this text? Were they writing as an individual or on behalf of an organization?		
PURPOSE What do you consider to be the overall intention for the text? Are there secondary intentions? Why do you think so?		
AUDIENCE Who is the intended audience for the data story and what are they supposed to do with this information? Who might be the secondary audience(s)? How does the author appeal to audience values or opinions?		
GENRE What kind of text is the data story (i.e., is it a website, a report, an infographic, a video, etc.)? Is the text static, dynamic interactive, or timeline-based?		
EXIGENCE What is the sociohistorical context for the data story?		
DATA SOURCE Who conducted the study/studies that this data story is based on and why?		
DATA ALTERATION How were the data manipulated from their raw form into the visualization that we see? Are details about the data alteration provided?		

continued on next page

TABLE 2.4.—continued

Questions to Guide Rhetorical Reading	Student's Response	Source(s) Consulted
DATA ANALYSIS What terms are central to the writer's argument (quantitative and otherwise)? How does the writer define the terms?		
DATA PRESENTATION What elements are emphasized through organization, color, emphasis, or other strategies? How is contrast used? What elements are aligned? How and why are elements positioned in relation to one another? How do the data, images, and design elements work together to draw the audience into feeling a particular way about the topic of the data story?		

Source: Angela Laflen.

over 8.5 million views. The source of "COVID Cases Since June" is a website called Dan's COVID Charts.

Dan's COVID Charts is not the kind of source that students are generally encouraged to use in academic research, and even on Twitter many people questioned the credibility of the chart and the methodology used to create it. Dan Goodspeed does not have traditional scholarly credentials; in fact, it is not immediately clear what his credentials are. The chart also cannot be easily validated using a domain name since Goodspeed publishes his charts at https://dangoodspeed.com. Students are often instructed to dismiss any source with a .com domain name. For these reasons, "COVID Cases Since June" presents an interesting case study for a rhetorical reading since it is a source of information that students would reject if relying on traditional criteria for evaluating information sources.

When a reader navigates to "COVID Cases Since June," the bar chart race begins automatically. It defaults to showing the race for "Most Cases," but readers can also click on "Fewest Cases" and watch how the race for fewest cases unfolds over time. Both versions of the race show twenty-six bars, so between the races for most cases and fewest cases, bars for all fifty states are

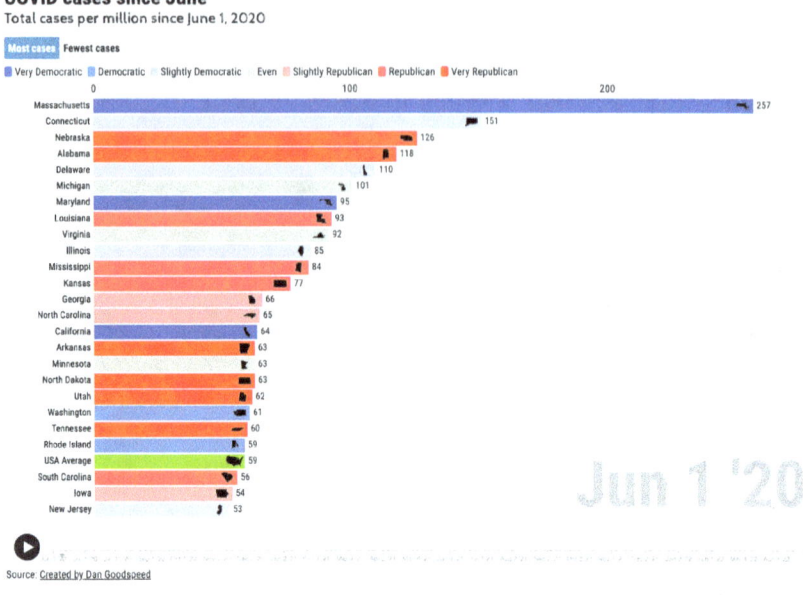

FIGURE 2.3. Screen capture from "COVID Cases Since June—Most Cases" from Goodspeed, Dan. n.d. "COVID Cases Since June." Dan's COVID Charts. https://dangoodspeed.com/covid/total-cases-since-june.

included, color coded by partisan leaning. Democratic states are represented by blue bars, with the intensity of the color indicating the strength of the state's partisanship. Republican states are represented by red bars, with the strengths of the state's partisanship indicated by the intensity of the color. Even states are represented by muted green bars, and the US average for case counts is represented by a bright green bar. Since twenty-six bars are included in both versions of the race, there is overlap between the last bar included in "Most Cases" and the last bar included for "Fewest Cases." The bars change position as their numbers go up or down, and while the "Most Cases" race begins on June 1, 2020, nearly evenly split between green/blue bars and red bars, the race becomes bright red by the final shot on April 30, 2022. The first day, shown in figure 2.3, has nine blue bars of varying shades, four green bars, and thirteen red bars. By the last day, twenty-one bars are red, with eleven of those dark red and only five bars are blue or green.

The race plays out in reverse for "Fewest Cases." The first day has fourteen red bars and eleven blue or green bars. The last day has six red bars and nineteen blue or green bars, with five of those being dark blue. One of Goodspeed's annotations on the chart notes that "the results suggest a strong correlation between a state's political leanings and its ability to employ proven science to slow the spread of COVID," a claim visually supported by the races.

Some of the information required to construct the rhetorical context for "COVID Cases Since June" is available within the target text itself. Goodspeed labels the bar chart to make it easy for readers to see the numbers being charted, and he also explains the sources for the data he used and how he altered the data presented in the chart. The language choices in "COVID Cases Since June" are also significant. In particular, the meaning of the charts depends on the definition of the words "case," "partisanship," and "proven preventative measures." Goodspeed explains two of these terms in detail. He explains that "The numbers are the total confirmed normalized* cases per million for each state since June. A '10,000' means 1% of the state's population has tested positive of COVID since June 1." He also explains that he assigned the partisanship of each state using the Cook Partisan Voting Index. The Cook Partisan Voting Index also color codes states to indicate the intensity of their partisanship; however, Cook does not label any state even. Goodspeed does not explain the thresholds he used to determine whether a state was "even," but it seems to be +1 or +2 within the Cook scale. He also explains the decision to begin with June 1: "It was around that time that countries worldwide that had been sucker-punched months before had the opportunity to apply proven preventative measures." Goodspeed does not explain what "proven preventative measures" means or consider what measures specific states implemented. This omission has the effect of suggesting that states grouped together by partisanship implemented or did not implement the same set of preventative measures, though there was in fact considerable variation even among the states assigned together to particular partisanship categories. Goodspeed flattens all differences among the states' responses to COVID other than partisanship.

A reader would likely begin laterally reading "COVID Cases Since June" by clicking on the "About Me" page on Goodspeed's website, which provides additional details about the author of the site. For more information about the text's purpose, genre, exigence, and data storytelling composing process, it is necessary to consult external sources. On the day that I used Google to search for the phrase "Dan's Covid Charts," the first three results included a link to Goodspeed's site and his GoFundMe page soliticing donations to support his website. The fourth search result listed was an interview with Goodspeed by his local newspaper that provided quite a bit more information about his purpose for creating the chart and the history of the chart. The seventh search result was a link to an analysis of Goodspeed's racing bar chart posted to the website Flowing Data that provided additional context for this type of chart. Other sources that appeared on the first page of search results included the Twitter post that went viral after sharing "COVID Cases Since June," an academic article that referenced Dan's COVID Charts as a source, and a university library guide that listed Dan's COVID Charts as a source for quantitative data related to the pandemic. Laterally reading "COVID Cases Since June" by opening up browser windows and searching for information about the chart and the website on which it is posted revealed a wide range of sources that provide context for Goodspeed, the type of chart he created, and the larger exigence for the chart. Perhaps most importantly, taking bearings in this way revealed that other scholars have cited Goodspeed's chart as a credible source for information about the pandemic, which suggests that the chart is worth reading more closely and perhaps using as a source for research purposes.

A rhetorical reading of "COVID Cases Since June" illustrates how Goodspeed's design choices and use of the bar chart races format draws the reader into accepting his argument that Republican-leaning states had a greater difficulty applying proven preventative measures to protect their population from COVID over time. Goodspeed accurately reports data to support his argument that Democratic-leaning states were better able to prevent the spread of COVID, although he does flatten out differences among states grouped together by partisanship. As a result, it is not clear that a reader could use the bar chart races to help them assess their own individual risk or determine which preventative measures proved most effective for particular states to limit the spread. Readers who would likely find the chart interesting include those looking to see how their state compared to others in terms of preventing the spread of COVID over time or those interested to see how state partisanship correlated to the spread of COVID over time. Although the data story is not one that bears traditional markers of credibility and would be easy to dismiss out of hand as a "bad" source as a result, it is a text that could be useful for some students depending on their research context.

"TOP 5 COUNTIES WITH THE GREATEST NUMBER OF CONFIRMED COVID-19 CASES"

"Top 5 Counties with the Greatest Number of Confirmed COVID-19 Cases" is a multi-series column chart that the Georgia Department of Public Health website posted in May 2020. Charts shared by government agencies such as the Georgia Department of Public Health are the kinds of sources that students are generally encouraged to think of as credible and use for research purposes. The author of the chart—a state government agency—has credibility associated with it, and the Georgia Department of Public Health has a .gov domain. During the COVID-19 public health crisis, state departments of health became vitally important sources of information as members of the public were desperate for reliable and up-to-date information about the pandemic and how to stay safe during it.

Like "COVID Cases Since June," the Georgia Department of Public Health's chart went viral, only the latter chart drew widespread attention because it appeared to intentially misrepresent data in order to support the argument that COVID cases were falling in Georgia's five largest counties. Moreover, the Georgia Department of Public Health posted several charts during this period that were flagged by journalists for communicating pandemic-related information in confusing or inaccurate ways, so this chart seemed to represent a problematic trend that contributed to public confusion about COVID and weakened public trust in government health organizations during the early days of the pandemic. This chart presents an interesting case study for a rhetorical reading because it illustrates the necessity of taking bearings through lateral reading even of data stories created by seemingly credible sources of information.

"Top 5 Counties" was originally posted to a page on the Georgia Department of Public Health's website titled "COVID-19 Status Report." This page included multiple graphs that are updated regularly. As shown in figure 2.4, the dates on the x-axis (the horizontal line) of "Top 5 Counties" are not listed in ascending or descending order. While numbers on the y-axis are presented in linear order from 0 to 50 to 100 to 150, the dates on the x-axis seem to be listed randomly, or perhaps to show a decreasing trend. For example, one series of dates on the x-axis are listed May 6, May 4, May 5, April 25. In addition, the counties are not presented in the same order as the reader moves from date to date but are also organized in descending order. Consequently, it is not possible to analyze the differences between values inside the categories in this chart. Although the chart creates a strong visual impression of decreasing case counts across all five counties over a two-week period, it is impossible to determine what the actual pattern for any given county is or across the counties as a whole based on this presentation of data.

The page on which the chart was originally published included an explanation of what readers would find on the page: "Information reported to DPH

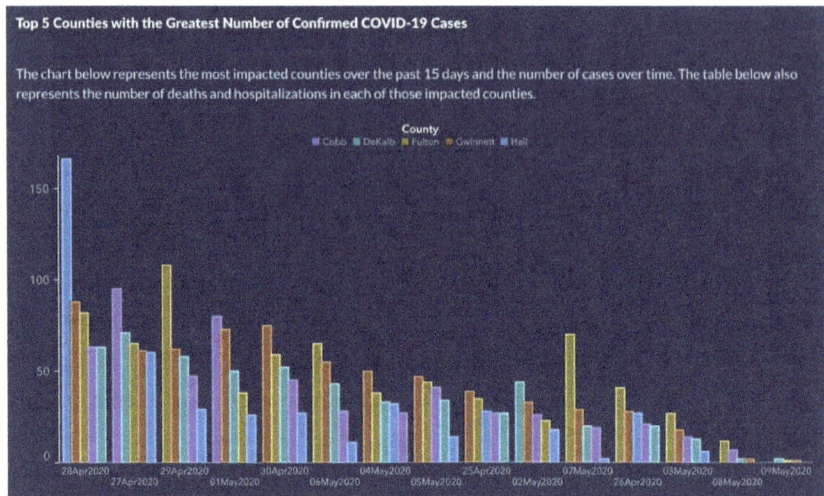

FIGURE 2.4. Misleading data visualization shared online by the Georgia Department of Public Health from Georgia Department of Public Health. 2020. "Top 5 Counties with the Greatest Number of Confirmed COVID-19 Cases." COVID-19 Status Report, May 2020. Accessed May 17, 2020. https://dph.georgia.gov/covid-19-status-report.

on the total number of COVID-19 tests, confirmed COVID-19 cases (PCR positive), antigen positive cases, ICU admissions, hospitalizations, and deaths attributed to COVID-19." Clicking on the "About DPH" tab on the navigation bar provided readers with more information about the Georgia Department of Public Health, "the lead agency in preventing disease, injury and disability; promoting health and well-being; and preparing for and responding to disasters from a health perspective." Very little information was available within the chart itself or the status report page to help readers construct the rhetorical context for "Top 5 Counties" because the chart was removed from the page following media coverage of its flaws.

In order to laterally read this text, a reader would quickly need to move to external sources. On the day that I used Google to search for "Georgia Department of Health 'Top 5 Counties with the Greatest Number of Confirmed COVID-19 Cases,'" the first two results included a link to Chegg assignments asking students to correct the faulty chart. The third result was a link to a Facebook post by the Georgia Department of Health that shared the chart originally on May 20, 2020. The fifth and sixth results provided links to Fox News stories covering the apology by the Georgia Department of Health for what it referred to as a "processing error" that resulted in the faulty chart. Later on the first page of search results was a link to a blog by a math professor analyzing the problems with the presentation of data in the chart. Taking bearings on "Top 5 Counties" revealed that the chart had been identified as having serious problems in its presentation of data and that the Georgia Department of Health established a pattern of communicating poorly (if not dishonestly) with the public during the early days of the pandemic, which suggests that readers should proceed with caution when working with any COVID-related information the agency provided.

A rhetorical reading of "Top 5 Counties" illustrates how the chart's creator presented data in a distorted way in order to make it appear that COVID cases were falling in the top five counties in the state of Georgia over a two-week period. Additionally, although "Top 5 Counties" does not represent data in an ethical way, it might still be a source that would be valuable for students to examine and cite in their research as a particularly clear example of the role that data distortion played in disseminating mis- and disinformation during the COVID-19 pandemic. Students would be better positioned to evaluate the usefulness of this source in the context of their own research based on a thorough understanding of the chart's rhetorical situation.

Students confront texts like "COVID Cases Since June" and "Top 5 Counties" regularly in their daily lives and are forced to make decisions about whether they are credible sources of information. Based on the traditional criteria for evaluating sources that are usually taught to students, they would tend to ignore a source like Dan's COVID Charts in favor of a source like the Georgia Department of Public Health. Having made that choice, they may not even bother to read "Top 5 Counties" more closely since it was published by a credible source, or if they did notice the problems with the presentation of data in "Top 5 Counties," they would be inclined to reject both sources as too flawed to bother using. The rhetorical approach to reading data stories equips students with strategies to help them efficiently and effectively read data stories to determine whether they might be good sources of information. This approach draws on the networked capabilities of the Internet to help students construct a rhetorical context for the data story they need to read and encourages students to use that rhetorical context to understand the rhetorical tactics used in data stories.

Conclusion

In the late 1980s, Haas and Flower (1988) recognized that "teaching students to read rhetorically is genuinely difficult" (182). Today, Overstreet (2021) argues that the difficulty is compounded by technological changes that increase reader distraction and render "prior reading practices defined by depth and linearity more difficult" (376). In a post-truth era, reading has become a complex task in which relying on traditional markers of reliability to determine the credibility of a source is no longer sufficient. The stakes of data literacy are incredibly high as mis- and disinformation increasingly come bearing the traditional markers of reliability and given the challenges of reading data stories. However, as Overstreet also points out, while technology has complicated literacy, it also "open[s] up new paths to comprehension" (376).

The model for a rhetorical approach to reading data stories that I present in this chapter seeks to open up a variety of paths that instructors can take to help students cultivate the skills of critical readers of data stories. This approach can be adapted for use in a wide variety of classes and with students who are new to or more experienced in reading data stories. Instructors may choose to focus only on introducing students to data storytelling by including information about the data-driven inquiry process and basic vocabulary for data visualizations. For students without any previous experience reading data stories, such an introduction will help them begin to cultivate their functional data literacy. Other instructors may devote more class time to modeling taking bearings of a data story through lateral reading and assign students to construct the rhetorical context for data stories. This type of focus will promote students' rhetorical data literacy in addition to functional literacy.

Incorporating data stories into writing and rhetoric classes can be a valuable way to engage students in rhetorical reading. By examining the ways data stories are constructed and the strategies they use to persuade their audience, students can learn to become more critical and informed consumers of information. Rhetorical reading can also help students develop their analytical skills and understand the power of data in shaping public discourse. Writing and rhetoric instructors who include data stories in the classroom can provide a unique opportunity for students to practice rhetorical reading and better understand the role that data play in narratives that shape public discourse.

3
Cultivating Critical Data Communication Skills

Olivia was an English education major with little previous experience working with data when she enrolled in my professional writing course. She hoped the course would be valuable in helping her apply for teaching positions and communicate with the parents of her students. When I introduced a critical data storytelling assignment to the class that I refer to as the Visual Argument Using Data As Evidence Project (the assignment description for which is included in chapter 4's appendix), she worried that her lack of experience creating data visualizations would prevent her from succeeding. At the outset of the project, she largely equated data storytelling with making graphs and recounted that she could not remember having made a graph during college because "most of the English classes I've taken haven't really required any type of data in my writing." On the other hand, she also explained that she generally enjoyed page design and looked forward to "being creative" while composing a data story. Ryo, a civil engineering major, enrolled in professional writing for reasons similar to Olivia: to develop the writing skills he perceived he would need to communicate with employers and colleagues. He described himself as a "maker" who "loved making and creating things to solve problems." Like Olivia, Ryo also equated data storytelling with graphs at the beginning of the project. However, he considered himself proficient at creating graphs. Not

https://doi.org/10.7330/9781646427437.c003

only did he work with data frequently in his engineering courses, but he had also taken a data journalism course in college. He expected the data storytelling project to be one of the easier assignments of the semester.

During the assignment, Olivia struggled with using data as evidence to support the argument she wanted to make in her data story, which she formatted as an infographic. She focused most of her time on the parts of the project she found interesting, which included creating and arranging textual and visual assets, and did not leave adequate time for collecting, analyzing, or visualizing data. As a result, the data displays she included in her infographic did not effectively support the larger argument she made and were not labeled clearly. When she submitted her project self-assessment along with her data story, Olivia described herself as satisfied with the visual design of her infographic but noted that she was dissatisfied with the way she had used data in the infographic: "Something in my brain just made it seem like, 'oh, they're just graphs, it should be okay.' And I overlooked that part." For his part, Ryo's general familiarity with working with data gave him a solid foundation for creating graphs to use in his data story, which he also designed as an infographic. However, he realized that the rhetorical dimensions of design also made composing a data story that would be meaningful to readers more complex than he expected: "I have come to realize that this project is more than just collecting data and making charts. The placement of each asset in the data story can make a huge difference." For Ryo, the challenge of data storytelling was not a matter of choosing among or creating graphs but of acting on the analysis of the rhetorical situation to design and compose a data story.

In reflecting on the assignment after the completion of the semester, both students recognized that their original conceptions about data storytelling were overly simplistic. Olivia explained that although she was not entirely happy with the data story she composed, she felt better prepared to analyze the data stories she encountered in daily life after having experienced the process of composing a data story. In particular, Olivia explained that she paid more attention to statistics when she encountered them online and felt the analysis skills she had developed as an English major were valuable in this context: "When you build your own data story, you start looking at or analyzing statistics in a deeper level when you see them. When you're just scrolling on social media, or when you're watching stuff on YouTube and a dataset comes up, it actually makes you analyze it more. Like I read a news article, or I watch an interview and someone brings up a statistic, and then I look it up, or I do my research on it, and if their sources are reliable. I've always been good at analyzing things. That's what we do as English majors." Ryo also observed that he had a deeper understanding of data storytelling after completing the assignment. He noted that his previous experiences working with data had not asked him to consider the rhetorical dimension of communicating about data and had oversimplified the process of data communication as a result: "In [the data journalism] class, we were just given data sets and asked to make different kinds of graphs and run tests. I haven't had to think before about how readers will understand my graphs or not. From making my own data story, I can see that this is more complicated than I ever thought about before."

Today data literacy instruction is often aimed at writers like Olivia, those who are not sure how to choose among graph types or use software programs to create graphs. Yet, students like Ryo, who have been trained to create data visualizations but lack rhetorical and critical understanding of the larger contexts in which data operates, can similarly benefit from data storytelling assignments. Although at the outset of the data storytelling assignment Olivia and Ryo both equated data storytelling with creating graphs, after completing the assignment they acknowledged that the data storytelling composing process was more complex than they had imagined. Additionally, although they began and ended the assignment in very different places regarding their technical and mathematical skills and future plans for using data, they both demonstrated growth in data and multimodal literacies. Olivia appreciated how her experiences analyzing texts, contexts, and audiences in other English classes were relevant to the work of crafting a data story, while Ryo recognized that the technical skills required to create graphs and run statistical tests were only one part of composing rhetorically effective data stories.

Olivia and Ryo represent the range of experiences working with data that students bring to multimodal assignments and the potential for data storytelling assignments to help students cultivate critical data literacy whether they have never or rarely worked with data before or have considerable experience working with data. As rhetoric and composition instructors develop assignments to help students cultivate their skills in communicating about and with data, we need to consider how critical data literacy pedagogy can benefit a range of students. Not only inexperienced students like Olivia but also more experienced students like Ryo derive benefits from an expanded view of data storytelling that moves beyond simply creating graphs and considers the larger rhetorical dimensions of data. At a time when the entire information environment is being reshaped by algorithmic and computational logics and datafied ways of knowing, we miss out on significant pedagogical possibilities if we do not investigate critical data literacy in our writing courses.

Drawing on my own experiences teaching data storytelling in a variety of writing classes as well as published scholarship by rhetoric and composition teacher/scholars, in this chapter I share a framework for designing critical data storytelling assignments. I begin by discussing the context for what is frequently referred to as the data literacy crisis, a "crisis" precipitated by the rapid and widespread transformation of information in the big data era. Next, I compare approaches to cultivating data literacy, which vary considerably despite generally embracing the concept of data storytelling as a way to make data actionable and discuss how the emphasis on data storytelling in rhetoric and composition scholarship makes this approach particularly suitable for use in a wide range of writing courses. I present my own model for a critical approach to communicating about data, along with a variety of pedagogical resources I have found useful in developing critical data storytelling assignments. To represent the range of possibilities for these assignments, at the end of the chapter I share assignment sheets for three critical data storytelling assignments and include a sample student response for each assignment.

Drowning in Data but Starving for Insight

In chapter 1 I discussed how big data has transformed information and information environments, impacting the ways that our students research, write, and think. Driving these changes is a desire by institutions ranging from governments to businesses and beyond to use the insights that big data can provide to improve—and where possible automate—decision-making. The desire to improve decision-making is evident in most arguments for the value of big data. For example, writing for *Harvard Business Review*, Andrew McAfee and Erik Brynjolfsson (2012) explain that "because of big data, managers can measure, and hence know, radically more about their businesses, and directly translate that knowledge into improved decision making and performance." Writing about the impact of big data on local government for PEW, Kil Huh, Amber Ivey, and Dan Kitson (2018) observe: "Every day, human services professionals in the public sector make complex policy decisions that affect citizens, such as how to improve service delivery, allocate budget dollars, and respond to crises. Increasingly, they use insights gleaned from massive amounts of data—originally collected by governments for reporting purposes—to make strategic decisions." In the context of higher education, Karen L. Webber and Henry Zheng (2020) argue that "the continuing importance of data analytics is not lost on higher education leaders, who face a multitude of challenges, including increasing operating costs, dwindling state support, limits to tuition increases, and increased competition from the for-profit sector. To navigate these challenges, savvy leaders must leverage data to make sound decisions."

The potential for big data to improve decision-making is based on the quantity of data available as well as new ways of accessing and interacting with data. It has been estimated that the total volume of data worldwide will reach 182 zettabytes in 2025 and 394 zettabytes by 2028 (Taylor 2025). These data are the result of "the omnipresence of computers in every aspect of human life, which means we're recording and capturing ever-increasing amounts of data" (Blevins 2013). While these data include *structured data*, such as transactions and financial records and semi-structured data, such as web server logs and streaming data from sensors, the vast majority of the data available—Griffith (2018) estimates 90 percent—are *unstructured data*, such as text, documents, and multimedia files. These data are unstructured because they are generated by Internet users who do not usually think of what they are doing as creating data. Lev Manovich (2012) explains that "pretty much everybody in the world who is using the web and/or mobile phones" is contributing to the creation of data, "both consciously and by leaving digital footprints" (470). People intentionally contribute to the creation of data by posting content online when they publish blogs, upload videos to YouTube or TikTok, share images on Instagram, Facebook, or other social media, and contribute to online discussion boards—whether or not they perceive of these activities as creating data. People unintentionally create data every time they engage in online activities, whether they are using a search engine, sending emails, following accounts on social media, sending texts over the Internet, or using apps.

At the same time, more people have access to more data than ever before. In this sense, big data "is less about data that is big than it is about a capacity to search, aggregate, and cross-reference large data sets" (boyd and Crawford 2012, 663). The process of datafication described in chapter 1 allows most of the information collected digitally to be made available for data analysis. As a result, it is possible to ask and answer questions that were difficult or impossible to explore in the past. Manovich explains that "the rise of social media along with the progress in computational tools that can process massive amounts of data makes possible a fundamentally new approach for the study of human beings and society. We no longer have to choose between data size and data depth. We can study exact trajectories formed by billions of cultural expressions, experiences, texts, and links. The detailed knowledge and insights that before can only be reached about a few people can now be reached about many more people" (462–463).

However, it has proven enormously difficult to mine big data for the insights that can lead to better and/or more efficient decisions. As a result, the metaphor most used by journalists and scholars to describe the era of big data is that of drowning in a sea of data. The adage "drowning in data but starving for information" is often attributed to the business author and consultant John Naisbitt (1982), who used a similar phrase in his book *Megatrends: Ten New Directions Transforming Our Lives* (26). In the twenty-first century, the adage and concurrent drowning metaphors have become commonplace in discussions of big data. For example, Seth Stephens-Davidowitz (2023) recently turned to the metaphor to introduce a study of decision-making he conducted for Oracle CloudWorld Tour: "People are drowning in data. This study highlights how the overwhelming amount of inputs a person gets in their average day—internet searches, news alerts, unsolicited comments from friends—frequently add up to more information than the brain is configured to handle." The drowning metaphor has also been extended in calls from leaders in government, business, and education to prepare students and members of the public to learn to swim in the sea of data by cultivating data literacy (Noyes 2015; Price Waterhouse Coopers and Business-Higher Education Forum 2017; US Department of Education 2021). Data literacy has come to be widely regarded as necessary to move from "drowning in data" to "swimming in insights," as Tableau engineer Mark Tossell (2021) recently put it.

Though data literacy used to be largely synonymous with statistical literacy, Mark Frank, Johanna Walker, Judie Attard, and Alan Tygel (2016) contend that "the Internet has fundamentally changed the game by potentially allowing anyone with Internet access to access a vast range of data sources" (5). Consequently, data literacy "is rapidly becoming a requirement to participate in modern life" (5). A fundamental component of data literacy is communicating about data. As a result of the explosive growth of data, people far removed from data science and statistics are now expected to be able to communicate about data. As Brent Dykes (2020) explains, "You no longer need to have the words 'data' or 'analyst' in your job title to be immersed in numbers and be expected to use them on a regular basis" (6). For this reason, Annika Wolff and colleagues (2016) describe communicators as one of the four types of people needing to use data literacy in "Creating an Understanding of Data Literacy for a Data-Driven Society." Communicators are those "who make sense of and tell stories about data for others to digest" (18), and Wolff and colleagues describe it as a more complex role than that of the readers discussed in chapter 2. While readers need to be able to read data stories to inform their own decision-making and avoid being taken in by mis- or disinformation, communicators have additional responsibilities associated with communicating clearly and accurately about data.

Recognition of the importance of data communication skills is evident in strident headlines that declare that data literacy is in crisis such as "The Impending Data Literacy Crisis Among Military Leaders" (Farina 2022), "Pandemic Exposes Data Literacy Crisis" (2021), and "Students' Data Literacy Is Slipping, Even as Jobs Demand the Skill" (Schwartz 2023). It is not difficult to find evidence supporting the notion that data literacy skill development has not kept pace with advances in big data. For example, in the report *Data Literacy: The Upskilling Evolution*, the Data Literacy Project (2022) reports that only 11 percent of employees globally feel confident in their data literacy skills (11), although 59 percent of those surveyed reported that they wanted to cultivate their data literacy skills in order to use data better on the job (12).

Recent developments in generative AI have led to increased interest in data literacy as a prerequisite for working with AI as well. While some have hoped that AI would automate data analysis and reduce the labor involved in working with data (Colenso 2024; Farmer 2024; Rasheed et al. 2024), in practice, AI makes the need for data know-how more important than ever before (Aizenberg and Van Den Hoven 2020; Dwivedi and Mahanty 2024; Nouri et al. 2024). Human oversight is required throughout the entire process of using AI for data analysis to ensure accuracy, and AI is so far unable to automatically generate conversational answers to nuanced questions about data (Kesari 2024). Not surprisingly, as the data literacy skills required to work with AI have been recognized, there have been further calls to develop data literacy education. For example, in the *Education Week* article "AI Is Making Data Literacy a 'Survival Skill' That Schools Must Teach, Experts Argue," Lauraine Langreo (2023) reports on research that found that as a result of "data literacy not being taught in schools," members of the public are unprepared for the present reality of AI or a future in which AI is incorporated even more widely into society. Although we might be rightly skeptical of the rhetoric of crisis surrounding data literacy, the identification of data literacy as a new frontline in what Bronwyn T. Williams (2007) has termed the "perpetual literacy crisis" (178) signals widespread anxiety that data literacy is now required to signal one's literacy.

In response to this perceived data literacy crisis, the last decade has seen the emergence of an entire industry dedicated to helping people learn to communicate about data. Increasingly, resources developed to help "novices learn to 'speak data'" (D'Ignazio and Bhargava 2016, 84) embrace the concept of data storytelling as one of the best ways to help communicators identify and convey big data insights, though the resources differ in the approaches they take to this concept. In rhetoric and composition, too, a focus on data storytelling has emerged as a way to include critical data literacy instruction in multimodal composition pedagogy. Rhetoric and composition scholars put particular emphasis on data storytelling as a type of critical practice, which encourages students to question the assumptions underlying datafied information environments and ways of knowing and to act on the analysis of rhetorical situations to design and compose data stories.

Approaches to Data Storytelling

Although the concept of a data story can be traced to the mid-twentieth century, the phrase did not become more commonly used until the twenty-first century. In the 2010s data storytelling was taken up frequently in business contexts as a pairing of information visualization with narrative structure or storyline in order to communicate clearly and memorably the insights gained from analyzing data with the goal of convincing the audience to make a decision or take an action. Consequently, many of the resources developed to help people learn to tell data stories are aimed at business professionals (Duarte 2013; Duarte 2019; Dykes 2020; Knaflic 2015).

Resources designed for business professionals frequently take a highly formalistic approach to storytelling that largely equates storytelling with use of particular narrative structures. Emphasizing narrative structure helps the writers of these resources to distinguish data storytelling from writing fiction. As Nancy Duarte (2019) reassures her readers in *Data Story: Explain Data and Inspire Action Through Story*, "We're not asking you to embrace fairy tales or incorporate any sort of creative fiction into your data process. Instead, you'll utilize stories with a structure so inherently powerful that others can recall and retell it" (5). In the best-known guides to data storytelling for business professionals, this "inherently powerful" structure is the three-act framework originally described by Aristotle in *Poetics*. Duarte (2019) explains that "this highly structured three-act framework ... organizes content according to the way our brains process information best" (64). In addition to Duarte's books *Data Story* and *Resonate*, Cole Nussbaumer Knaflic's 2015 book *Storytelling with Data: A Data Visualization Guide for Business Professionals* also draws on Aristotle's theory of drama, encouraging writers to "use this idea of a beginning, middle, and end—taking inspiration from the three-act structure—to set up the stories we want to communicate with data" (171).

However, not every writer of a resource designed for business professionals agrees that the three-part structure is the best way to structure data stories. More recently, Dykes (2020) critiqued Aristotle's tragedy structure for being "too simple, as it didn't provide enough direction on how to construct a story," and offered his own four-part "Data Storytelling Arc" adapted from Freytag's Pyramid to encourage data storytellers to structure data stories so they move from the setting, to rising insights, to an aha moment, to ending with a solution and next steps (163). Although the resources created to help business professionals compose data stories do highlight different approaches to organizing narratives, most of them present "essentially formal understandings, focused on the shape of the product rather than the craft or process of composing those stories" (Danner 2020b).

Rhetoric and composition scholars such as Patrick Danner have pushed back against formalist approaches to data storytelling while also recognizing data storytelling as a potentially valuable way to prepare students to communicate about data. "Storytelling might be a worthwhile way to conceptualize this activity," writes Danner, "but if so, we should emphasize the verb form here—*how people craft stories*—and impart those lessons to students and practitioners alike" (2020b). In rhetoric and composition, data storytelling refers to the process involved in composing data stories, which places emphasis on rhetorical choice-making over formal narrative structure. Rhetoric and composition scholars have described the rhetorical choice-making involved in inventing (Beveridge 2015; Danner 2020a; Danner 2020b; Laflen 2021; Wolfe 2010; Wolfe 2015), arranging (Fanning 2020; Sorapure 2010; Wolfe 2015), and delivering (Danner 2020b; Sorapure 2010) data stories. In rhetoric and composition scholarship, the emphasis is on critical and rhetorical engagement with data stories, and critical data storytelling assignments in rhetoric and composition courses are therefore frequently exploratory and experimental as a result, including numerous opportunities for students to reflect on their interactions with data and on the affordances and constraints of data. As Madeleine Sorapure and Austin Fauni (2020) explain, the purpose of including data in most writing courses is not to produce data scientists capable of creating sophisticated data visualizations but rather "capable readers, writers, students, and citizens—and, now more than ever, people who can ask and answer genuine questions with and about data."

Not all rhetoric and composition scholars who write about including data-based assignments in the classroom describe these as data storytelling assignments, but references to "telling a story" (Bay and Atherton 2021; Beveridge 2017) often slip into articles that don't specifically mention data storytelling. I consider all data-based assignments that encourage students to engage data rhetorically, critically, and reflectively to be critical data storytelling assignments because this aids in identifying common guiding principles and practices across assignments that are characterized by the diversity of approaches they take to engaging data in the classroom. This includes articles that discuss data-based assignments in relation to information visualization (Danner 2020b; Fanning 2020; Laflen 2020; Laflen 2021; Sorapure 2010; Wolfe 2015), data-driven research about networked writing (Beveridge 2017), critical data literacy pedagogy (Bay and Atherton 2021), and digital humanities methods of macroanalysis (Hoag and Emmelhainz 2021). Not surprisingly, technical and professional communication courses serve as the context for a number of these articles since data visualization has long been a staple of professional and technical communication instruction (Bay and Atherton 2021; Laflen 2022; Pigg, Hannah, and Stone 2018; Wolfe 2015, 344–45). However, increasingly scholars discuss incorporating data literacy instruction into courses focused on digital writing (Beveridge 2017; Danner 2020b; Hoag and Emmelhainz 2021; Sorapure 2010), public rhetorics (Bay and Atherton 2021), and even first-year composition (Fanning 2020; Laflen 2021). Taken together, this work evidences a growing consensus that practices for communicating about and with data need to be studied and shaped and that writing and rhetoric courses are appropriate places to do so. Within this emerging pedagogy, "the collecting, processing, and visualizing of data . . . should be understood as *both* statistical *and* rhetorical in nature" (Beveridge 2017, emphasis in original).

The critical data storytelling assignments described in rhetoric and composition scholarship vary widely in terms of length and complexity. Sometimes these assignments take place during only a single class or two, while others run the length of a semester. Some of them employ custom software, while

Cultivating Critical Data Communication Skills : 87

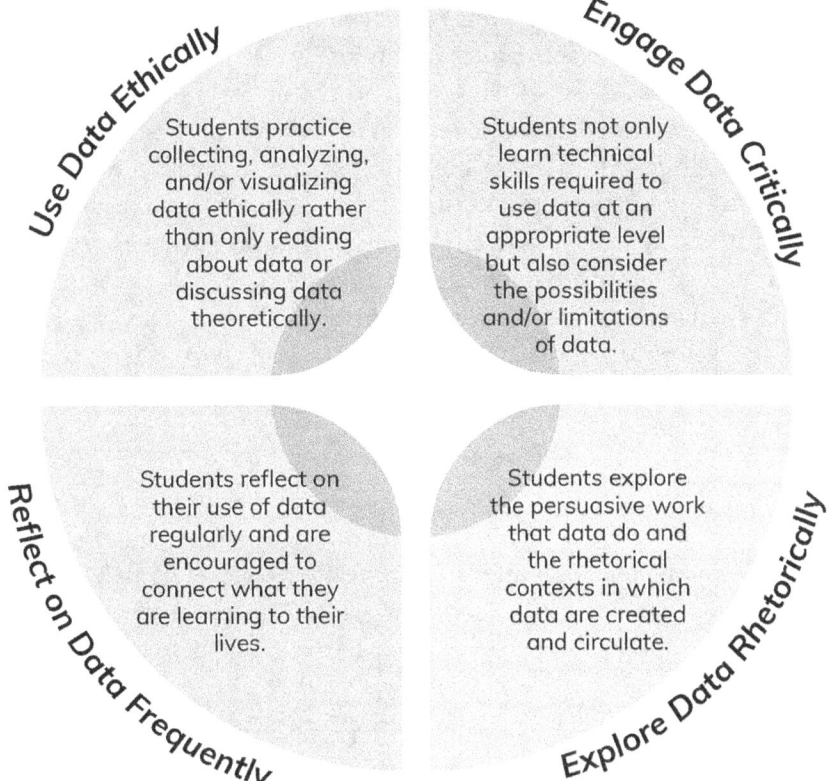

FIGURE 3.1. Guiding principles for critical data storytelling assignments.

others use only free, consumer-level technologies. Similarly, though some assignments ask students to use sophisticated math and statistics, more commonly the data storytelling included in composition courses require the use of little to no math. Sources of data also differ drastically: students might be provided by the instructor with fictional or real data to work with, asked to identify an available data set, or tasked with collecting data themselves. At every step of designing a data storytelling assignment, instructors can choose options with more or less complexity, and given the level of students in the course and the assignment purposes, any choice might be appropriate to help cultivate students' functional, critical, and/or rhetorical data literacy and meet course learning objectives.

Although there may be no limit to the ways in which critical data storytelling assignments can or even should be included in writing instruction, a common set of principles are legible across the range of critical data storytelling assignments that rhetoric and composition scholars/teachers have discussed and that I have used to design assignments for my own students. These principles ensure that data storytelling assignments promote critical and rhetorical engagement with data regardless of exactly what type of assignment an instructor designs. These four guiding principles are shown in figure 3.1. They distinguish the critical approach to data storytelling operative in rhetoric and composition. Rather than focus on particular narrative structures or even on preparing students to use specific technologies, tests, or tools, the emphasis of these assignments is on considering the possibilities and limitations of data, the rhetorical contexts in which data operate, and how students understand the relationship between what they are learning about data and their future plans and goals.

A Critical Approach to Data Communication

The four guiding principles inform my model for a critical approach to communicating about data, which is shown in table 3.1. This model can be adapted for use in a wide range of courses and with diverse groups of students to promote an agentive, critical orientation toward data regardless of exactly what kind of critical data storytelling assignment an instructor designs. It includes recommendations for how instructors and students can work together to explore using data ethically to make persuasive arguments and to examine the assumptions on which datafied ways of knowing are based.

Critical data storytelling assignments provide opportunities for students to use data ethically for exploratory or persuasive purposes. Including opportunities to use data distinguishes storytelling assignments from the type of rhetorical reading assignments discussed in chapter 2, for which students might write about data but do not usually gain experience using data. Since many students have never experienced the data storytelling composition process for themselves, it is important that they have the chance to do so to better understand the labor and choice-making involved in creating these texts. However, what it means to "use data" varies widely across assignments. In upper-level or graduate courses, students are often tasked with designing data-collection procedures (Bay and Atherton 2021) or working with the large data sets characteristic of big data (Beveridge 2017). In lower-level courses or courses with more entry-level students, instructors frequently ask students to work with small data sets containing personal data (Pennell 2014; Sorapure and Fauni 2020) or with data sets provided by the instructor (Fanning 2020;

TABLE 3.1. Critical data literacy pedagogy for critical communicators

Characteristic	Classroom Strategies	Goals
Understand how to use data ethically to make persuasive arguments or explore topics	· Introduce technical skills required to use data at an appropriate level. · Introduce ethical practices for collecting, analyzing, and/or visualizing data. · Practice using data to make an argument or explore a topic.	1. Foster students' digital literacies. 2. Help students recognize the ethical dimensions of working with data. 3. Recognize how data serve useful exploratory and explanatory purposes.
Question the assumptions underlying datafied information environments and ways of knowing	· Introduce characteristics of and assumptions underlying datafied ways of knowing and information. · Discuss relevant tactics and strategies for navigating datafied information environments and ways of knowing. · Examine the affordances and constraints of data in sample data texts.	1. Recognize how datafied information and ways of knowing differ from other forms of knowledge and the strengths and limits associated with datafied knowledge production. 2. Begin to identify effective strategies for using, critiquing, or resisting datafied information environments and ways of knowing.
Act on the analysis of contexts and audiences to design and compose data stories	· Model analyzing the rhetorical situations of data stories. · Practice designing and composing a data story appropriate to its rhetorical context.	1. Develop facility in using data to respond to a variety of situations and contexts. 2. Understand and use a variety of technologies to address a range of audiences. 3. Match the capacities of different data sources and visualizations to varying rhetorical situations.

Source: Angela Laflen.

Wolfe 2015), which sometimes even include fictional data for students to practice using (Danner 2020b). Evidence suggests that students do not need to use data at a sophisticated level to benefit; even gathering small personal data and hand drawing visualizations provides critical insight into the data storytelling process (Simpson 2020; Sorapure and Fauni 2020). Students' experience using data ethically in whatever way they do so creates a context in which they can question the assumptions underlying datafied information environments and ways of knowing and act on the analysis of the rhetorical situation to design and compose their own data stories.

Choosing Among Options for Collecting, Analyzing, and Visualizing Data

The critical communicators model can serve as a heuristic to assist instructors with choosing among the array of options available for collecting, analyzing, and visualizing data as they design assignments for use in their local contexts. As indicated by the incredible variation in critical data storytelling assignments that rhetoric and composition instructions have designed, there is not a one-size-fits-all data storytelling assignment that instructors can turn to. Instead, instructors should adapt sample critical data storytelling assignments or design their own by considering their "classroom context, including such factors as the skills of students and teachers, availability of technology, and curricular goals" (Sorapure 2010, 69). The model helps to ensure that any assignment an instructor designs will provide opportunities to cultivate functional, critical, and rhetorical data literacies, regardless of the specific options that an instructor chooses for a given assignment. The planning questions shown in figure 3.2 further support the design of critical data storytelling assignments. In addition to listing questions that rhetoric and composition instructors inevitably face when designing critical data storytelling assignments, figure 3.2 charts common ways that instructors have chosen to answer these questions in their assignments based on the level of student they are working with and desirable level of complexity. This resource can be used to think through the ethical issues inherent in assignments involving data and to choose among options available for collecting, analyzing, and visualizing data. The answers to these questions are best determined by careful consideration of the local context in which the course will be taught and the instructor's goals for including the assignment.

Because all the available options for collecting, analyzing, and visualizing data can be overwhelming, it is helpful to know what other instructors have used with students for data-based assignments. Scholars in rhetoric and composition have road-tested a number of different tools, sources of data, and genres, some of which show promise as low-bridge, entry-level options that can be used to introduce data storytelling to students. Daniel Anderson (2008) refers to free, consumer-level technologies as "low-bridge technologies" (42), and he argues that using low-bridge technologies in multimedia instruction "ameliorates difficulties that can shut down flow," even as "the challenge of

FIGURE 3.2. Questions to guide critical data storytelling assignment planning.

composing with unfamiliar forms opens pathways to creativity and motivation" (44). Though Anderson does not consider data visualizations, some visualizations also function as "low-bridge" options. Students will already be familiar with the most common types of data visualizations, such as bar graphs and pie charts (Mathivanan and Devi 2021), so these common data

TABLE 3.2. Road-tested options for critical data storytelling assignments

I need to choose…	Other instructors have used…	Examples
Data Visualizations	Graphs	Bar chart, line chart, column chart, pie chart, timeline, map, motion chart, word cloud, network graph, time series analysis, frequency graph
	Lists	Frequency list
	Tables	Pivot table, frequency table, descriptive statistics table
Genres	Interactive	Map, website, motion chart
	Static	Infographic, white paper/backgrounder, usability test report, social media post, public service announcement, speculative design, annual report, slideshow, poster, fact sheet
	Timeline-based	Film, video, timed slideshow, visual podcast, animation
Sources of Data	Government data	Data.gov
	Personal data	Dear Data
	Open data	Pew Research Center Datasets, YouGov, Google Cloud Public Datasets
	AI design tools	DALL-E, Midjourney, Stable Diffusion, Adobe Express/Spark

continued on next page

visualizations, which are also easy to create and work with using accessible programs, can serve as low-bridge data visualizations. Evidence suggests that using low-bridge technologies and visualizations in a critical data storytelling assignment can still provide major benefits to students (D. Anderson 2008; Sorapure 2010). As a result, students' experiences using data in composition and rhetoric courses primarily serve as a catalyst for their critical engagement with data rather than as a step toward mastering the technical elements of data storytelling. Choosing the most accessible and lowest cost options available—in terms of time and money—is therefore preferable in most cases.

Some of the options that have proven useful in rhetoric and composition course contexts are shown in table 3.2. This list is not comprehensive, nor is it intended to be. Instead, it serves as a starting point that identifies some of the options that other writing and rhetoric teachers have used in their assignments. Some of these options are free, some are not, and some offer free trials that might be available to students.

TABLE 3.2—*continued*

I need to choose...	Other instructors have used...	Examples
Tools	AI privacy policy analysis bots	Polisis, Pribot
	AI writing platforms	ChatGPT, Jasper, Anyword, Grammarly, Rytr
	Business intelligence software	Tableau
	Chatbots	ChatGPT, Google Gemini, Bing AI, Claude, YouChat
	Design software	Canva, Piktochart, Visme, Adobe Illustrator
	Global development statistics tool	Gapminder
	Spreadsheet software	Microsoft Excel, Google Sheets, Numbers
	Survey development software	Google Forms, Survey Monkey, Qualtrics
	Text analysis software	Voyant, AntConc, Text Analysis and Visualization Portal (TAPoR)
	Tracking detection tools	Trackography, Panopticlick, Thunderbeam-Lightbeam for Chrome, Disconnect
	Video editing software	Apple iMovie, YouTube, Windows Video Editor, Vimeo Create, Movie Maker Online
	Web mapping platforms	Google Maps, ArcGIS StoryMaps, StoryMapJS

Source: Angela Laflen.

Sample Critical Data Storytelling Assignments

In this section, I share assignment sheets for three road-tested writing assignments that I have used in my writing courses to encourage my students to engage critically with data. These assignments, which focus on playing with data, producing small data, and arguing with data, range in length from three class sessions to an entire four-week course unit. Each of them uses low-bridge technologies and data visualizations, and together they demonstrate the range of ways that data can be included in writing courses. I have also included an example of how a student responded to each assignment.

ASSIGNMENT: PLAYING WITH DATA

DRAFTING DATA VISUALIZATIONS TO PRACTICE INVENTING DATA STORIES

INTRODUCTION

Every data set can be used to tell a variety of data stories. Writers *invent* data stories through the choices they make about what data to visualize and how to visualize them. This assignment asks you to create three different data visualizations using institutional student enrollment data. Think of each data visualization you create as a different way of telling a story about the students who attend our university. You may create any kind of data visualization you want such as the types we talked about in class: a bar graph, pie chart, line graph, etc., and you may use any spreadsheet program you have access to such as Excel, Numbers, or Sheets to create your data visualization. This assignment will help you practice working with data and creating data visualizations and familiarize you with the process writers use to turn data into stories.

LEARNING OUTCOMES
- Select data for use in data visualizations.
- Use a spreadsheet program to create and label data visualizations.
- Recognize how data function rhetorically in multimodal texts.
- Provide feedback to classmates on drafts of their data visualizations.
- Reflect on the strengths and weakness of the data visualizations drafts you created and on the affordances and constraints of data visualizations generally.

READINGS THAT SUPPORT THE ASSIGNMENT

Patrick Danner, "Storytelling With and Around Data" (*Kairos*, 25.1, 2020).

Patrick Danner, "Story/telling with Data as Distributed Activity" (*Technical Communication Quarterly*, 29.2, 2020).

Johanna Drucker, *Graphesis: Visual Forms of Knowledge Production* (Harvard UP, 2014).

Angela Laflen, "Preparing Students to Read and Compose Data Stories in the Fake News Era," *Teaching Critical Reading and Writing in the Era of Fake News* (Peter Lang, 2020).

Mike Markel and Stuart A. Selber, *Technical Communication*, 13th edition. (Bedford/St. Martin's, 2020).

Joanna Wolfe, "Teaching Students to Focus on the Data in Data Visualization" (*Journal of Business and Technical Communication*, 29.3, 2015).

HOW THIS ASSIGNMENT WORKS

This is a three-part assignment that will take place over three class sessions.

Part 1: Invent | Part 2: Draft | Part 3: Review and Reflect

Part 1: Invent

Identify statistically supportable stories in a data set.

> **PURPOSE**: To understand that every data set can be used to tell a variety of stories and practice *inventing* stories based on a data set.
> **AUDIENCE**: Yourself, your classmates, and your instructor
> **FORMAT**: Discussion and exit ticket
> **DETAILS**: In-class activity

During class, we will discuss different types of data visualizations and the process through which data are translated into data visualizations, using examples. We will spend time looking at institutional data provided by the university, which includes student enrollment data, and learning about how to read the data set and use a spreadsheet program such as Excel or Sheets to work with it to create different types of visualizations. Your "exit ticket" reflection activity for this class will be to describe the approach you'd like to take to inventing data stories based on the institutional data set: would you like to invent 3 different stories or a single story visualized in 3 different ways? Describe the stor(ies) you think might be supported by the data set. Finally, brainstorm a list of the different kinds of visualizations that could help you to usefully tell the stor(ies) you want to tell using the data set. Consider the strengths and weaknesses of the visualization options for the particular story you want to tell and rhetorical situation in which you are working.

Part 2: Draft

Create data visualizations.

> **PURPOSE**: To practice selecting data for use in data visualizations and using a spreadsheet program to create and label data visualizations.
> **AUDIENCE**: Your classmates and your instructor
> **FORMAT**: You may choose to create any type of data visualization for this assignment (such as a bar graph, table, column chart, etc.); upload the drafts of your 3 visualizations as a single or separate pdf or jpg file(s), along with a short

description of the visualizations you drafted and which one you think is best and strongest and why, to Canvas.

DETAILS: In-class activity

During this class, you will input or upload the data you want to use to tell the story/stories about student enrollment into a spreadsheet program. Then you will create at least 3 different data displays. Title and label each visualization clearly and correctly. Once you have completed your visualizations, save or copy, download, or take a screen shot of them and submit whatever file type you create to Canvas. In the Canvas assignment submission text box, write a brief description of the visualizations you drafted and discuss which one you think tells the best or strongest story and why.

Part 3: Review and Reflect

Participate in peer review and reflect on your learning.

PURPOSE: To provide feedback to classmates on drafts of your data visualizations and reflect on your understanding of how data function rhetorically in multimodal texts and on the affordances and constraints of data visualizations generally.

AUDIENCE: Your classmates and your instructor

FORMAT: Peer review will take place in class among a small group of students; reflection should be 2–3 paragraphs of written text.

DETAILS: In-class activity

You will have time in class to share your data visualizations with a small group of classmates and to discuss all the drafts. You should provide feedback on the strengths and weaknesses of the different visualizations and offer useful feedback for improvement. Questions to discuss include:

1. What kind of graph or chart is each data display? Is the type of graph or chart used well-suited to the type of data presented?
2. Does each data display have a clear focus?
3. What level of interpretation has the writer used for each of the data displays? Could the level of interpretation be changed to make the focus or presentation of data clearer?
4. Are the data displays clearly titled and labeled? Has the writer displayed percentages or real numbers or something else? How can you tell what type of data is represented? Can you tell how large the sample size was from which data were drawn?
5. What kinds of annotations could the writer add to provide useful context that would help you better understand each data display?

6. Are the data displays designed to make reading and understanding easy? Consider the use of fonts, colors, shapes. Do any parts of the data displays need to be larger or smaller?
7. Do you see any distracting spelling or grammar errors?

You will also have time in class to draft a reflection on the feedback you received and on your understanding of how data function rhetorically in multimodal texts and on the affordances and constraints of data visualizations generally. Some questions to consider in your reflection include:

1. What strengths and weaknesses did your readers identify for each data visualization draft? Were these the same strengths and weaknesses you identified originally?
2. Which of the data visualizations you created do you think tells the best or strongest story? What makes this visualization the best? What changes would you make to this visualization if you were to continue working on it?
3. What were your visualizations able to show clearly and what were they not able to show clearly (perhaps because some information had to be condensed or omitted)?
4. What affordances and constraints can you identify for data visualizations? In other words, what do they communicate well and in what ways are they limited as forms of communication?

STUDENT RESPONSE

I have included the playing with data assignment most often in professional writing courses, using a variety of data sets. The example shown in figure 3.3 was created by a student in an upper-level technical writing course. Working with institutional enrollment data published online by the university, the student created three different data visualizations—map, bar graph, and pie chart—to tell a story about how the university drew students primarily from the local region.

ASSIGNMENT: PRODUCING SMALL DATA

A PERSONAL DATA DOCUMENTARY PROJECT TO PROMOTE SELF-AWARENESS AND CONNECTION WITH OTHERS

INTRODUCTION

In this course, we are focusing on digital literacies and what it means to write in online spaces. You likely already know that as you use the Internet, you leave behind a digital trail. Every person and interaction can be measured, mapped, and counted; these measurements are called data. Online, the data that are collected about you are used to create an online profile that determines what you see online—from advertisements to news stories. You can also use data collected from your life yourself to see patterns that you might not otherwise notice. Noticing these patterns can help you to understand yourself better, relate to others, and become an even better observer of your own life.

For this assignment, you will practice manually gathering, analyzing, and visualizing your own personal data. In doing so, you will face some of the same decisions that data visualization designers encounter in their work and have the opportunity to think about how to make personal data meaningful to an audience of your classmates. You'll also think about how data collected from life can give you insight into yourself and serve as a basis for connecting with others.

LEARNING OUTCOMES

- Practice manually collecting personal data.
- Translate data into a hand-drawn visualization.
- Write a key that explains to readers how to decipher the visualization.
- Reflect on how data can be used to foster self-awareness and connection with others.

READINGS THAT SUPPORT THE ASSIGNMENT

Joanna Drucker, "Humanities Approaches to Graphical Design," (*DHQ: Digital Humanities Quarterly*, 5.1, 2011).

Giorgia Lupi, "How We Can Find Ourselves in Data," https://www.ted.com/talks/giorgia_lupi_how_we_can_find_ourselves_in_data (*TED*, March 2017).

Giorgia Lupi and Stefanie Posavec, *Dear Data* (Princeton Architectural Press, 2016).

Giorgia Lupi and Stefanie Posavec, http://www.dear-data.com/theproject (website, n.d.).

Giorgia Lupi and Stefanie Posavec, *Observe, Collect, Draw! A Visual Journal* (Princeton Architectural Press, 2018).

Jeffrey Shaffer and Andy Kriebel, *Dear Data Two* (website, 2015–2016).

Jill Simpson, "Visualizing Data: A Lived Experience," *Data Visualization in Society* (Amsterdam University Press, 2020).

Jill Simpson, "Visualizing Mental Illness" (openDemocracy, 2017).

Madeleine Sorapure and Austin Fauni, "Teaching Dear Data" (*Kairos*, 25.1, 2020).

HOW THIS ASSIGNMENT WORKS

This is a four-part assignment that will take place over two weeks.

Part 1: Gather | Part 2: Experiment | Part 3: Compose | Part 4: Reflect

FIRST VISUALIZATION

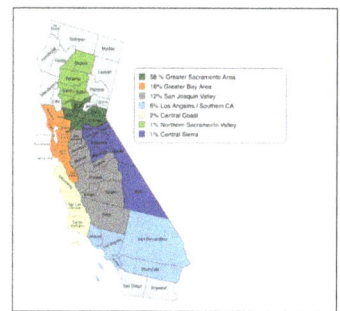

SECOND VISUALIZATION

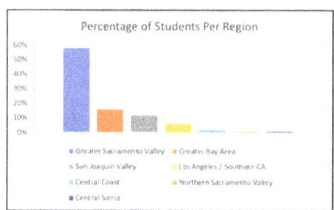

THIRD VISUALIZATION

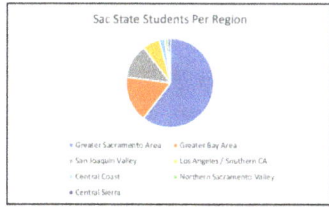

EXCERPT FROM STUDENT REFLECTION

The map is focused less on percentages of students, and more on the location of where the students are from. This type of delivery works well when the audience is interested in visualizing the collective space of the data, rather than just the specific numbers. In this case, we see that Sac State students come from most of California. I included percentages in the legend to add extra context, though this type of graph wouldn't be the ideal type of demonstration for comparison of percentages alone.

Both the bar graph and the pie chart are good for comparing data. In this case, the pie chart is less ideal because the percentage of Sac State students from California is not equal to 100%, making the data in the pie chart look slightly skewed. The pie chart also doesn't contain a guiding percentage (though it could); however, the pie chart can already be difficult to interpret and serves best when minimal information is present. Both charts offer the clearest comparison of data because the higher percentages take up more space. Their downside is the visibility of low-percentage numbers, which reads better within a bar graph. In other words, the bar graph is best when wanting to compare specific percentages. And while this still applies to the bar chart, the pie chart works well when wanting to compare broader ideas like "most" and "least."

FIGURE 3.3. Student response to playing with data assignment from Davis 2024.

Part 1: Gather

Collect personal data.

> PURPOSE: To understand the kinds of questions that can be explored using personal data and how to choose among variables to answer those questions.
> AUDIENCE: Yourself, your classmates, and your instructor
> FORMAT: Discussion and brainstorming activity
> DETAILS: In-class activity

During class, we will discuss what data are and why they matter. We will also talk about the purpose and methods of personal data documentary projects, looking at examples from *Dear Data* and "Visualizing Mental Illness." As a class, we will brainstorm a list of questions that could be explored using personal data and the variables that we could observe to collect data related to those questions.

You will have time to brainstorm 3–5 questions you would be interested in exploring using your own personal data and 3–5 variables for each question that you might observe related to that question. You will decide which question and variable seem most promising to begin with for the project.

Before the next class session: gather your data. You may manually gather data any way you want. Some possible ways to gather data include using paper, your phone's calendar, note-taking apps, notebooks, or taking photos.

Part 2: Experiment

Sketch first ideas.

> PURPOSE: To expand your visual vocabulary by sketching and experimenting with first ideas for a visualization based on your personal data.
> AUDIENCE: Yourself, your classmates, and your instructor
> FORMAT: At least two hand-drawn sketches
> DETAILS: In-class activity

Bring to class the personal data you collected. In class, I will provide drawing materials including colored pencils, pens, markers, and paper that we will use to experiment with a variety of visual communication strategies including color variation, symbol variation, thickness and length, left and right, shape variation, abstract art, nature imagery, astronomical diagrams, and visual metaphors.

You will have time in class to sketch and experiment with first ideas you have for visualizing the personal data you collected. Before starting to visualize, spend some time with your data, searching for patterns and trying to understand it at a deeper level. Often, it is helpful to simplify the data by grouping them into larger categories based on what will best communicate the story. Starting with the patterns you discovered in the data, decide what the main story is for the drawing. Explore ideas by sketching and playfully experimenting with form, color, and materials in a freehand fashion as you decide the visual elements that will represent every part of the data. Think about whether a particular metaphor might help you communicate your ideas to your readers clearly.

Before the next class session: Draw the final picture: After sketching and testing ideas for a visualization in class, create your drawing. Make it as beautiful and understandable as you can.

Part 3: Compose

Translate personal data into a visualization and key.

> PURPOSE: To understand how to translate data into a visualization and key that will help readers to understand the main story.
> AUDIENCE: Yourself, your classmates, and your instructor
> FORMAT: Hand-drawn visualization and key
> DETAILS: In-class activity

You will bring your drawing to class, during which you will be paired with 2–3 other students. Without explaining your drawing, you will share it with your classmates, who will discuss how they interpret the drawing and what they think it means. You will record their discussion to learn what additional information they need in a key to understand the drawing.

You will have time in class to draft a key to explain your drawing.

Part 4: Reflect

Situate the assignment in the context of course readings and future goals.

> PURPOSE: To reflect on your understanding of the readings, your experience of gathering, analyzing, and visualizing personal data, and your intentions for future practices and goals.
> AUDIENCE: Yourself and your instructor
> FORMAT: You can choose the format for your reflection. It can be written or audio or video recorded. You can employ a formal or informal tone.
> DETAILS: Submit through Canvas.

Reflect on the process of collecting your personal data, organizing it, and creating a drawing and key to translate it for yourself, your classmates, and your instructor. Situate your process in the context of relevant readings from the course syllabus and class discussions. What choices did you have to make as you gathered, analyzed, and visualized your personal data? How did you consider your readers' needs and try to connect with them through the choices that you made? How did the process of gathering, analyzing, and visualizing your data help you better understand yourself? If it did not, what kind of data might have provided insight for you? Has your thinking about data changed because of the assignment? How will you think about or use data in the future based on your experiences during this assignment?

STUDENT RESPONSE

I have included the producing small data assignment in my digital writing course. To create the personal data portrait shown in figure 3.4, the student

PERSONAL DATA PORTRAIT

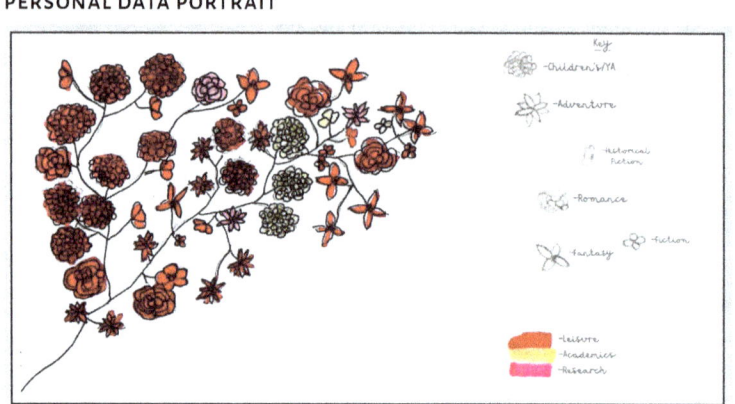

EXCERPT FROM STUDENT REFLECTION

The process amazed me once I started gathering data along the way. Before I started, I wondered what the best way was to describe every book I read, and what context I read them. Simple to break down since I only read them in these three contexts: leisure, academic, and research. The hardest part was to display the genres. At first, I thought it could be like a dish, each one presenting a dessert or meal; however, it didn't go into the full scope of the uniqueness of each genre until I realized the best way to describe my reading habits was through flowers. Books, like flowers, have a unique way of presenting themselves. This led to making flower designs, making the adventure genre have these sharp petals while my children's and young adult books were in this hydrangea shape. Then I chose the colors: red for leisure, pink for research, and yellow for academics, mainly because it was logically representative of flowers in real life, and it would make my data really stand out.

The process made me realize that I read a lot of books in my leisure time than for academic and research purposes (which usually was more for my personal writing practice). I think that reading in the context of my leisure time was a way to let my mind go quiet. Allowing my mind to embrace what was on the pages and words, instead of looking for something—I was truly in the moment. Finding that in my data is what made it so beautiful and unique, like the drawn flowers on the paper. When I look back on my data in the future, I want to expand more on what I read! Perhaps reading more adventure or having a new flower on that tree that would represent sci-fi, petals blocky and stiff.

FIGURE 3.4. Student response to producing small data assignment. Source: Dobbins 2023.

counted the books in her personal collection at home and created a visualization by hand to represent the genre of each book and the reason she had read it, whether for leisure, school, or her own personal research.

ASSIGNMENT: REVISING A FLAWED DATA STORY

AN INFOGRAPHIC ASSIGNMENT TO PRACTICE ETHICAL DATA-BASED ARGUMENTATION

INTRODUCTION

We have discussed the problem of mis- and disinformation circulating online in class. Inaccurate and misleading data often exacerbate—intentionally or not—the problem of mis- and disinformation. This assignment will give you the opportunity to revise a flawed infographic that communicates data in an inaccurate way.

I have provided a variety of flawed infographics that we will discuss in class as examples, and you may choose to use one of these for the assignment. However, you may also choose another flawed infographic to work with. If you do choose another infographic, make sure that:

1. It is static (as opposed to timeline-based or interactive)
2. It has an obvious error in its use of data (such as using fabricated or cherry-picked data) or its design (data displays are improperly labeled, or it violates basic page design principles) rather than an error in statistical calculation that will require advanced knowledge of statistics to correct.
3. You share it with me ahead of time so I can make sure it will work for the assignment.

Your goal in the assignment is to revise the flawed infographic so that it presents an ethical data-based argument for an audience of college students. Since your own rhetorical situation almost certainly differs from the original context in which the infographic was created, you may decide how extensively the flawed infographic needs to be revised to suit the new rhetorical situation (in terms of its argument, use of evidence, data displays, design, language used, etc.). Most importantly, be sure that you correct the problems with data in the original infographic and do not introduce any new data errors during the revision process.

LEARNING OUTCOMES

- Recognize common errors in infographics and how these contribute to the spread of mis- and disinformation.
- Recognize the extent to which infographics are designed and use data to be persuasive.
- Identify credible data using library and Internet research.
- Create accurate graphs using a spreadsheet program.
- Understand the genre conventions for infographics.
- Contextualize data displays in an infographic.
- Provide feedback to classmates on drafts of their infographics.
- Reflect on your work during this assignment and what you learned.

READINGS THAT SUPPORT THE ASSIGNMENT

Aaron Beveridge, "Looking in the Dustbin: Data Janitorial Work, Statistical Reasoning, and Information Rhetorics" (*Computers and Writing Online*, 2015).

danah boyd and Kate Crawford, "Six Provocations for Big Data" (*A Decade in Internet Time: Symposium on the Dynamics of the Internet and Society*, 2011).

Alberto Cairo, *How Charts Lie: Getting Smarter about Visual Information* (W. W. Norton and Company, 2019).

Alyin Caliskan et al., "Semantics Derived Automatically from Language Corpora Contain Human-Like Biases" (*Science* 356, 2017).

Angela Laflen, "Quantitative Literacy in the Composition Classroom: Using Infographics' Assignments to Teach Ethical and Effective Data Use," *Literacy and Pedagogy in an Age of Misinformation and Disinformation* (Parlor Press, 2021).

Peter Lawrence, "The Mismeasurement of Science" (*Current Biology* 17, 2007).

David Lazer et al., "The Parable of Google Flu: Traps in Big Data Analysis" (*Science* 343, 2014).

Cathy O'Neil, *Weapons of Math Destruction* (Crown Press, 2016).

Edward Tufte, *The Visual Display of Quantitative Information* (Graphics, 1983).

Jevin West, "How to Improve the Use of Metrics: Learn from Game Theory" (*Nature* 465, 2014).

Joanna Wolfe, "Rhetorical Numbers: A Case for Quantitative Writing in the Composition Classroom" (*College Composition and Communication*, 61.3, 2010).

WTF Visualizations, https://viz.wtf/ (website, n.d.).

How This Assignment Works

This is a unit-long assignment divided into 4 parts that will take place over 4 weeks.

Part 1: Plan | Part 2: Revise | Part 3: Review | Part 4: Reflect

Part 1: Plan

Analyze a flawed infographic and determine how to revise it.

PURPOSE: To set project goals that demonstrate awareness of your rhetorical situation including the availability of research sources and technological resources.

AUDIENCE: Yourself and your instructor

FORMAT: 2-page rhetorical analysis and revision plan; mockup

DETAILS: Submit to Canvas Assignments on _____

We have examined a range of infographics to draft evaluation criteria for infographics. While some of these infographics share credible information for the purpose of improving readers' decision-making, others use data in a variety of problematic ways we have discussed in class. For this assignment, choose one of the flawed infographics to revise from the examples distributed in class or from your own search for flawed infographics (you may even find one waiting in your social media feed—there are many flawed infographics circulating online).

Draft a 2-page rhetorical analysis and revision plan. Use the rhetorical analysis questions below to guide your analysis.

- Who conducted the study that this data story is based on and why?
- How were the data manipulated from their raw form into the visualization that we see? Are details about the data alteration provided?
- What terms are central to the writer's argument (quantitative and otherwise)? How does the writer define the terms? Who would disagree with the way the terms have been defined, and why? Would the writer's argument change if the definition of the term(s) changed; if so, how?
- Who is the audience for this data story and what are they supposed to do with this information? How do the data, images, and design elements work together to draw the audience into feeling a particular way about the topic of the data story?
- What story does this data story tell? What organizational pattern(s) did the writer use to tell that story? How would using a different organizational pattern change the argument?
- After identifying the flaws in the infographic, develop a revision plan for it. Describe your rhetorical intentions for the document and the evaluation criteria that your revision needs to meet.

Create a mockup for the revised infographic. A *mockup* is a visual outline of a project. It should include the proposed layout, colors, images, fonts, data visualizations, and recurring elements such as headers. Include as much of the textual content as possible. You may create your mockup by hand, on paper, or digitally, using a program like Word, PowerPoint, or Canva.

Part 2: Revise

Revise the flawed infographic so that it presents an ethical data-based argument.

> **PURPOSE**: To revise an infographic that presents an ethical data-based argument.
> **AUDIENCE**: Yourself, your classmates, and your instructor
> **FORMAT**: Infographic
> **DETAILS**: Submit through Canvas on _____

Use whatever program you wish to create a revision of the flawed infographic. Your goal is to revise the flawed infographic so that it presents an ethical data-based argument for an audience of college students. You may decide how extensively to change the argument, use of evidence, data displays, design, language, length, and other elements of the original infographic to suit your rhetorical situation. Most importantly, be sure that you correct the problems with

FIGURE 3.5. Misleading infographic titled "Planned Parenthood Federation of America: Abortions Up... Life-Saving Procedures Down" from GOP Oversight. "Planned Parenthood's Taxpayer Funding—Part 1." YouTube Video, 2:28. September 29, 2015. https://www.youtube.com/watch?v=3V2YRZCh84I&t=2642s.

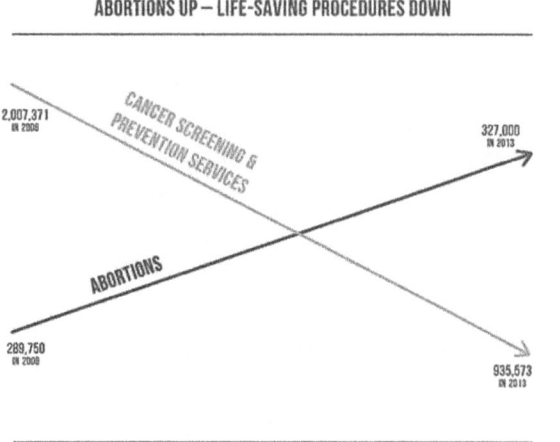

data in the original infographic and do not introduce any new data errors during the revision process.

Part 3: Review

Participate in peer review of drafts.

> **PURPOSE**: To understand how other readers perceive of the meaning and persuasiveness of your infographic.
> **AUDIENCE**: Yourself and your classmates
> **FORMAT**: In-class small-group activity
> **DETAILS**: Bring to class on _____

You will have time in class to review the revised infographic of a small group of classmates. You will use our consolidated evaluation criteria to provide feedback on and assess their infographic, and you'll receive feedback on your own revision.

Part 4: Reflect

> **PURPOSE**: To understand how other readers perceive of the meaning and persuasiveness of your infographic.
> **AUDIENCE**: Yourself and your instructor
> **FORMAT**: 1–2-page written reflection
> **DETAILS**: Submit to Canvas on _____

After you have received peer feedback on your infographic, write a 1–2-page reflection that discusses the process of revising an infographic. Connect your

STUDENT'S REVISED INFOGRAPHIC

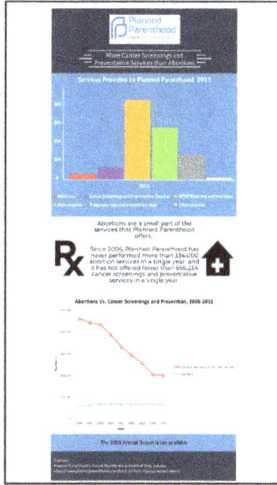

EXCERPT FROM STUDENT REFLECTION

I have completed the infographic revision assignment for this class, and I have learned a lot about the process for creating an infograph. I chose to revise the Planned Parenthood graph we looked at in class. Originally I was just going to correct the graph and add some context and imagery related to it but I extended the revision to change the original argument. So instead of arguing that abortion services are up like the original graph did, I was struck by how more other types of services Planned Parenthood offers than just abortions and that became my argument.

When I first started the infographic project, I was intimidated by trying to read data. However, looking through the data slowly I started to understand what the data was trying to represent. After picking out what data sets to use for my revision I started to brainstorm how I was going to represent the data I had chosen. What really helped me with the process of selecting how I was going to structure my infographic was the examples that you provided us for the reading assignment. I realized that infographics have a lot of leeway when it comes to how they are structured.

With these factors in mind I thought that the most difficult aspect of this project was sewing all the parts of my infographic together. What made this aspect so difficult was conveying my main argument clearly and concisely. I think I made this harder on myself by changing the argument from the original graph. Nevertheless, this project taught me valuable skillsets to practice which can help me in my future career.

FIGURE 3.6. Student response to revising a flawed data story assignment from Williams 2017.

experience back to the larger concepts we are learning about in class such as how mis- and disinformation circulates online, and explain how this assignment informed your understanding of communicating ethically. You may want to respond to some or all of the following questions: Why did you choose to revise the particular infographic that you worked with? What argument did the original infographic present? What changes did you make to the infographic during your revision? What specific choices did you make while creating your revision to support your own argument? What were the affordances and limitations of making an argument in the form of an infographic? What were the affordances and limitations of the programs you used to create your infographic? How does your work on this project connect with other things we have been reading and learning in class?

STUDENT RESPONSE

I have included the revising a flawed infographic assignment most often in professional writing courses, using a variety of different flawed infographics. Figure 3.5 shows a misleading infographic about Planned Parenthood services that a student chose to revise, and figure 3.6 shows the student's revision and an excerpt from their project reflection. This student turned to Planned Parenthood's annual reports for data to use in his revised infographic, but based on the data he found, he decided to revise the argument presented in the infographic. His revised argument is that Planned Parenthood is far more than abortions; abortions are actually a small percentage of the total services the organization offers. He also updated the data used in the infographic by adding data for 2014 and 2015 (the original infographic only included data through 2013). He did retain the dual axis line graph from the original infographic but corrected the y-axis so the numbers are charted more accurately. He also changed the colors used for the line graph, so red indicates the number of cancer screenings, and blue denotes abortions. He removed the arrow at the end of the line graph from the original and added dots for more precision to the line graph. He also created a new data display: a bar graph comparing the numbers for different services offered by Planned Parenthood. This student used the color pallet that Planned Parenthood uses, shades of blue, and he added icons associated with medicine.

Conclusion

Including critical data storytelling assignments in writing courses represents an exciting way to foster students' data and multimodal literacies. These assignments help to equip students with the skills necessary to navigate datafied information environments and engage the data stories they encounter online more critically. Although the possibilities for these assignments can be overwhelming as they are endless and constantly evolving, the resources provided in this chapter are intended to serve as a starting point for instructors new to including data storytelling in their courses and those who wish to try something new.

4
Responding to and Assessing Students' Data Stories

Joe was a freshman in my first-year writing course during the semester I first included a research infographic, and he welcomed the assignment as a change from the traditional academic writing assignments that he did not enjoy. He was also interested in learning about a new genre that he had not written before despite seeing infographics frequently in his daily life. Joe decided to write about college student safety issues in his infographic and chose to include graphs because he associated infographics with the presentation of numeric information and believed graphs to be a way to replace written text. Joe was not the only student to use data in his infographic that semester, or even to struggle in using data, but his submission was memorable to me nonetheless. It helped me recognize how unprepared some of my students were to work with data in their infographics and also how unprepared I was to respond to and assess critical data storytelling assignments in the context of first-year writing. Figure 4.1 shows the introductory section of Joe's infographic, in which he introduced his topic and provided background information.

Although I was used to working with students on presenting data and creating graphs in the context of professional writing courses, I had not previously received student submissions in first-year writing that were

https://doi.org/10.7330/9781646427437.c004

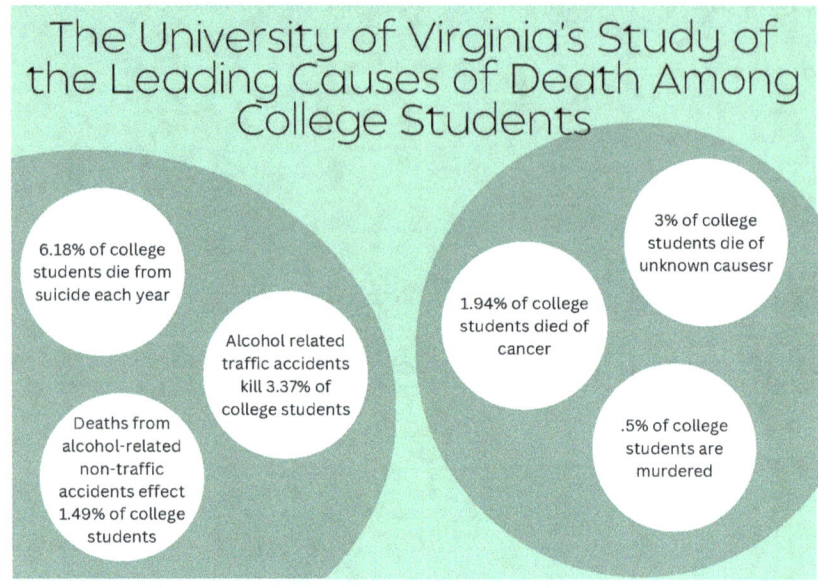

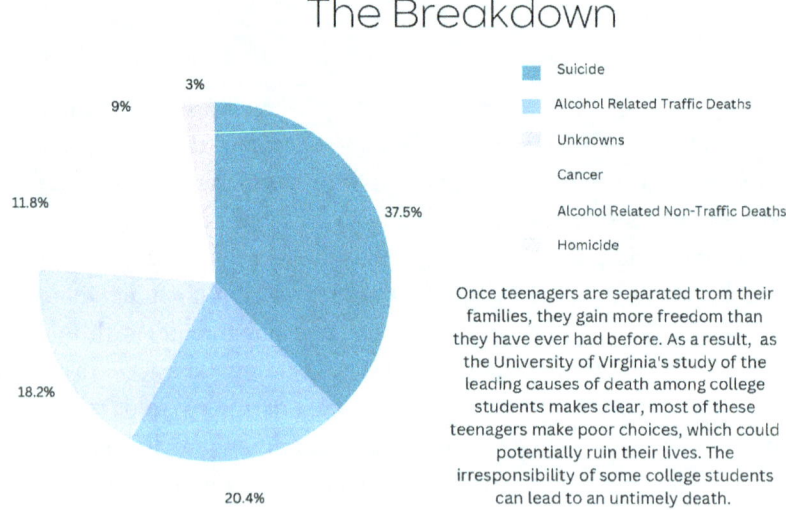

FIGURE 4.1. Student sample of an infographic from Robbins 2015.

comprised almost entirely of data. The lessons I provided in class and the rubric I devised for the assignment—which focused on rhetorical issues such as the infographic's argument, organization, and use of evidence—did not fully account for issues like these. Joe had incorrectly reported the mortality rates listed in one study that included a limited number of college students as percentages of the total population of college students. As a result, his numbers were completely inaccurate; for example, he stated that 6.18 percent of all college students died from suicide, while the study population was limited to 1.6 million students from 157 four-year colleges. Of this population, only 254 students died. Of the 254 students who died, 6.18 percent of these deaths were due to suicide (approximately 16 deaths). The other percentages included in the top section are similarly erroneous. Since Joe largely relied on these numbers to introduce his argument, which he elaborated in the next section as "most college students make poor choices," some of which lead to death, the entire argument was specious. Joe did report the percentages from the report accurately in the second section of his infographic in a pie chart, but since he did not label the pie chart or provide any context for the chart, it is impossible for readers to know what this pie chart meant or how to read it.

Joe's draft illustrates that he was uncertain of not only what the numbers he reported meant but also what information a reader would need to understand and interpret the numbers he presented. In other words, Joe needed to develop critical and rhetorical awareness about how to use data in the context of making an argument in addition to the functional data literacy skills required to understand and report the numbers from his source correctly. Where would Joe have cultivated these abilities prior to the infographic assignment in my course? What course would have given him prior experience composing multimodal data stories? At the time, I suppose I thought that Joe's math courses might have given him experience working with data. In any case, I had not prepared my students to write about data in their infographics because my multimodal pedagogy did not adequately account for data literacy. I did not yet have a sense for what the development of data literacy looked like in students with widely varying backgrounds and skills in using data or how to help students cultivate data literacy beyond preparing them to create readable graphs.

A large part of my learning how to incorporate data storytelling into multimodal composition pedagogy has focused on learning how to respond to and assess students' data stories in ways that foster data literacy growth. Few, if any, rhetoric and composition instructors are currently trained to include critical data literacy in writing instruction. Even as multimodal composition pedagogy becomes more common in writing instruction (Chen 2021; Khadka and Lee 2019b), discussion of data literacy is rarely included in materials intended to prepare instructors for designing or assessing multimodal assignments. Instructors of professional and technical communication do have access to more resources for preparing students to work with data, but these resources often present such a narrow, technical view of data as to imply that quantitative arguments are "arhetorical" (Wolfe 2010, 439). As a result, when it comes to preparing instructors to design and assess data-based assignments in writing courses, support is frequently either nonexistent or goes little further than emphasizing the ability to create and format simple graphs and tables. And though being able to produce readable graphs is an important part of students' functional data literacy, the critical and rhetorical possibilities for communicating with data extend far beyond the ability to create graphs.

My own formal training as a graduate student did not include multimodal pedagogy, let alone data literacy. Similar to Meredith Zoetewey and Julie Staggers's description of early pedagogical experiences with multimodality, my experience as a student was largely limited to assignments asking me to "make a website" (Zoetewey and Staggers 2003, 136). If the site could function, it was a success. This influenced the way I taught multimodal composition to my students as well, with little sense of the larger purpose of multimodal assignments or how to scaffold students' learning through these assignments. In teaching professional writing too, I emphasized functional literacy over rhetorical or critical literacy, focusing instruction on helping students create texts that worked, whether those were websites or graphs. Over time, I sought professional development opportunities to learn to teach multimodal writing more effectively. In particular, after my first experience assigning the research infographic in first-year writing, I began digging into the literature on data literacy. What I learned about the need to cultivate critical data literacy changed the way I taught multimodal composition not only in first-year and digital writing courses but in professional writing as well, as I adopted multiliteracies pedagogy in all my courses. In addition to helping students become users of technologies and producers of data stories, I sought to help them become questioners of data stories, to be able to rhetorically read and use the available means of composing data stories to achieve various communicative purposes and to develop a critical orientation toward the data stories they counter in their daily lives through frequent analysis of discourse and composing in a variety of modalities.

In writing about her experience of learning to assess her students' multimodal projects, Jody Shipka (2009) observes that "having had opportunities to receive and respond to hundreds of these complex multimodal productions over the past nine years has allowed me to remain a student in my classes. And that has been a very good and productive thing" (W345). This has been true of my experience receiving and responding to the data stories my students have created and submitted for my writing courses since 2015 as well. The opportunity to read and respond to these texts has helped me become a better reader of data stories generally and pushed me to develop the pedagogy needed to prepare students to compose data stories and for me to assess them. In conjunction with developing the critical data literacy pedagogy model that I share in this book, I have also systematically studied the impact of this pedagogy on my students' data and multimodal literacies. Shortly after my first promising (but not entirely successful) effort to include the research infographic assignment in first-year writing, I applied for IRB approval to systematically collect student artifacts to help me develop and refine the critical data literacy model that I present in chapters 1–3 of this book. When I moved to a larger and more diverse university on the west coast, I applied for and received IRB approval to continue the study there. In 2020, I received approval to modify the study to collect introductory bio data surveys from student volunteers to learn more about students' backgrounds and previous experiences working with data and to interview volunteers to better understand students' data literacy practices following their completion of a data storytelling assignment in my course. What I have learned about students' development of data literacy from this research has guided the ways I respond to and assess students' work on critical data storytelling assignments.

Chapter 4 shares an instructive approach to responding to and assessing students' data stories aimed at preparing students to both evaluate and compose data stories simultaneously. The chapter opens by defining instructive assessment and contextualizing it within multimodal pedagogy. I report results from my research of students' development of data literacies that indicate the extent to which critical data storytelling assignments require students to engage in a process of trial and error and risk failure as they acquire the new skills necessary to complete these assignments. I discuss specific instructive assessment strategies I use to help students understand criteria for evaluating data stories and how to assess their own and others' work, and I share one example of a data storytelling assignment from a first-year writing class to demonstrate how these strategies can support students in the data literacy learning process. The chapter closes by considering how instructive assessment can be used with different grading schemes and by offering recommendations for using instructive assessment with critical data storytelling assignments.

Assessment as a Teaching and Learning Tool

Data stories present new challenges for writing and rhetoric teachers. Teachers might rightly wonder the extent to which they will be required to become experts in data analysis and data storytelling themselves to respond to and evaluate students' data-based arguments and texts and whether their expertise in alphabetic or even multimodal literacies are sufficient for helping students to compose these texts. How can instructors know when they understand data storytelling well enough to help students and evaluate their work? I have found that I did not need to master data storytelling myself before including these assignments in my courses. Instead, I have made assessing data stories central to my pedagogy. Centering assessment freed me from serving as the sole or primary judge of my students' data stories—a role I was not comfortable playing—and positioned me as a co-learner with students in ways that have made it possible to adapt to changing technologies and conventions. My approach to assessing students' data stories reflects my understanding that, as digital writing specialist Chanon Adsanatham (2012) has expressed it, "learning to evaluate the effectiveness of a text is an important part of being able to write and read well," and as a result "it is a crucial skill students need to acquire to succeed as writers" (153).

Writing assessment leader Brian Huot (2002) has termed this approach to assessment "instructive evaluation," which he defines as evaluation "tied to the act of learning a specific task while participating in a particular literacy event" (170). Instructive evaluation involves students in the process of evaluation, helping them to become aware of what they are working to create and "how well their current drafts match the linguistic and rhetorical targets they have set for themselves, targets that have come from their understanding of the context, audience, purpose and other rhetorical features of a specific piece of writing" (170). Instructive evaluation centers assessment in a class as students are involved in setting the targets they are trying to meet based on their rhetorical purposes for the text and then have multiple opportunities to evaluate how their work in progress meets those targets and refine the targets as needed as they proceed. Since my primary motivation for including data storytelling in my courses is to help students become better readers and communicators of data stories, it is essential that they have opportunities to learn to evaluate the effectiveness of data stories so they can better determine the extent to which data stories that they or others have written accomplish their rhetorical purposes.

The instructive approach to assessment that I use for critical data storytelling assignments reflects a similar emphasis on using assessment to help students learn to read and compose multimodal texts within multimodal pedagogy. Assessment has been a particular point of difficulty since the multimodal turn in writing studies in the 1990s, contributing to the slow uptake of multimodal pedagogy in composition more widely (Reilly and Atkins 2013; Wood 2019, 255). In their study of how instructors implemented multimodal pedagogy in their writing program, for example, Elizabeth A. Murray, Hailey A. Sheets, and Nicole A. Williams found that a significant number of instructors were "uncomfortable assigning multimodal projects specifically because of assessment concerns" (Murray et al. 2009, 67). Madeleine Sorapure (2006) explains that "an uneasiness with assessing something other than a written text" had even led to a common practice of assigning a multimodal project but then basing the assignment grade almost entirely on a textual essay or reflection that accompanies the multimodal text (3). The discomfort that instructors frequently seem to feel about using traditional approaches to assessment to evaluate students' work on multimodal projects indicates the extent to which traditional approaches are not well aligned with the larger values and affordances of multimodal pedagogy.

Traditional approaches to assessment generally separate assessment from the writing process, with assessment largely confined to the end of the writing process when instructors use instructor-generated grading criteria to assign a grade to a final product. Huot (2002) has long emphasized that this separation represents a missed opportunity in composition pedagogy as including assessment throughout the writing process of any text makes assessment a powerful mechanism for helping students learn to evaluate their own and others' writing. In the case of multimodal pedagogy, the separation is particularly problematic as students often come to multimodal composing with little idea of how to evaluate multimodal texts or how their own work will be evaluated. Shane Wood (2019) argues that as a result, "traditional frameworks of assessment ultimately undermine the affordances of multimodal pedagogy because of their emphasis on product singularity, not process-based labor" (260). While multimodal pedagogy emphasizes process and experimentation, traditional frameworks instead reward alignment with particular standards, which has been found to discourage students from experimenting in their writing out of the fear of failure (Reilly and Atkins 2013).

A number of scholars have worked to reimagine how assessment can be used to help students better understand multimodal conventions and genres and how their own work will be evaluated. These approaches vary widely. Shipka (2011) emphasizes the importance of self-assessment and "rhetorical sensitivity" in multimodal evaluation by asking students to compose a "statement of goals and choices" along with their final project, which she used to assess their work (113). Adsanatham (2012) describes the use of student-generated grading criteria to grade multimodal video compositions. Wood (2019) argues that labor-based grading contracts complement "values within multimodal pedagogy: cultivating process, encouraging student agency, embracing risks and failure, emphasizing genre flexibility, embracing multilingualism, and creating rhetorical awareness" (256). Christa Teston, Brittany Previte, and Yanar Hashlamon (2019) recommend placing a dynamic feedback model at the center of multimodal pedagogy to foreground "the ways writing in the world is conditioned by material-discursive factors in constant flux" (205). Despite the differences among these assessment approaches, each seeks to involve students more actively in assessment procedures throughout the process of composing a multimodal text. Rather than serving as a final step in the process of producing a multimodal work, assessment develops or takes place iteratively throughout the entire process of creating a multimodal text as other course activities are organized around assessment.

Instructive Assessment and Critical Data Storytelling Assignments

The same qualities that make instructive assessment well-suited for multimodal assignments also make it well-suited for fostering critical data literacy with data storytelling assignments. Huot (2002) argues that instructive assessment is a particularly powerful tool for literacy learning since it prepares students to both evaluate and compose texts simultaneously (170). Just as students often come to multimodal composing with little understanding of how to evaluate these texts, they also usually come to data storytelling without knowing how to evaluate data stories or how their own work will be evaluated. In part, this is because math instruction does not usually prepare students to evaluate data-based arguments, but rather, to perform mathematical operations—or at least students do not perceive of math courses as having prepared them to evaluate such arguments. This became apparent in the survey and interview data I collected for my study of students' data literacy practices and development. For this part of the study, I collected introductory surveys from 129 students in six different classes taught since 2020, each of which included a critical data storytelling assignment (two sections each of first-year writing, professional writing, and digital writing), followed at the end of the semester by interviews with fifteen participants drawn from the classes. In the introductory surveys, all the students reported previously having completed math coursework, with 71 percent of them having studied statistics, but only 40 percent of students said they were somewhat or strongly comfortable using data. In fact, even my students who did describe themselves as comfortable working with data often followed up in open-ended responses on the survey or during interviews to explain that while they feel comfortable completing mathematical operations, they have no previous experiences evaluating or composing data stories. As one of the students I interviewed, who had an associate degree in math, had completed many math courses and had rated herself as very comfortable using data explained during an interview, "There's a difference in the way we used data in the writing class because we were supposed to put the numbers into context versus just report them. I hadn't done that before in any of my math courses." Consequently, students often used words like "nervous" or "worried" to describe their feelings at the outset of the data storytelling assignment because they were not sure what they are being asked to do or how their work will be evaluated. One of my students who rated herself uncomfortable working with data—a senior majoring in child and adolescent education—recalled that, "when I was first told that we would have to be making a data story for the class it made me really nervous. I was worried that I would fail this assignment since I didn't even know what a data story was."

Because few students have prior experience with critical data storytelling assignments, these assignments require them to "reach beyond their current expertise" in several ways (Reilly and Atkins 2013). From analyzing data I collected during interviews with fifteen student volunteers from a variety of writing classes after they have completed a data storytelling assignment, I discovered that there are four common difficulties students encounter while completing these assignments, listed here in order of most to least common: (1) difficulty making graphs, (2) difficulty using multimodal text editors like Canva, (3) difficulty planning and managing the time involved in creating a data story, and (4) difficulty designing and coordinating the multimodal assets used in their projects. Students further delineated a number of specific difficulties associated with making graphs, including locating data, choosing among graph types, choosing the best interpretive level for data, and labeling graphs. Notably, the difficulties that students described are primarily issues of functional data literacy. Students also identified a range of strategies that

> **BOX 4.1. Students' Difficulties and Recovery Strategies in Their Own Words**
>
> **MAKING GRAPHS**
>
> The most common difficulty students mentioned was making graphs. There were four different ways students mentioned struggling to make graphs.
>
> 1. **LOCATING DATA.** As Grace, a business major in a first-year writing course, explained, "I wish I could have found more information to help me with the second graph, because I was only able to find salary information from like the past two decades; it simply says the number has doubled since 2000. But if you look at the graph that might just make you think it's a linear progression, and I don't know whether it actually was! That's definitely a challenge, like finding year-by-year statistics."
>
> Grace also described how she handled this difficulty by "contextualizing the data you do have and making sure that readers know what might be missing."
>
> 2. **CHOOSING AMONG GRAPH TYPES.** Haley, a childhood and adolescent education major in a professional writing course, recalled how "before I decided on the kind of graph that I wanted to use, I was looking at some of the other features that Canva offers, and I was trying to do use another kind of graph. And then it didn't really look appealing, like it didn't make the positive progression I wanted to show clear. Obviously, when you see my graph now you can see that progression, but in the other graphs I tried using, it was very difficult to see that as someone from the audience just looking at it. So it wasn't doing anything for my infographic and I had to make several different graphs before I was able to make the progression clear."
>
> Haley used a process of trial and error to overcome this difficulty: "Canva has an option where you can see other types of graph formats. So I would click in the different ones. And I was like, 'Oh, this one looks a lot better.' So that's what I ended up doing to choose which graph to use."
>
> 3. **CHOOSING THE BEST INTERPRETIVE LEVEL FOR DATA.** Ajay, a political science major in a first-year writing course, explained, "What didn't work well were my graph designs. I found coordinating the right amount of information in order to clearly show information to be my weak point."
>
> Like Haley, Ajay "overcame this by trial and error, changing one thing and seeing how it looked."
>
> 4. **LABELING GRAPHS.** Katherine, a computer science major in a digital writing course, struggled with determining how detailed to make her labels and annotations: "You had mentioned a couple times that I should put little labels and explain what the X&Y means and stuff like that. Because I was just so comfortable like, 'Yeah, I know what this is because I made the graphs.' So really putting myself in like I guess the audience's shoes was I think harder for me."
>
> She found peer review valuable for better understanding her audience's needs: "During peer review my group mates were saying like, 'Okay, I can kind of see the point of your other graphs, but like, I don't really see the point of the third one.' I could see what they meant and how it didn't make sense without more explanation."
>
> **USING MULTIMODAL TEXT EDITORS**
>
> Students also reported some difficulties using unfamiliar text editors like Canva to create their data stories. According to Jordan, an English major in digital writing, lack of familiarity was at the root of this difficulty: "I don't know how to really finesse the application that allows me to produce graphs and such."

> Jordan turned to Internet resources and instructor-created resources for help: "I remember watching the videos Canva provides to help you make graphs. I think you also included some instructional videos as well and those helped with guidance for that."
>
> **PLANNING AND MANAGING THE TIME INVOLVED IN CREATING A DATA STORY**
> Because students were generally unfamiliar with the process of composing a data story, some of them also struggled to manage their time effectively throughout the assignment. Luke, an English major in a professional writing course, was one of these students: "I underestimated how long this project would take because these were so many parts involved in it.... I was going to try to clean the revision up more because I could see some other ways to make it better, but I ran out of time."
>
> Although Luke did not overcome this difficulty in time for the assignment, he did suggest that he was able to learn from failure to avoid the problem in a future assignment: "You have this vision of how you want everything to go, but then you have to find things that you can actually use from your sources. So that gets a little challenging from a time perspective. But I think it is very doable if you plan for the time to build a good asset collection. And it was pretty cool because I knew to do that for my final project, so it turned out better."
>
> **DESIGNING AND COORDINATING THE MULTIMODAL ASSETS USED IN THE PROJECT**
> Although mentioned least often by students, design issues and coordinating multimodal assets were reported as a difficulty by a few students. Faith, a communications major in a first-year writing course, recalled struggling with design: "I'm not a designer, by any means. I didn't have any trouble putting information in the data story, but I did not know how to design. I had to ask my peers, 'Does this look right? Do these colors match?'"
>
> Faith relied on both peer review and model texts to navigate the design challenges she faced: "Seeing my peer's drafts and looking at models to see other people's ideas helped me out because I was really struggling in the beginning with my first draft. It was kind of not the greatest. I think just seeing some other people's ideas, I was like, 'Okay, I can actually add my own little twist to make it look good.'"

helped them to recover from or move past the difficulties they faced including (1) being transparent about the limitations of data, (2) trial and error, (3) participating in peer review, (4) watching Internet and instructor-created tutorial videos, (5) learning from failure, and (6) utilizing models. Box 4.1 provides more details about the difficulties and recovery strategies that students reported in their interviews.

Students' descriptions of their difficulties with critical data storytelling assignments indicate the extent to which they are learning the expectations for data stories at the same time as they are practicing this new type of communication. As a result, data storytelling projects require trial-and-error and frequent opportunities for peer and instructor feedback as students learn what is involved in composing these texts. However, the fact that students encounter predictable difficulties in completing critical data storytelling

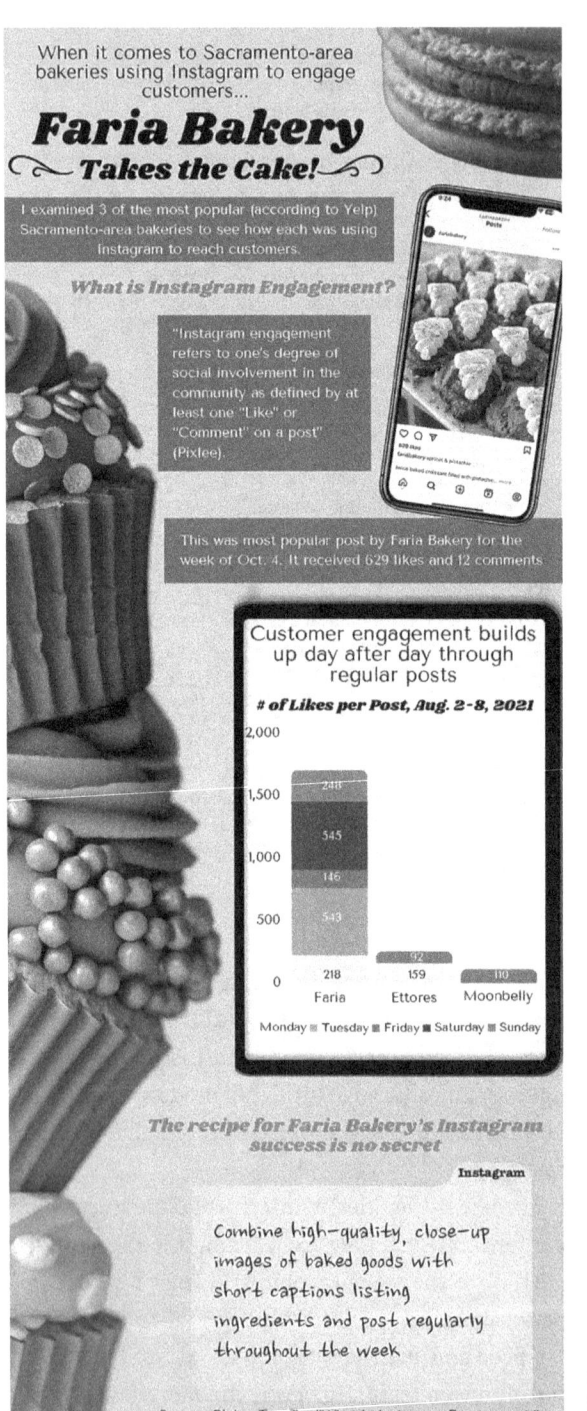

FIGURE 4.2. Sample infographic composed alongside students.

assignments is no reason not to assign these texts. Working through the difficulties they encounter in completing a data storytelling assignment is key to students' development of data and multimodal literacies. The difficulties that my students list—learning to choose appropriate graph types and label those graphs so others can understand them, manipulate programs, revise using reader feedback, manage time, and combine multimodal elements to communicate with readers—are learning outcomes for data storytelling assignments.

To support students' exploration of data storytelling, instructors need to use an assessment framework that does not penalize them for failures that occur during the composing process. Digital writing scholars Colleen A. Reilly and Anthony T. Atkins (2013) explain that "creating digital texts often requires that students learn new skills, which simultaneously requires that they take risks and experience failure." Wood (2019) points out that "assessment must mirror the nature of these assignments in order for the pedagogy to truly embrace failure. The assignment cannot lend itself to failure while the assessment punishes students for their choices" (250). In the case of critical data storytelling assignments, it is important that students have opportunities to work through the planning and drafting process so they can adjust their research question and topic, their design, and their choice of graphs as they proceed. It is also necessary for students to have adequate time to troubleshoot the inevitable issues that arise in locating and working with data and programs. Most importantly, students need to learn how to evaluate data stories so they can determine where their work meets evaluation criteria. In Huot's words, "Before students can learn to revise rhetorically, they need to assess rhetorically" (170).

Learning to Respond to and Assess Data Stories

The literature on multimodal assessment is full of stories of instructors describing themselves as learners of new forms of composing and expression at the same time they are learning to evaluate students' work. Sonya C. Borton and Brian Huot argue that "this feeling of being a learner *and* a teacher—of learning to teach a multimodal class *while recognizing that we lack the* same certitude and sense of expertise that we bring to more conventional courses—not only helps us bridge the gaps between teachers and students . . . , it also helps us to contextualize assessment" (Borton and Huot 2007, 103, italics in original). Learning to respond to and assess my students' data stories has required me to learn to compose these texts alongside them. Although I do not consider myself an expert in data analysis or storytelling, I do complete the data storytelling assignments I set in my courses along with my students, often working one or two steps ahead of them in order to identify technological or other challenges they will shortly encounter (see figure 4.2 for an example). Based on my own experience completing the assignment, I provide additional instruction as needed. Working alongside my students gives me valuable insight into the challenges involved in composing data stories, while allowing me to model the data storytelling composing process for students and have my own texts and drafts to use as examples in class. Other scholars have similarly recommended composing multimodal texts alongside students, especially when an instructor is new to multimodal composition (Borton and Huot 2007; Moran and Herrington 2003). In answer to the question "how do teachers know when they have acquired *sufficient experience composing and understandings of* multimodal texts to help students?" Borton and Huot respond that so long as an instructor is employing instructive assessment, there is no need to delay teaching these assignments: "Working carefully and thoughtfully with students in identifying and articulating the challenges that authors encounter when composing multimodal texts—may help teachers close the gap between their alphabetic and multimodal composing experiences" (103, italics in original). I have found that the same is true for data storytelling as well.

Instructive Assessment Strategies for Critical Data Storytelling Assignments

In my experience of working with students on critical data storytelling assignments, I have noticed that when I ask students for their initial impressions of data stories, they usually are quick to home in on issues of design. I think this is because they feel they have some basis for evaluating the design of the texts. Students may not know whether the use of data or the argument presented is appropriate, but they do know that they prefer certain colors and color palettes and that particular fonts are easier or more difficult to read. However, students' focus on issues of design can mask the fact that they often have few other strategies available to help them assess data stories, which makes reading and composing these texts challenging. One of the best ways I have found to help students learn to assess data stories is by providing opportunities for them to generate, use, and reflect on evaluation criteria that will be used to assess their work.

Including students in the development and use of evaluation criteria is a form of community-based assessment pedagogy, which has a long history in composition studies. As an example, Ed White (1994) has recommended that students participate in developing the grading criteria that they and the instructor would then use to assess and evaluate their work (18–19). Asao Inoue (2005) has similarly argued for including students in the assessment of their writing, explaining that "students must leave my course with the beginnings of a theorizing (or at least an understanding) of their own writing and assessment practices. They can't get this if I assess their writing for them" (210). And Adsanatham (2012) has extended the practice to multimodal assignments, explaining that while this approach offers "many pedagogical advantages for both the learners and the instructor," the most important advantage is "that in the end, students became more informed and critical readers and authors of digital multimodal rhetoric" (168–169). Adsanatham also underscores how important it is to scaffold students' work on evaluation criteria generation assignments since students have often not been included in the assessment process in the past. In this section, I describe scaffolding assignments that I use to provide opportunities for students to generate, use, and reflect on the evaluation criteria that will be used to assess their and others' data stories.

RHETORICAL READING

In chapter 2, I discussed strategies for rhetorical reading of data stories, which have value not only for helping students to become critical readers of data stories but also as scaffolding activities for helping students learn to identify qualities associated with different types of data stories and with strategies for representing data generally. In my courses, I introduce rhetorical reading early in the semester as a method for students to choose among sources of information by identifying whether a source could be useful for them in a given context. When I introduce a data storytelling assignment, I ensure that we spend at least a week rhetorically reading the same kinds of data stories that students will be composing, whether these are infographics, websites, white papers, or something else. As we read the stories, I ask students to use the critical questions for data stories presented in table 2.3 in chapter 2 to guide their reading. Rhetorical reading helps to prepare students with knowledge of the genres and conventions of the kinds of stories they will be composing so they can contribute to generating evaluation criteria.

DRAFTING AND TESTING GRADING CRITERIA

After students have participated in rhetorical reading several data stories like those they will be composing, I ask them to generate evaluation criteria within the context of their assignment. As a class, we spend time reading the assignment description and discussing the assignment's rhetorical purpose. I share sample evaluation criteria that have been published in articles by Teston et al. (2019) and Borton and Huot (2007) and by previous classes of students. I provide the following guidelines for students to use as they draft evaluation criteria: The criteria must clearly define the features of an effective data story, address the data source, alteration, and analysis, consider how data were presented using multiple modes of communication, and be thorough and thoughtful. These guidelines are intended to help students think rhetorically and to demonstrate how students' rhetorical reading of data stories can help them to evaluate the arguments presented in those stories.

Students then test the criteria they have developed by using them to grade a sample data story, and based on this test and peer and instructor feedback that they receive on their criteria, they revise the criteria. Adsanatham (2012) explains that this process "allows students to refine and revise their knowledge about the makeup of an effective text, leading to a more complex understanding about writing conventions and stronger grading criteria" (158). After students have refined their grading criteria, I consolidate them into a single document that eliminates redundancy and groups similar points together under a single heading. The class then has the chance to practice using the consolidated evaluation criteria to grade a sample data story and we make further revisions based on that test.

SETTING RHETORICAL INTENTIONS AND GOALS

After we have created consolidated class evaluation criteria, I ask students to draft a statement articulating the intentions and goals they have for their data storytelling assignment in the context of their rhetorical situation, including the evaluation criteria. In addition to considering the audience, purpose, and genre of their text, they also discuss how they intend to use data to meet the evaluation criteria. I have not used one particular form or genre for the purpose of students setting their intentions and goals. Rather, I usually adapt this part of the assessment process to suit the course and assignment. I have asked students in my professional writing courses, for example, to draft a proposal in which they discuss their intentions and goals. Although the questions I ask students to address vary by course and assignment, core questions include the following:

1. What assignment requirements and evaluation criteria does your text need to meet? How will you meet them? How will you know that you have met the assignment requirements and evaluation criteria?
2. What do you want this piece to accomplish beyond meeting assignment requirements and evaluation criteria?
3. What sources of data have you identified? How are the data you plan to use appropriate to your project's rhetorical situation? How do you plan to visualize data for readers?
4. What specific rhetorical, material, methodological, and technical choices did you make to accomplish the goals you described above?

COLLABORATIVE PEER REVIEW

Students also use the consolidated evaluation criteria to provide peer feedback to their classmates on drafts of their data stories. In addition to receiving feedback from their peers about how their data story could be revised to better meet evaluation criteria, they also find it valuable to see how other students have approached the same assignment and worked to meet the same evaluation criteria. Students conduct peer review using either Eli Review or our course LMS to share drafts with one another and record feedback. Because their feedback is digitally archived, I am also able to review the feedback that students provide and give them "feedback on their feedback" to ensure they understand the evaluation criteria and help them further improve their evaluative skills.

SELF-ASSESSMENT

Self-assessment can be included at any point during the drafting and revising process, and I connect self-assessment to evaluation criteria by specifically asking students to consider the extent to which their writing meets evaluation criteria. I assign a self-assessment after students submit drafts of their project, and this self-assessment—along with peer review—becomes the basis for a revision plan that students draft. I assign self-assessment again at the end of a project when students submit their revised project, in which context the assignment serves as an example of what Kathleen Blake Yancey (1998) terms "reflection-in-presentation," to refer to "the process of

CONTENT AND ORGANIZATION

	COMPLETE	NEEDS REVISION	MISSING
1. The text is suited to its purpose, audience, and context.	☐	☐	☐
2. The text effectively employs the conventions associated with a specific multimodal genre.	☐	☐	☐
3. Multimodal elements work together in the text to make the writer's argument clear and interesting.	☐	☐	☐
4. The text is concise but thorough.	☐	☐	☐
5. Design elements (such as font, colors, sounds, style of images, etc.) are used consistently throughout.	☐	☐	☐

USE OF SOURCES AND DATA

6. Sources and assets used in the text are properly cited or credited.	☐	☐	☐
7. The text provides information about the author of and purpose for data and other evidence.	☐	☐	☐
8. The text provides information about how data presented were cleaned and analyzed.	☐	☐	☐
9. Graphs are easy to read and clearly labeled.	☐	☐	☐

READER EXPERIENCE

10. The text is well designed and easy to read/watch.	☐	☐	☐
11. The text is accessible to users.	☐	☐	☐
12. The text has been proofread for correctness and clarity.	☐	☐	☐

FIGURE 4.3. Sample consolidated evaluation criteria.

articulating the relationships between and among the multiple variable of writing and the writer in a specific context for a specific audience, and the associated texts" (14). For group projects, self-assessment provides a moment to gather feedback on the group's work and team member evaluations. Self-assessment can capture the learning that often takes place through the process of trial and error.

One Example

Although I have outlined in general terms how I use instructive assessment strategies in teaching data storytelling, I include an example here from a data storytelling assignment that I used in a first-year writing course focused on academic literacies (see this chapter's appendix for the assignment description). For their visual argument using data as evidence assignments, students were asked to research an issue of relevance to an audience of college students and then develop a persuasive visual argument that uses data as evidence related to that issue. The topics that students chose for their assignments included social media and college student mental health, the costs of college, professionalizing college athletics, student activism, and so on. They could choose whatever multimodal form they thought would be most effective for their topic and audience. Projects took the form of podcasts, video essays, websites, infographics, and narrated slide shows, among others. The primary goal of this assignment was to encourage students to use rhetorical concepts such as audience awareness and visual rhetoric to work through the process of planning, drafting, and revising a visual argument that meets student-generated evaluation criteria for data stories.

Prior to introducing the assignment, students had practiced rhetorically reading a variety of different types of sources and text throughout the semester, and they had gathered sources of information related to their topic, including scholarly and "wildcard" sources (Singer 2019). I also assigned readings related to composing multimodal texts and data stories drawn from those listed on the assignment sheet. When I announced the assignment, the class looked carefully at the goals for the assignment, discussed the rhetorical purpose of a visual argument using data as evidence, and thought in practical ways about the needs of the audience. Students then used their understanding of this rhetorical situation to develop evaluation criteria for the assignment (see figure 4.3). They used their criteria to evaluate sample data stories of different types, after which students made additional changes to their criteria and submitted them to a class discussion board. I compiled the criteria into a single document.

After the evaluation criteria document was compiled, students drafted a pitch presentation for the assignment, including a discussion about the form they wanted their data story to take and conventions associated with that form, the data they planned to include and how they wanted to incorporate it, what they hoped the revision would achieve, how they planned to combine

SELF-ASSESSMENT OF DATA STORY

Directions: Please fill out the following self-assessment form and submit it to Canvas Assignments. First, please comment on what you've done well and what you still want to improve on during revision. Then, tell me whether you think that the labor you have put into this assignment earns a "complete" or "incomplete" grade.

Note: If you have completely ignored one of the following grading criteria, your paper is likely "incomplete."

Done Well	Grading Criteria	Revision To-Do's
	Criteria #1 Does the text show the writer's awareness of their rhetorical situation and is it suited to the rhetorical situation?	
	Criteria #2 Does the writer clearly define terms that are important to their topic or argument?	
	Criteria #3 Does the text meet or successfully resist the conventions associated with a specific multimodal genre?	
	Criteria #4 Does the text show the writer's awareness of the strengths and limitations of the multimodal elements used?	
	Criteria #5 Is the text concise but thorough?	
	Criteria #6 Are design elements (such as font, colors, sounds, style of images, etc.) used consistently throughout the text to create a unified appearance?	

FIGURE 4.4a. Sample self-assessment form, first page.

modes to achieve their goals, and what programs they planned to use to create the story. Students received peer and instructor feedback on the plans shared during their pitch presentations. They then drafted an initial version of their text focused on their design ideas. These versions took the form of a thumbnail for students creating a static or interactive text and a storyboard/script for those creating a timeline-based text.

Done Well	Grading Criteria	Revision To-Do's
	Criteria #7 Are sources and assets used in the text clearly cited or credited?	
	Criteria #8 Does the text describe the context for data and other evidence in enough detail that readers can determine if the information is credible?	
	Criteria #9 Does the text describe how data were cleaned and analyzed in enough detail that readers can determine if the information is credible?	
	Criteria #10 Are graphs easy to read and clearly labeled?	
	Criteria #11 Is the text accessible to users?	
	Criteria #12 Has the text been proofread for correctness and clarity?	
Based on the above criteria, is your paper "Complete" or "Incomplete"? Explain your reasoning.		

FIGURE 4.4b. Sample self-assessment form, second page.

Students brought laptops to class throughout the course of this assignment to facilitate class workshops on using technology, creating graphs, and page design principles. I met with students one-on-one during class time and outside of class as needed to troubleshoot technical issues and discuss their progress.

Drafts of the visual arguments took the form most appropriate—mockups or wireframes—and students shared these drafts with one another using the

CONTENT AND ORGANIZATION

	COMPLETE	NEEDS REVISION	MISSING
1. The text shows the writer's awareness of their rhetorical situation and is suited to the rhetorical situation.	☐	☐	☐
2. The writer clearly defines terms that are important to their topic or argument.	☐	☐	☐
3. The text meets or successfully resists the conventions associated with a specific multimodal genre.	☐	☐	☐
4. The text shows the writer's awareness of the strengths and limitations of the multimodal elements used.	☐	☐	☐
5. The text is concise but thorough.	☐	☐	☐
6. Design elements (such as font, colors, sounds, style of images, etc.) are used consistently throughout the text to create a unified appearance.	☐	☐	☐

USE OF SOURCES AND DATA

	COMPLETE	NEEDS REVISION	MISSING
7. Sources and assets used in the text are clearly cited or credited.	☐	☐	☐
8. The text describes the context for data and other evidence in enough detail that readers can determine if the information is credible.	☐	☐	☐
9. The text describes how data were cleaned and analyzed in enough detail that readers can determine if the information is credible.	☐	☐	☐
10. Graphs are easy to read and clearly labeled.	☐	☐	☐

READER EXPERIENCE

	COMPLETE	NEEDS REVISION	MISSING
11. The text is accessible to users.	☐	☐	☐
12. The text has been proofread for correctness and clarity.	☐	☐	☐

FIGURE 4.5. Sample revised evaluation criteria.

discussion board tool in our course LMS, Canvas. They tested the student-generated evaluation criteria on their own drafts, using the criteria for peer review and to complete the self-assessment shown in figure 4.4 that led to a revision plan. Based on the peer review, final changes were made to the grading criteria (see figure 4.5).

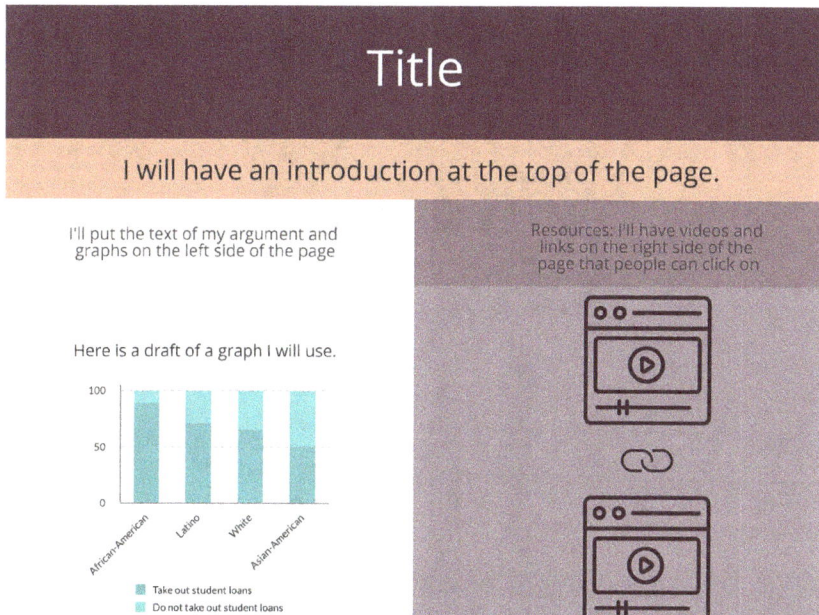

FIGURE 4.6. Sample student thumbnail from Ibarra 2021a.

Students shared their revised drafts with one another during a project showcase. They submitted final project labor logs, reflection videos, and self-assessment cover letters along with their revised drafts to Canvas as well.

STUDENT RESPONSE

Ajay was a first-semester freshman majoring in political science when he completed the visual argument assignment. He had completed algebra, geometry, statistics, precalculus, and calculus in high school. Like the majority of my male students, he described himself as comfortable working with data. Ajay was also very interested in learning more about working with data, since he thought this would be useful in his political science courses. Ajay's experience with the visual argument assignment reflected his unique background, and I do not intend to suggest that he is representative of all students who completed the assignment or of students in general. Instead, I offer the example of this student response to illustrate what the process of "trial and error" can look like as students "reach beyond their current level of expertise" to complete critical data storytelling assignments and how instructive assessment can support students' learning through this process.

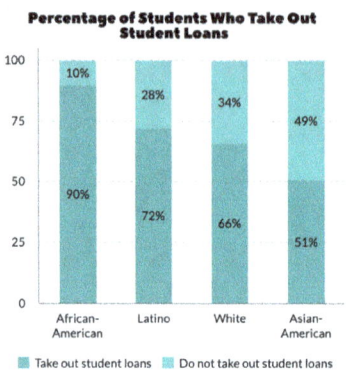

FIGURE 4.7. Sample student mockup of "graphs" page from Ibarra 2021a.

Ajay decided to create a website focused on arguing that college loans contribute to racial inequality, a topic he was personally interested in as a student who had taken out loans to attend college and was working part-time to reduce the need for loans as much as possible. He outlined an ambitious plan for his website in his pitch presentation. He wanted to tackle multiple topics related to the issue of college costs and create a highly interactive website

Responding to and Assessing Students' Data Stories : 133

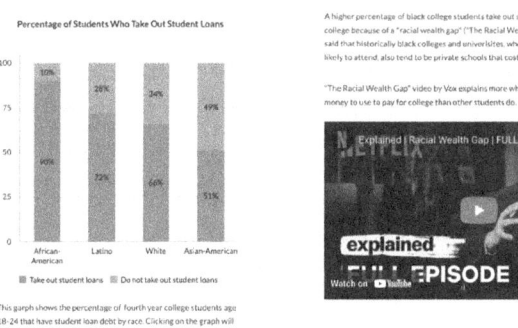

FIGURE 4.8. Sample excerpt from a student website from Ibarra 2021b.

with graphs that users could explore and adjust based on their interests. As he described his initial plans,

> I will go through a story of how college loans impact black students during and after college. I want to have graphics that are interactive, giving more information once a cursor hovers over the top of it. I want to emphasize the different areas of life that are being affected by college loans. The areas that I will cover will be limited internship and research opportunities during college due to need to work, difficulty of paying college loans after college, impact of college debt on long-term financial stability, how students of different races are affected, and political resistance to forgiving student debt.

Ajay created the thumbnail shown in figure 4.6 for his website using Piktochart. His thumbnail outlined his plans for a single web page; he indicated several ways that readers would be able to interact with the content on the page through the inclusion of links and videos to click on that would take them to other sources of information. He drafted one static graph that he wanted to use on the web page as well, a stacked bar chart that he also created using Piktochart.

Based on the feedback Ajay received on his pitch and thumbnail, he reflected that:

My plans aren't very clear. My classmates pointed out how my objective wasn't very clear. I have taken note of this and will remember to work on it when I have a clear head space. As far as my design, I received a few comments about its clarity as well. One comment wanted me to clarify what the graph was about. It was suggested to use different labels, particularly relabeling the percentages with specific numbers, and a more detailed explanation of what those labels meant. In sum, I need to make sure that when I do my website to make sure that my graphs and argument are clear.

Ajay used Google Sites to create the mockup of his website shown in figure 4.7. For the mockup, he created two pages—an introductory page and a page he named "Graphs." The graphs page included little text and only four images: one of which was a slightly revised version of the graph Ajay created for his thumbnail, one photo Ajay copied and pasted from the Internet, and two graphs that Ajay copied from the Internet.

When Ajay assessed his mockup using the student-generated evaluation criteria, he recognized that it did not fulfil several criteria; the "Graphs" page specifically did not meet criteria 5, 6, 7, and 8. Ajay's determination that his mockup did not yet meet the grading criteria for the visual argument assignment was supported by the peer feedback he received as well. His classmates advised Ajay to (1) add linguistic elements to contextualize his argument and the data presented for readers, (2) avoid use of copyrighted found assets on his site, (3) credit information sources clearly, and (4) strengthen visual cohesion by using design elements consistently. Based on this self-assessment and peer feedback, Ajay drafted a revision plan. He outlined the following plans for revision: "Overall, I need to work on my argument. I thought the graphs I used were easy to understand on their own and kind of made the argument clear enough, but my readers say that isn't so. I also need to make my own graphs and use the same colors for them. Then I need to use images that I have permission to use and include citations for them and all of my sources. Finally, I need to make sure that my grammar is correct."

During revision, Ajay added two additional pages to his website, created his own assets to use in the project, and added text to provide instructions to readers and context for the data included (see figure 4.8). In his self-assessment cover letter, Ajay concluded that his revision met the assignment's evaluation criteria. "My original goal of the revision was to make a comprehensive and simple website. I found that the most challenging part to do this were the graphs, as they were difficult to manipulate. With patience I was able to succeed in making a clear and simple website. I spent nearly 20 hours working on the revision. Part of this was due to the learning curve of graphs. Yet overall, it is finished on time and I think it meets the grading standards, which my draft did not."

Ajay's work on the project was a constant process of trial and error, as he learned through experimentation how to perform functional tasks such as creating and labeling graphs and how to develop a rhetorically sound argument that accounted for the genre conventions of websites, the affordances of data and different modes of communication, and the needs of his readers. Even though we had read about and discussed the copyright issues involved in choosing assets for use in data stories and this had come up when we generated evaluation criteria for the assignment as well, Ajay did not fully understand the implications of this issue until he had to choose assets for use in his own project. He also had difficulty determining what information readers would need to understand the graphs he included and the overall argument he wanted to make. Continually assessing his own and his classmates' work rhetorically using the criteria that the class generated for the assignment provided a structure that helped Ajay revise his website rhetorically as well.

Adapting Instructive Assessment for Use with Different Grading Schemes

In addition to helping students learn how to assess their own and others' data stories, including students in the process of developing and using evaluation criteria also provides an opportunity to help them understand how their work will be graded. Regardless of the type of grading scheme that an instructor uses, students need opportunities to practice using the same grading scheme the instructor will use to assign grades. For example, if an instructor will use points to grade the data story, then students should be asked to assign points to their own and others' drafts in order to understand how points will be allocated during grading.

In my writing courses, I normally use labor-based contract grading. This means that I work with students to delineate how their grade in my course will be determined, and rather than assigning points or letters to their formal assignments, I indicate whether an assignment has "met the grading criteria," "needs revision," or is "missing." Students can continue revising formal assignments marked "needs revision" as many times as necessary until the assignment is marked "met the grading criteria" until near the end of the semester when they curate and submit a digital portfolio of their work throughout the class. To help my students understand how their work will

> **BOX 4.2. Recommendations for Instructive Assessment of Data Stories**
>
> - Spell out the rhetorical purpose for including a data-storytelling assignment in your course.
> - Work alongside students to complete data-storytelling assignments.
> - Introduce rhetorical reading of data stories early in the semester and give students practice reading these texts throughout the semester.
> - Involve students in generating and testing evaluation criteria for data stories.
> - Use class time and individual meetings with students to troubleshoot technical issues and work on their data stories.
> - Set deadlines for each part of the assignment and help students practice assessing their own and others' work in progress using evaluation criteria.
> - Provide regular opportunities for students to reflect on evaluation criteria and the data-storytelling composing process and to self-assess their learning and how well their work in progress meets evaluation criteria.
> - Familiarize students with the grading scheme that will be used grade their assignment and encourage them to practice using the grading scheme to assess their own and others' work in progress.

be graded, I ask them to determine whether their own and their classmates' initial and revised drafts have met the grading criteria or still need revision when they complete peer review and self-assessment assignments. Although it might seem that providing unlimited opportunities for students to revise formal assignments to meet evaluation criteria would add unduly to the time and labor involved in grading, I have found that when my students are involved in generating, using, and reflecting on the evaluation criteria that I use to assess their work, most of them are able to meet these criteria when they submit their work for grading. An additional revision is usually enough to help those who initially receive a score of "needs revision" to meet the evaluation criteria. In my experience, it is usually one or two students at most who require multiple revisions of an assignment to meet the grading criteria.

Although I believe that labor-based contract grading is particularly well-suited to the affordances of multimodal composing and data storytelling, an argument Wood (2019) makes in more detail in "Multimodal Pedagogy and Multimodal Assessment," it is still possible to use instructive assessment with other types of grading schemes, whether these are point based, use percentages, or something else. Instructive assessment can even be used when instructors do not have the freedom to design their own grading heuristics and procedures. In some program or course contexts, instructors will be required to use particular rubrics for grading purposes, as Murray et al. (2009) have described. In this case, students can still be asked to develop evaluation criteria for data stories that the instructor can use to provide formative feedback throughout the project, and students should still have the opportunity to practice using the mandated rubric to assess their own and others' writing in order to better understand the criteria that will be used to assess their work.

Conclusion

Assessment need not be a barrier to including critical data storytelling assignments in writing courses. Instructors do not have to master data analytics and data storytelling to usefully respond to and assess students' work but can instead draw on the power of instructive assessment to help students assess their own and others' work. In fact, when students have the opportunity to generate, use, and reflect on the evaluation criteria that will be used to assess their work, assessment can be a valuable mechanism for helping students improve their functional, critical, and rhetorical data literacies. I have offered examples of a range of ways that instructors can include instructive assessment in critical data storytelling assignments in this chapter (see box 4.2). Most of these already constitute common pedagogical practices in writing classes, including the use of student-generated evaluation criteria, peer review, and self-assessment assignments. Additionally, I cannot overemphasize the value of completing data storytelling assignments alongside students. Working through data storytelling assignments along with my students has helped me to understand the challenges students face in completing these projects, better design and scaffold data storytelling assignments, and respond to and assess students' work more confidently—and empathetically.

Appendix

ASSIGNMENT: ARGUING WITH DATA

DEVELOPING A VISUAL ARGUMENT USING DATA AS EVIDENCE

INTRODUCTION

We have been learning about digital literacies and what it means to write multimodal texts. Increasingly, composing multimodal texts requires writers to use data because more data are available to work with today and data are often used to guide decision-making. Because data do not speak for themselves, they must be analyzed and interpreted to make sense. It has also become relatively easy to make visual arguments using data as evidence because design programs like Canva and Piktochart make it simple for people to include data displays in multimodal texts. However, there are a lot of bad data circulating online today because people introduce errors (accidentally or deliberately) when analyzing or interpreting them. This project will help you practice "making data speak" by creating data displays accompanied by text and other visuals to make a persuasive argument for a specific audience.

For this assignment, you will research a local issue of relevance to an audience of college students and then develop a persuasive visual argument that uses data as evidence related to that issue. Your goal is to design a visual argument that will be persuasive in the context of your rhetorical situation. So choose a format for your project that will help you reach your audience, whether that is a static text like an infographic, a linear text like a public service announcement video, or an interactive text like a storymap. Regardless of the format, choose credible data to use as evidence that your readers will accept as useful and persuasive, and design data displays that your audience will be able to read and understand.

LEARNING OUTCOMES
- Set project goals that demonstrate awareness of your rhetorical situation.
- Choose credible sources of information, including data, related to an issue of local relevance.
- Use appropriate planning tools (storyboard, mockup, wireframe) to plan the layout and content for the visual argument.
- Work through the process of planning, drafting, and revising a visual argument.
- Provide useful feedback to classmates on drafts of their visual argument.
- Reflect on your understanding of the relationship between digital literacy, multimodal composing, and using data as persuasive evidence, taking into consideration your experiences during the assignment.

READINGS THAT SUPPORT THE ASSIGNMENT
Cheryl E. Ball et al. *Writer/Designer: A Guide to Making Multimodal Projects*, 3rd edition (Bedford/St. Martin's, 2022).

Jenae Cohn, "Understanding Visual Rhetoric," *Writing Spaces*, vol. 3 (Parlor Press, 2020).

Melanie Gagich, "An Introduction to and Strategies for Multimodal Composing," *Writing Spaces*, vol. 3 (Parlor Press, 2020).

Angela Laflen, "Learning to 'Speak Data': Data Literacy and Multimodal Composition Pedagogy." *Multimodal Composition: Faculty Development Programs and Institutional Change* (Routledge UP, 2022).

Angela Laflen, "Strategies for Analyzing and Composing Data Stories," *Writing Spaces*, vol. 5 (Parlor Press, 2023).

Carlos Salinas, "Technical Rhetoricians and the Art of Configuring Images," (*Technical Communication Quarterly*, 11, 2002).

Madeleine Sorapure, "Information Visualization, Web 2.0, and the Teaching of Writing" (*Computers and Composition*, 27.1, 2010).

Joanna Wolfe, "Rhetorical Numbers: A Case for Quantitative Writing in the Composition Classroom" (*College Composition and Communication*, 61.3, 2010).

HOW THIS ASSIGNMENT WORKS

This is a unit-long project divided into seven parts that will take place over six weeks. We will draft evaluation criteria that will be used to assess the assignment together as a class.

Part 1: Evaluation Criteria | Part 2: Pitch | Part 3: Design | Part 4: Draft | Part 5: Review | Part 6: Revise | Part 7: Assess

Part 1: Evaluation Criteria

Generate and test evaluation criteria for data stories.

PURPOSE: To generate and test evaluation criteria that demonstrate your rhetorical understanding of data storytelling.

AUDIENCE: Yourself, your classmates, and your instructor

FORMAT: Discussion board posts and replies

DETAILS: Submit Part 1 through Canvas on _____; submit Part 2 through Canvas on _____

PART 1. Develop the criteria that should be used to grade the sample data stories you have read/watched this week. These criteria must be clear and specific, and they must demonstrate your rhetorical understanding of data storytelling. Before developing them, please review the models I've provided. Your criteria must address the following categories:

- Data Source
- Data Alteration
- Data Analysis
- Data Presentation

For each category, specify what needs to be met. Make a list of at least 3 things. For instance, under data source, what are some of the things you would look for? Under data alteration, what might be some important things we need to "take bearings on" to determine how the data was altered? Please avoid vague statements such as the data source is credible; the images look nice, etc. Specify what you mean by credible and nice. Do you mean that the data source is properly cited, or that it was created by an author that the reader is likely to believe is trustworthy?

Post your finished work to our course discussion board and provide useful feedback (i.e., feedback that describes, evaluates, and suggests) on at least 3 of your classmates' criteria. Depending on the kind of feedback you receive on your criteria, you may need to further revise them. If revision is necessary, revise and re-post your work by the date on the course calendar.

PART 2. Choose one of the sample data stories shared in class and grade it using the criteria you developed. In the Part 2 discussion board, post the grade that you think the sample deserves. Then use your criteria to justify why it should receive that grade. Also, explain where the sample falls short and what it does well.

Part 2: Pitch

Describe plans for meeting rhetorical situation and evaluation criteria.

> PURPOSE: To set project goals that demonstrate awareness of your rhetorical situation including the availability of research sources and technological resources.
> AUDIENCE: Yourself and your instructor
> FORMAT: Slideshow outlining project goals and explaining how the format and content of your idea might come together in the final project.
> DETAILS: Presentation in class on _____

In class we have been talking about developing visual arguments, using data as evidence, and the arguing with data assignment you will complete. You have had time to brainstorm ideas and approaches you might use. We have also spent time talking about how to evaluate data stories and generated criteria to use in evaluating data stories. As you begin to formalize your plans for the project, it will be helpful to receive feedback on your ideas. In class on _____ you will share a 3–5-minute pitch that explains how the content and form of your idea might come together in the final project. Your goal is to convince your classmates and instructor that you understand the issue you have chosen to work with and have a plan for approaching it and can successfully accomplish the project you are pitching. Create a slideshow using PowerPoint, Google Slides, or a similar program to share your pitch with the class. Be sure to address the following in your pitch:

1. What is the rhetorical situation for your visual argument?
2. What is your topic?

3. What genre will you use for your project?
4. How will you design your project in relation to your topic?
5. What assignment requirements and evaluation criteria does your text need to meet? How will you meet them? How will you know that you have met the assignment requirements and evaluation criteria?
6. What do you want this piece to accomplish beyond meeting assignment requirements and evaluation criteria?
7. What sources of data have you identified? How is the data you plan to use appropriate to your project's rhetorical situation? How do you plan to visualize data for readers?
8. What specific rhetorical, material, methodological, and technical choices did you make in order to accomplish the goals you described above?
9. What else do you need to know to complete your project?

Part 3: Design

Lay out an initial version of the text.

> **PURPOSE**: To work through the complexities of arranging content
> **AUDIENCE**: Yourself, your classmates, and your instructor
> **FORMAT**: For static and interactive texts: a thumbnail; for timeline-based texts: a storyboard/script
> **DETAILS**: Bring to class on _____

Bring to class the initial version of your text, which will take the form of a thumbnail if you are creating a static or interactive text and a storyboard/script if you are creating a timeline-based text. A *thumbnail* is a small, quickly sketched design idea. A *storyboard* is a sequence of drawings that presents the movement, spatial arrangement, and soundtracks of objects of characters in shots, screens, or scenes, and a *script* is a draft that allows you to specify what will actually be said or shown in a timeline-based text. You may create your initial version by hand or digitally. Aim to represent all of the content you plan to include in your text in the initial version so you can work through the complexities of arranging that content. But you do not need to create a highly polished thumbnail or storyboard/script. Simply sketching your thumbnail or storyboard is fine for this stage of the project. You will have the chance to share your initial version with small groups of your classmates and the instructor and to receive feedback on this early version.

Part 4: Draft

Compose a first draft.

> **PURPOSE**: To compose a first draft that brings the content and format of the project together

> **AUDIENCE**: Yourself, your classmates, and your instructor
> **FORMAT**: For static and interactive texts: a mock-up; for timeline-based texts: a rough cut
> **DETAILS**: Bring to class on _____

Bring to class a first draft of your project for testing with classmates. The type of draft you produce will depend on the type of project you are creating. For static and interactive texts, you should draft a mock-up. For timeline-based projects, you should draft a rough cut. Do include drafts of the data visualizations you plan to include in your project.

A *mockup* is a visual outline of a project. It should include the proposed layout, colors, images, fonts, data visualizations, and recurring elements such as headers. Include as much of the textual content as possible. You may create your mockup by hand, on paper, or digitally, using a program like Word, PowerPoint, or Canva. A *rough cut* represents the first attempt at building a timeline-based project by putting the pieces into sequence. Your rough cut may be missing important elements such as background soundtracks, navigation, etc.

Part 5: Review

Participate in peer review and self-assessment of drafts.

> **PURPOSE**: To understand how other readers perceive of the meaning and persuasiveness of your visual argument
> **AUDIENCE**: Yourself and your classmates
> **FORMAT**: In-class small-group activity
> **DETAILS**: Bring to class on _____

You will bring your mockup or rough cut to class on _____. You will have time in class to use our consolidated evaluation criteria to assess your draft. During the remainder of class, you will have a chance to review the drafts of a small group of classmates using the consolidated evaluation criteria as a guide and receive their feedback on your draft.

For homework, draft a revision plan for your text based on your own self-assessment and the peer feedback you receive.

Part 6: Revise

Strengthen and polish the visual argument.

> **PURPOSE**: To revise a persuasive visual argument that uses credible data as evidence
> **AUDIENCE**: Yourself, your classmates, and your instructor

FORMAT: You may use any format for your project that will help you reach your audience

DETAILS: Submit through Canvas on _____

Based on the feedback you received on your draft as well as your own plans for the project, finish developing your persuasive visual argument that uses data as evidence. Be sure to cite the research sources you used for the project in some way—whether this means by using hyperlinks, adding a references list to the project, embedding your text on a page that also lists references, or something else. Also, give proper credit to the creators of any multimodal assets you used for the project that you did not create yourself.

Part 7: Assess

Critically examine your work.

> **PURPOSE**: To self-assess your visual argument and your work throughout the assignment in the context of course readings, the goals you set for yourself in your pitch, and your future plans
>
> **AUDIENCE**: Yourself and your instructor
>
> **FORMAT**: Write a cover letter for your visual argument addressed to the instructor
>
> **DETAILS**: Submit with your visual argument revision through Canvas

Along with your revised visual argument, you should submit a cover letter addressed to your instructor that reflects on your experience composing a visual argument using data as evidence and assesses your argument and your work on the assignment. Base your assessment on course readings and discussions, the goals and intentions you originally set for your project in your project pitch, and the consolidated evaluation criteria that will be used to grade your assignment. Consider the strengths of your argument and work process as well as areas that could be improved. How do you understand the relationship between this assignment and your future plans and goals? Does your text meet the evaluation criteria? Should your text be graded "meets grading criteria" or "needs revision" and why?

5
Using Data as a Tool to Improve Teaching and Learning

In the early 2000s, I began using a learning management system (LMS) to provide my response to student writing in all my courses, whether they were face-to-face, fully online, or hybrid. I was motivated to move response online primarily because this assuaged my concerns about losing student work and whether students could read my poor handwriting. Over time, I came to appreciate the digital archive of student work and instructor feedback that both my students and I could access when we exchanged their papers online. I also valued the convenience of being able to collect and return work on days and at times when class was not scheduled to meet. Though I found online response to be convenient and valuable overall, one question plagued me: were students actually looking at the feedback I returned to them online? This, of course, is a question that most writing instructors wonder about from time to time, and it is not unique to online response. However, when I returned hard-copy papers to students in class, I could see them riffling through their papers on the way to finding their grade on the assignment at the end. I could not be sure that the students read the marginal or summary comments closely—or even at all—but I knew that they had at least seen that there were comments on the paper. However, in the course LMS, the default setting was to post students' grades on an assignment using a gradebook tool and then to attach a

https://doi.org/10.7330/9781646427437.c005

"feedback file" or insert marginal comments separate from the grade. I wondered how many students actually looked at those feedback files or marginal comments—or even knew they existed—when they could see their grades separately.

During this time, I was learning more about LMSs and the various tools they offered, including the site statistics tool that passively captures a wide variety of information about students. I learned that the site statistics tool recorded whether students opened the feedback files I was attaching with my feedback on their writing. So I decided to conduct a test. I had been using the course gradebook to return grades. The following semester, I did not use the course gradebook. I typed students' grades in at the end of their feedback files, similar to what I had done when handwriting feedback on student papers with the grades written on the last page of an assignment. Then I compared the results. Not surprisingly, they indicated that students did not access feedback files as often when they could see their grade in the gradebook. More surprisingly, I also saw that a percentage of students were not opening feedback files in either case. The results of this test were significant enough that I then developed a full-fledged research study with a colleague that eventually included data for sixteen different classes of students, eight that used the course gradebook and eight that did not (Laflen and Smith 2017). The full study confirmed and expanded the results of my initial test. Even before I conducted the full study, though, my original test gave me a pretty solid basis for making decisions about how to use the LMS gradebook tool in my courses.

In fact, what I learned from that test motivated me to change my entire response approach to ensure that all my students saw and knew how to use the feedback I wrote for them. I eventually adopted the instructive approach to assessment that I described in chapter 4 so that assessment is centered in my courses and not merely something that happens at the end of the writing process when students submit their work for a grade. This not only meant working with students to develop evaluation criteria but also prioritizing my own feedback on their drafts earlier in the process and giving students time in class to look at and respond in writing to the feedback I provided on their work. I met with them more frequently to provide in-person feedback, and eventually I moved to labor-based contract grading.

Although I had previously been interested in instructive approaches to assessment, I was not motivated to make sweeping changes to my response practices until I had the hard data from my own classes showing me that my students were less likely to read feedback posted alongside grades in the course LMS and that some students were not looking at feedback provided on finished work. In this case, data helped make the limitations of a traditional approach to evaluating student writing so visible that the need for change was clear.

This example represents the potential for using classroom data to answer questions that emerge during teaching and lead to changes that benefit students. Significantly, my decision to conduct the test was not motivated by some top-down administrative imperative to use data to improve teaching and learning and, at least in its early phase, did not require the use of sophisticated or complex data-analysis tools. After I finished grading, it took a few hours to import the site statistics data from the LMS into Excel and clean it up so I could compare data from the two semesters. At that point, I just looked at the percentage of students in each class who opened feedback files, observing that a lower percentage of students in the course that used the gradebook tool opened the feedback files. Only later, during the full-scale study, did my colleague and I run statistical tests on the data to determine if the differences between the classes were "statistically significant."

Most of this book has focused on preparing students to navigate the changes that big data has brought to information and ways of knowing. The same forces of datification that have transformed the information environment in which our students read, research, and write have also transformed the environment in which we teach. Navigating a datafied teaching environment requires teachers to make more complex decisions about their teaching practices and how to promote student learning than ever before. Many of these decisions stem from constantly evolving classroom issues caused by technology. Educational technologists Donatella Persico and Francesca Pozzi explain that "the fast development of technological tools and the evolution of their affordances is making it very difficult for individual educators to be always updated on the potential of technology and its strategic use in education" (232). However, even teachers who avoid using or limit their use of technology must still make numerous decisions about how to help students whose "needs are changing, because their learning habits and strategies change due to pervasiveness of digital tools in our society" (Persico and Pozzi 2015, 232).

As one example, consider the choices that writing instructors face about how to provide formative feedback to students. New response modalities (i.e., audiovisual feedback) and response tools and technologies (e.g., LMS feedback tools, automated writing assistants, and commenting tools in software programs) offer numerous ways for writing instructors to provide formative feedback on student writing. And instructors' choices do matter. Previous research has found that different response modalities (i.e., electronic text and audiovisual feedback) affect the feedback that instructors provide as well as student perceptions of it (Cavanaugh and Song 2014; Cunningham 2019; Ice et al. 2010; Orlando 2016; Turner and West 2013; Warnock 2008). However, most often, the programs used to facilitate instructor response only provide instructions on how to make the technology work without explaining the pros and cons of using various options for response. It takes time for full-scale research studies to be conducted and for scholars to arrive at consensus about best practices. In the meantime, technology continues to change, and teachers face a new set of choices.

In addition to decisions about how to use technology in the classroom and support students whose learning needs have been shaped by technology, teachers also must decide how to respond to arguments about teaching and learning that claim authority based on being data-driven and evidence-based. For example, many administrators have come to use what is referred to as a DFW rate, a rate which refers to the percentage of grades of D or F or of students withdrawing from the course entirely, as a proxy measure of teaching effectiveness. Teachers with a high DFW rate (usually greater than 20–30 percent depending on the institution) for their courses are determined to be ineffective teachers, with implications for that teacher's tenure and promotion review or continuing employment (Flaherty 2018). As a result of administrators choosing to use DFW rates to measure teaching effectiveness, teachers are increasingly encouraged or even required to adopt practices intended to lower DFW rates in their courses—even when there are few data to indicate that the practices will make a difference to DFW rates, let alone student learning. As an example, Susan Lang and Craig Baehr have described receiving a letter from their institutional research office identifying several sections of first-year writing with a high DFW rate and recommending strategies that might lower the rate (Lang and Baehr 2012, 186). However, in their capacity as writing program administrators, Lang and Baehr knew that most of the recommended strategies were already practiced in the writing program and therefore could not be at the root of the high DFW rates for those courses (186).

Developing skills as rhetorical readers and critical communicators can help teachers to navigate the increasingly complex choices they face about how to use technology, support students whose learning habits and strategies have been shaped by technology, and respond to data-based arguments about teaching and learning. Although data are not suitable for answering every question that arises, Laura Aull (2021) has described how data can function as a "mirror" to hold up to current pedagogical practices to see how to improve them and to ensure that they are equitable. She explains how data analysis can "expose patterns that teachers and students are already responding to that otherwise remain beneath our discursive consciousness (Barlow; Lancaster Stance and Reader Positioning)" (86). Aull also argues that by exposing these patterns and making classroom practices more transparent, data analysis "can reflect back what we value and accordingly help us question it" (85).

My experience testing the use of the gradebook tool in my course LMS illustrates how data can function as a mirror of teaching practices. Even before I collected data about how often students opened feedback files, my students were already responding to the different feedback configurations facilitated by the LMS. I was also to some extent aware of their response, which is why I felt concerned that they might not be opening the feedback files in the first place. Working through the data storytelling composing process by collecting and analyzing data from site statistics made visible the pattern in students' behavior that I had only vaguely perceived before. It also prompted me to question and ultimately change my response practices to better align with my pedagogical values.

Lang and Baehr similarly describe using data to get to the root of the high DFW rates for some of the classes in their writing program. Lang and Baehr used rhetorical reading strategies to look outside of the DFW report they were presented with by their administration to construct a more complete rhetorical situation for the DFW data. Examining the assignments, grades, and commentary for students who failed or withdrew compared to students who completed the courses helped them to see a pattern of DFW students submitting significantly fewer assignments and submitting more late assignments than other students. Both groups of students received similar grades on the assignments that they did submit on time. Furthermore, Lang and Baehr could see that students began to struggle to submit assignments during the third through sixth weeks of the semester (189). Discovering these patterns helped Lang and Baehr to push back against the recommendations by the office of institutional research and prompted reflection on how the writing program was supporting students and teachers. Lang and Baehr revised their teacher training practices to emphasize working with students on their time-management skills and employed other strategies to help students understand the importance of submitting work on time (189–190).

Although in these examples different kinds of data were collected and analyzed using very different techniques to answer questions that arose in the context of specific classroom and institutional contexts, in both cases data helped to cut through complex decisions and arguments about teaching. These data brought to consciousness patterns that teachers and students were already responding to and in doing so made critical reflection and pedagogical change more productive and better focused.

In this chapter, I explore how rhetoric and composition teachers can use data for teaching purposes. The chapter begins by considering calls from within the field of rhetoric and composition for instructors to cultivate data literacy and the kind of data literacy described as being necessary for rhetoric and composition teachers. I also examine some of the concerns that surround data use, in particular those that focus on the use of data to monitor students and teachers. Next, I discuss how the concept of data literacy for teachers (DLFT) can be adapted by college instructors to cultivate the rhetorical reading and critical communication skills that help teachers to use data as a tool for teaching and learning. Then I share resources that instructors can use to cultivate their own data literacy and design data inquiries, and I present an extended example of a classroom data inquiry. The chapter closes with recommendations for using data in teaching contexts.

Context for Writing Teachers' Use of Data

Since the early 2000s, rhetoric and composition scholars have called on writing teachers to use available data so they are prepared to "respond critically to reports of research that will be used to decide how they will teach, what they will teach and to what ends" (Anson 2008, 28). For example, Joe Moxley (2008) urged writing teachers to enact what he calls "datagogies" in the writing classroom (182), which refers to "a process of making informed, repeated curriculum changes in response to real-time data and dialogs among teachers, teachers [sic], and administrators" (Dixon and Moxley 2013, 242). Although Moxley (2008) acknowledged that doing so would require teachers to "broaden the nature of our work, our conception of what constitutes texts and how to prepare our students as citizens and critical thinkers," he cautioned that "unless rhetoricians become more involved in designing datagogies, they will lose their voices and authority as teachers" (200). In the years since, the pressure to adopt data-driven, evidence-based teaching practices has only increased and, along with it, the need for rhetoric and composition instructors to use quantitative methods as evidence to maintain authority about how writing is taught at the college level (Adler-Kassner 2017; Lang and Baehr 2012, 192; Moxley 2013).

Calls for writing teachers to use data to inform teaching practices reflect a growing interest within the field of rhetoric and composition in using data to support the field's views of teaching writing (Lang and Baehr 2012, 174). This interest represents a return to using data-driven methods that fell out of use due to the "oft-referenced social turn in Composition," a major feature of which was "resistance to anything approaching the 'positivistic position of modern science'" (Miller and Licastro 2021, 5). While early work by compositionists such as Janet Emig (1972), Sondra Perl (1979), and Linda Flower and John Hayes (1980) relied heavily on quantitative methods to examine writing processes and practices, the field moved sharply toward nonempirical, frequently anecdotal forms of evidence from the 1980s to the early 2000s. As a result, by the early 2000s, publication of what Richard Haswell (2005) has termed "RAD," for replicable/aggregable/data-supported studies of teaching, declined across all of the composition journals published by the National Council for Teachers of English (*College Composition and Communication, College English, Research in the Teaching of English*).

The reliance on nonempirical forms of evidence left the field of rhetoric and composition vulnerable to attacks from those who called into question programs and practices. Chris Anson (2008) explains that it was challenging for rhetoric and composition administrators to fend off these attacks since "much teaching and administration of composition is not overwhelmingly supported by research, or supported by a preponderance of research" (20). Anson called for a return to more data-driven methods as a way to change "the public discourse about writing from belief to evidence, from felt sense to investigation and inquiry" (12).

The return to data-driven research in rhetoric and composition has been facilitated by new sources of data and technologies that make working with data more accessible than in the past. Lang and Baehr (2012) explain that "current tools and data sources . . . now offer opportunities to automate, replicate, and add a new level of empiricism to our research" (176). These resources have made it possible for rhetoric and composition researchers, administrators, and teachers to access and analyze data to address longstanding issues in teaching writing such as student writing habits (Jamieson and Moore Howard 2013), assignment genre (Aull 2015), and instructor feedback

(Dixon and Moxley 2013), among others. At the same time, big data creates new questions to explore related to student privacy (Beck et al. 2021; Beck and Hutchinson Campos 2021; Kulak 2021; Reilly 2021), algorithmic biases (Bakke 2020; Gallagher 2020), building sustainable data infrastructures (Ball et al. 2021; Phelps 2021), and more.

Though rhetoric and composition scholarship has clearly indicated that writing teachers should use data to inform their teaching, this scholarship has not always described in detail the data literacy skills writing teachers require to work with data in classroom contexts. Nevertheless, a basic outline of what writing teachers' data literacy might look like in practice is possible to discern. For example, Anson provides an extended description of a data inquiry process for teachers that is "grounded in classrooms": "A teacher who begins reflecting on how writing prompts determine certain aspects of her students' writing might learn about early work that tested the impact of variations in the background information given in similar writing prompts (e.g., Hoetker and Brossell 1986, 1989; Hoetker and Ash 1984). In turn, this research could trigger several informal classroom investigations, which in turn might increase the teacher's awareness and critical instructional ability. Potentially, further questions can open doors to larger and more formal research studies. In this way, the consumption of research affects the nature and quality of instruction by encouraging sharper observation and deeper reflection" (31). Anson's description indicates that teachers need to be able to understand and apply the results of empirical research studies as well as to improve their knowledge and teaching practice through conducting classroom investigations. Both of these tasks require functional and rhetorical data literacy in addition to disciplinary and pedagogical knowledge.

More recently, scholars have emphasized the importance of teachers' critical data literacy as well. In particular, it is important for rhetoric and composition teachers to be critical users of classroom technologies that collect student data and create new opportunities for monitoring students and teachers (Beck 2016; Beck and Hutchinson Campos 2021; Beck et al. 2021; Crow 2013; Johnson 2021; Kulak 2021; Reilly 2021). In educational contexts, data have long been used to surveil students and teachers. Today, technology extends the possibilities for surveillance as *dataveillance*, which Selena Nemorin (2017) defines as "the systematic monitoring of individuals and/or groups through personal data networks in order to regulate or govern behaviours" (248). For example, using DFW rates as a proxy measure of teaching effectiveness illustrates how data can be employed to surveil instructors.

Teachers' use of data and digital technologies that collect information for teaching purposes is complicated by dataveillance. Rhetoric and composition scholars have highlighted several concerns that bear directly on teachers' use of data, including the intersections of digital surveillance and big data connected to writing program portfolios (Crow 2013), the history and practice of surveillance and privacy in writing classrooms (Beck 2016), and the use of grades as surveillance data (Johnson 2021), among others. These scholars also call on instructors to take more responsibility for how student data are collected and used in their classrooms.

Dataveillance makes the critical use of data by teachers urgent. As a result, recent scholarship describes the critical, data literate writing teacher as one who:

1. asks questions about classroom technologies, how they change authority, and how student data are collected and used (Beck 2016; Johnson 2021, 65; Moxley 2008, 183)
2. assumes agency over how technology is used in the classroom and student success rather than simply accepting top-down administrative decisions about how to implement technology and measure student success (Adler-Kassner 2017, 337; Duin and Tham 2020)
3. recognizes and evaluates the ideologies that underly classroom technologies (Beck et al. 2021; Greenwood et al. 2019; Moxley 2008, 195)

Taken together, descriptions of teachers using data in rhetoric and composition scholarship emphasize the need for teachers to have functional, rhetorical, and critical data literacy skills (see box 5.1).

Despite the importance of data literacy to writing instructors, data literacy is still not regularly included in the training graduate students receive to prepare them to teach college writing. Fortunately, writing teachers can turn to a growing number of resources that have been developed at the national level to foster data literacy. Since 2011, Dartmouth College has sponsored a summer institute specifically to support scholars in developing data-driven research projects (Donahue 2010). The International Conference on Writing Analytics, dedicated to "actionable data for teaching and learning writing," has met annually since 2014 and launched a journal publishing research articles, the *Journal of Writing Analytics*, in 2017. Journals such as *Kairos*, *Computers and Composition*, and *Composition Forum* also regularly publish articles related

> **BOX 5.1. Characteristics of a Data Literate Writing Instructor**
>
> Data literate writing instructors draw on functional, rhetorical, and critical data literacies to:
> - understand and apply the results of empirical research studies in the classroom.
> - conduct classroom data inquiries to improve their knowledge and teaching practice.
> - question classroom technologies, how they change authority, and how student data are collected and used.
> - assume agency over student success and how technology is used in the classroom.
> - recognize and evaluate the ideologies that underlie classroom technologies that collect student data.

to teaching students how to use data and have even devoted special issues to data-related topics. *Kairos* published a special issue, "Data Visualization in Composition," in 2020, and *Computers and Composition* has published two special issues focused on data: "Composing Algorithms: Writing (with) Rhetorical Machines" in 2020 and "Rhetorics of Data: Collection, Consent, and Critical Digital Literacies" in 2021. These resources help teachers understand the stakes of and possibilities for using data for teaching purposes and serve a vital role in fostering rhetoric and composition teachers' data literacy.

Professional organizations and journals have also responded to recent developments in generative AI and recognition of the need to incorporate these developments into writing instruction by developing resources aimed at preparing instructors to work with AI, including the publication of the *MLA-CCCC Joint Task Force on Writing and AI Working Paper: Overview of the Issues, Statement of Principles, and Recommendations* in 2023 and additional working papers since then. Because generative AI would not exist and cannot function without data, most resources focused on helping instructors learn how to work with AI also focus, either explicitly or implicitly, on working with data.

Data Literacy for Teachers

Even if writing teachers accept the argument that they should use data in the classroom and cultivate their own skills as rhetorical readers and critical communicators, it can still be daunting to use data for teaching-related purposes. The amount of data and range of technologies and tools available to teachers are overwhelming and threaten to make what could be a useful resource for teachers unusable given the time constraints teachers already face. Data literacy for teachers (DLFT) is the key to using data effectively for teaching purposes without becoming overwhelmed by them. DLFT refers to "the ability to transform information into actionable instructional knowledge and practices by collecting, analyzing, and interpreting all types of data (assessment, school climate, behavioral, snapshot, longitudinal, moment-to-moment, and so on) to help determine instructional steps" (Gummer and Mandinach 2015, 2). Education researchers Edith S. Gummer and Ellen B. Mandinach, who coined the acronym DLTF, have reported extensively on K–12 teachers' development of data literacy in several studies. Although K–12 teachers' training to teach and experiences using data are not identical to college writing instructors, research by Gummer and Mandinach in addition to other education researchers, offers the most detailed view available of how teachers cultivate and use data literacy for teaching-related purposes and provides a framework for using data in classroom contexts that can be adapted for use by college instructors as well.

Central to DLFT is the notion that teachers' disciplinary and pedagogical knowledge must inform their use of data. Rather than being led by the availability of data or technology, teachers first judge that data might provide useful information and then design a data inquiry to help them use data to address a question or issue they have identified in teaching. Understanding the limitations of data—a key characteristic of critical data literacy—is necessary to be able to determine whether data might be useful in addressing a problem or question. Rob Kitchin and Tracey P. Lauriault remind us that all data only "provide oligoptic views of the world: views from certain vantage points, using particular tools, rather than an all-seeing, infallible god's eye view" (Kitchin and Lauriault 2015, 465–466). Data cannot answer every teaching-related question or solve every teaching-related problem, and anecdotal and nonempirical evidence continue to have value in educational contexts, especially when limited data are available or information about individual perceptions and experiences is necessary. As an example, Alex C. Lange, Antonio Duran, and Romeo Jackson (2019) note that anecdotal and nonempirical research were central to the initial development of best practices for supporting LGBTQ students in higher education (512). To use data effectively, teachers need to be able to account for the limitations of data in judging whether data are available or can be collected that can make visible patterns in our classrooms that we may not be able to see clearly otherwise and that can inform our decision-making.

If a teacher determines that data can be useful to address a teaching-related question or problem, they can make good use of data regardless of their background or comfort level working with data. In their study of K–12 teachers at various stages of their career, from pre-service to in-service, Jori S. Beck and Diana Nunnaley (2021) found that teachers' abilities to use data fall along a spectrum from novice to expert. Developing and expert users are characterized as having the types of skills that Annika Wolff et al. (2016) associate with communicators on their own data literacy spectrum, including being able to "understand the overarching situational context," "identify relevant and appropriate data sources," "organize and manage data, knowing the importance of ethical and responsible protection of data," and "examine and analyze data" (Beck and Nunnaley 2021, 2). Because teachers bring their disciplinary and pedagogical expertise to bear on teaching-related data and the data inquiries they conduct, DLFT does differ from the more general data literacy skills needed by communicators. DLFT constitutes a more specific type of professional data literacy. Nevertheless, teachers have widely varying backgrounds and comfort levels working with data, and whether they are novice or expert users, data can be useful to help teachers address the questions and problems they face in the classroom.

More important than any teacher's background using data are the beliefs and dispositions that a teacher brings to using data. Beliefs and dispositions that Mandinach and Gummer (2016) found to support DLFT include:

- Belief that all students can learn
- Disposition to think critically about teaching
- Belief in continuous inquiry cycle for improvement
- Belief in collaboration
- Disposition to adapt communication about and with data appropriately for different audiences.
- Belief in using data to inform teaching
- Belief in the value of data to communicate to others
- Disposition to use data ethically (60–64)

Interestingly, of the eight beliefs and dispositions that Gummer and Mandinach identify as important for supporting DLFT, only three of them directly relate to using data. The other five relate more generally to beliefs and dispositions about learning and teaching, indicating once again how important teachers' pedagogical knowledge and values are to their use of data. While any teacher can cultivate skills in using data through training and practice, teachers who fundamentally do not, for example, believe that all students can learn or who do not have a disposition to think critically about teaching are not any more likely to value examining their teaching using data than they are through any other method of analysis.

Though data cannot and should not supplant the other kinds of knowledge teachers bring to the classroom and their work with students, they can serve as a valuable resource to teachers who are open to using them. For college-level rhetoric and composition instructors, DLFT helps to fill in the gap between generally recognizing that instructors should use data and identifying what such use looks like.

Designing and Conducting Data Inquiries for Teaching Purposes

In practice, using data for teaching purposes usually involves an inquiry cycle, shown in figure 5.1. This cycle involves five steps, which teachers often work through iteratively as they return to earlier steps as needed to refine their research question, collect more data, or analyze data in different ways. The steps include identifying problems/framing questions, using data, transforming data into information, transforming information into decision, and evaluating outcomes.

Knowledge of the inquiry cycle can help teachers to use data in ways that are appropriate for their rhetorical situation and make the best use of available data and resources to examine teaching practices and student learning. The rest of this section describes the components of the data inquiry cycle, while recognizing that data inquiries are highly rhetorical, and, as such, decisions about how problems/questions are framed and how data are collected, analyzed, interpreted, and used for decision-making need to be determined by each teacher in the context of their class and institution. To highlight how contextual factors shape a data inquiry, I also provide an extended description of one data inquiry that I conducted in a professional writing course. I do not offer this example as an idealized model but rather as an example of the rhetorical application of the data inquiry cycle.

To help guide decision-making throughout a data inquiry, instructors should identify and reach out to relevant stakeholders and potential partners such as colleagues, the director of their IRB, information and educational

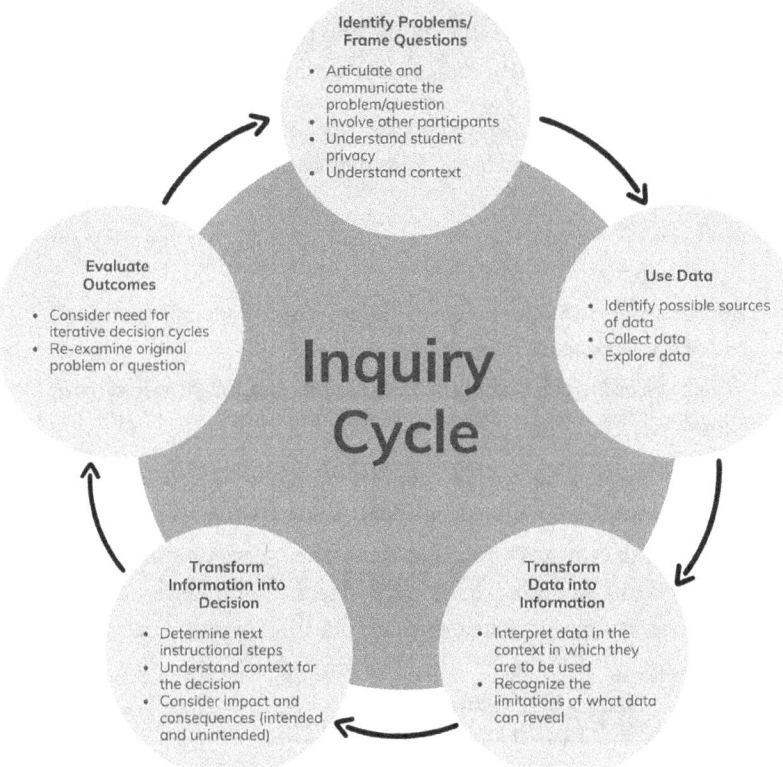

FIGURE 5.1. Data inquiry cycle adapted from Mandinach and Gummer 2016, 48.

technology staff members, statisticians, administrators, and others who have access to data or knowledge that could be useful. Working with potential participants while planning a data inquiry can help make the inquiry as strong as possible since participants can sometimes provide useful feedback on the question and methods that are being used or information about resources available within the local context and the type of inquiry that will be best suited to the context in which a teacher is working.

IDENTIFY PROBLEMS/FRAME QUESTIONS

The data inquiry cycle begins with a teacher identifying a specific teaching-related problem or question that needs to be addressed, and box 5.2 lists questions that can guide a teacher's work through this step. To start a data inquiry, it is important to identify not only a specific problem or question but also key constructs of interest and ways to measure the constructs.

Identify a Teaching-Related Problem or Question

The possibilities for questions that might lend themselves to a data inquiry in a writing classroom are nearly endless. A few examples include:

- If I [make a particular change] to my course, what will be the effect?
- What prior writing knowledge do students bring to first-year writing courses?
- In what ways does the use of [a particular technology] in the classroom affect students' research skills?
- How effectively do students demonstrate critical data literacy at the end of the semester?
- Which voices are being amplified through the readings I assign in my course?

The best questions will be "socially important and highly relevant to improving our understanding of education processes, distribution (access), effects, and quality" (Loeb et al. 2017, 18). Questions often focus on differences, gaps, characteristics and qualities, the impact of teaching practices, and curriculum. The process of developing a research question is also iterative, with the question changing, often becoming more refined, as the teacher begins preliminary data collection or exploration.

Recently, I was motivated to conduct a data inquiry after I made an instructional change in my professional writing course: In fall 2021 I replaced a more traditional project in the course with a course-based undergraduate research experience (CURE). My decision to add a CURE to my class was based on my learning about research indicating that CUREs are a high-impact teaching practice, especially beneficial for the racially and economically diverse students who might otherwise not have the opportunity to participate in undergraduate research such as the students who populate my courses at Sacramento State (American Association of Colleges and Universities 2022). The CURE I included in my course required students to conduct authentic research in professional writing by interviewing professionals and transcribing those interviews to include in a class database that all the students could then use to address a particular research question. I was concerned that the interview and transcription components were taking students longer to complete than the traditional research had, and I wanted to make sure that I had not added unduly to students' workload outside of class by adding the CURE to the course. The question I initially wanted to answer through the inquiry was, "Is the CURE in my professional writing course too time-consuming for students?"

> BOX 5.2. **Questions to consider when identifying problems/framing questions.**
>
> TO IDENTIFY PROBLEMS AND FRAME QUESTIONS
> - Articulate the problem/question.
> - Involve other participants.
> - Understand student privacy.
> - Understand context.
>
> QUESTIONS TO CONSIDER
> 1. What other stakeholders are involved in the data inquiry?
> 2. What is the (classroom, program, department, institutional, disciplinary) context in which the inquiry is taking place?
> 3. What specific teaching-related question or problem do you hope to address by conducting a data inquiry?
> 4. How are the key constructs of interest?
> 5. How can data be used to measure the constructs of interest?
> 6. How can you be sure that students' privacy is protected and ownership of their data is respected throughout the inquiry?
> 7. How will students benefit from the data inquiry?

Identify Key Constructs of Interest

After a teacher formulates a question, it is important to identify the key *constructs* of interest, that is, those ideas, attributes, or concepts that will be measured. Though it can be challenging to clarify the constructs to be measured, it is necessary to have a clear conceptualization to guide the inquiry (Loeb et al. 2017, 19). Table 5.1 illustrates the complexity involved in clarifying the constructs of interest for even a seemingly simple question.

For the data inquiry I conducted in my professional writing course, my original question emphasized a component, "too time-consuming," that proved difficult to define. How could I determine what the proper amount of time for students to spend on a research project outside of class was? What if both the CURE *and* the traditional research project were too time-consuming; how would I know this? How could I measure the component "time-consuming?" Because the component "time-consuming" was difficult to define, I revised my research question to be: "Are my professional writing students spending more time on the CURE than they did the traditional research project?" This revision clarified that "time" was the component I wanted to measure and

TABLE 5.1. Example of the complexity of describing constructs

How many first-year writing students are at our university?

Component	Issues to be clarified
How many	Does "how many" refer to head count or to full-time equivalency (FTE)?
first-year writing	Are stretch sections of first-year writing included or only one-semester sections? Or shortened summer sections of the course? Are correctional institutions that offer first-year writing courses also included?
students	Does "students" include only fully matriculated students? What about non-degree students?
are	At what point in time should the answer be valid? At the point of admission to the university? At the beginning of the semester?
at	Does this include students who take first-year writing in remote settings? What about students who take first-year writing somewhere else and transfer it in?
our university	Does this include only a particular campus or the entire university system the campus is a part of?

Source: Based on an example template from Loeb et al. 2017.

proposed a simple comparison of how much time students spent on the CURE and how much time they spent on the traditional research project.

Determine How to Measure the Construct

Once a teacher has defined the construct to be described, they must determine how it can be measured. Different types of data will be appropriate to answer different research questions, and some teachers prefer to use one type of data over another. Often the data that a teacher would like to use is not available, and the teacher has no choice but to use data that are available (assuming that they are still relevant) (Dahlman 2021). When ideal data are not available—which is usually the case—teachers must rely on *proxy data*, which refer to data that relate to, but are not a direct *measure* of, a construct. As an example, it can be difficult to measure student engagement in a course directly, so proxy data are generally used instead to measure student engagement. Proxy data are, by definition, imperfect, but they are commonly used out of necessity when they are a reasonable substitute or approximation. When using proxy data, the teacher should make sure that the proxies are relevant for answering the research question and be aware of their imperfections as measures of the underlying construct. In the case of student engagement, some LMSs compute an "engagement score" for each student using page clicks or logs-ins as proxy data, but these are not especially valid proxy measures for engagement since students can click on pages and log into an LMS without being really engaged in a course. More appropriate proxy measures for student engagement would be measuring the number of questions that students ask or how many times they view an instructional video.

In the case of my data inquiry, the possibilities for measuring "time" were severely limited as I did not have any way to directly observe and record the amount of time students spent working on the CURE in fall 2021 or on the traditional research project in spring 2019—especially since I was conducting the data inquiry after the conclusion of both semesters. Fortunately, I do ask students to keep a weekly labor log in which they record the number of hours they spend working on course tasks outside of class. Though these data were not ideal since they relied on students to accurately self-report their time and represented estimates of time rather than precise measurements, they were a reasonable approximation of the time students spent on the project, and they had the advantage of being recorded at the same time students completed the project rather than recalled after-the-fact.

USE DATA

The next step in the inquiry cycle is to use data. Using data involves identifying potential sources of data, collecting or acquiring data, and exploring data. box 5.3 lists questions that teachers should consider to guide their use of data.

Identify Possible Sources of Data

Some of the most common sources of data for teachers to work with are shown in table 5.2. This list is not comprehensive, nor is it intended to be. New sources of data emerge all the time as do tools for working with data. Generally, it is best to gather a range of data from different sources to get a fuller picture of the teaching and learning happening in the class and to compare the information from each kind of evidence to ensure that it is consistent.

I used classroom data for the data inquiry I conducted in my professional writing course. Specifically, I identified students' weekly labor log assignments as a source of data to help me answer my question. Labor logs, as shown in table 5.3, are spreadsheets that students create and update weekly

> **BOX 5.3. Questions to consider when using data.**
>
> **TO USE DATA**
> - Identify possible sources of data.
> - Collect data.
> - Explore data.
>
> **QUESTIONS TO CONSIDER**
> 1. What data sources are available that will provide the most relevant information given the question/problem you want or need to address?
> 2. What file format will you use to save your data?
> 3. How will you chunk or segment the data for analysis?
> 4. Where will you store data?
> 5. How will you ensure that data are stored securely?
> 6. What kind of data exploration will help you to best answer your research question?
> 7. How can data visualizations help you to explore the data?

in Google Sheets to record their work on course activities. Students keep a record of when and where they complete specific course activities and how long the activities took to complete. They also enter an "engagement rating" to record how engaged they felt by each activity, and they can enter notes on their labor log as well. The primary purpose of labor logs is to help students identify patterns in their own work that are helpful or harmful to them. Labor logs also provide useful information to me about how long particular activities are taking students and which activities students find more and less engaging. I grade labor logs only on completeness, not on how much time students spend on class or how much labor they record during a given week.

Since I have used the same labor log assignment for several years in my professional writing courses, I had data available from the last semester in which I used a traditional research project, spring 2019, that I could compare to data gathered from students' labor logs during the first semester I included the CURE, fall 2021.

Collect and Clean Data

Collecting data is necessary before a teacher can explore them. The work involved in collecting data will vary depending on the source of data as well by

TABLE 5.2. Sources of data for teaching-related data inquiries

Sources of Data	Examples	What kind of data might be available?
Classroom data	Assessments, assignments, grades, observations, surveys, interviews, student records	Student writing, instructor feedback, peer feedback, grades, classroom observation notes, attendance data, student demographics, student self-reports
Communication tools	Discussion forums and email systems	Discussion posts and replies, emails
eReaders and media viewers	Unizin consortium's Engage eReader	Page views, use of markup and interactive features
Instructional software programs	Eli Review	Course-level and student-level performance
Learning management systems	Canvas, Blackboard, D2L, Google Classroom	Student logins, visits to pages and other resources within the LMS, posts to discussion forums, performance on quizzes and tests, completion of assignments, and more
Publishers	McGraw Hill, Pearson, Follett	Adaptive data
Social learning platforms	Edmodo, Perusall, SC Training, Schoology	Page views, student activity, comment submission time, performance on quizzes and tests, and more
Student information systems	Wisenet, Academia ERP by Serosoft, PeopleSoft Campus Solutions	Academic activity such as course registration and class attendance, advising interactions, financial aid
University dashboards	Student success dashboards, Institutional research dashboards, Academic enterprise dashboards	Admissions, student enrollment, graduation and retention, degrees awarded, outcomes, and more

Source: Angela Laflen.

the software or platform that a teacher plans to use to explore data. Some of the considerations teachers may face as they prepare data for analysis include how to divide data into chunks or segments to explore, what file format to use to save data, and whether to store data locally on their computer or on the cloud.

Collecting data for use in my data inquiry meant copying data that students had originally submitted using Google Sheets and pasting it into a new spreadsheet that I created in Excel (I could have used Google Sheets to explore

TABLE 5.3. Sample student labor log for 1 week

Duration (in hours)	Date	What you worked on for this session	Which kind of session? Reading, writing, research, collaboration, something else?	Start time	Where did you work?	Engagement rating 1–5; 1 is very low and 5 is very high	Comments
3.5	11/1/21	Reading assigned chapters; watching instructor video	Reading; watching lecture video	2:00 pm	Panera	4	I was less focused when reading the assigned textbook; I need to find a way to focus
4	11/3/21	Using Piktochart to make graphs	Research and writing and troubleshooting	3:50 pm	Panera	5	It is hard to make graphs
2	11/4/21	Recorded and uploaded to Canvas; updated labor log	Writing and recording	1:00 pm	Home bedroom	5	

Source Angela Laflen.

these data, but I am more familiar with using Excel). I only copied over data (1) from the five weeks of the semester during which students worked on the relevant projects, (2) for students who had submitted their labor logs for all five weeks, and (3) for log entries that the students indicated were related to working on the research project, omitting entries related to other assignments such as readings or watching course videos.

After data are collected, the teacher needs to take time to clean them up before exploration. This process involves removing white spaces, duplicate

TABLE 5.4. Example of data before and after cleaning

Before cleaning	After cleaning
30 min	0.5
3.5 h	3.5
1 hour	1
1 hour 30 minutes	1.5
0.5	0.5
2 hr	2
28 MIN	0.5
1/2 Hours	0.5
4	4
3 1/2 hrs	3.5

Source: Angela Laflen.

TABLE 5.5. Excerpt from Excel spreadsheet

Spring 2019	Fall 2021
7.75	17
25.5	33.15
7.1	23.25
17	7.2
18.5	17
8	24.25
29.21	16.5

Source: Angela Laflen.

records, and basic errors. Cleaning data before exploration is always necessary to ensure that they are correct, consistent, and usable. Most aspects of data cleaning can be done using software tools, but a portion of it must be done manually. To clean data for use in my data inquiry, I made sure all the numbers were formatted the same way to make comparison possible. As an example, consider all the different ways two hours was formatted in the labor logs: 2, 2 hours, 2 hour, 2 hr, 2 hrs, 2hrs, 2hr. Each variation had to be replaced by "2" in the spreadsheet before data exploration. The same was true of all the variations in how students wrote numbers. Table 5.4 shows an example of data before and after cleaning. Although I could use find and replace functions to assist with cleaning the data, I still had to manually check that the numbers were formatted correctly.

It was necessary for the data to be formatted consistently to use the data-analysis tools in Excel to add up the numbers that each student reported spending on the project, which I did using the autosum function in Excel. I then created a new spreadsheet into which I copied over the hours per student per class, as shown in table 5.4.

Explore Data

After data have been collected and cleaned, they are ready to be explored. Data exploration is focused on getting to know the data. To get to know data, it is important to look deeply at the data from multiple perspectives, to combine

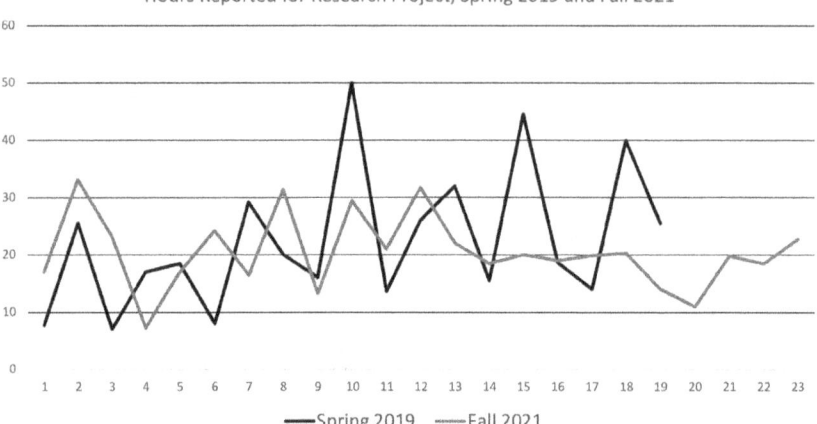

FIGURE 5.2. Line graph comparing the hours students reported spending on a research project in spring 2019 and fall 2021.

and present information to aid a range of different understandings, and to illuminate a number of possible relationships between teaching and learning. This involves differentiating, sorting, comparing, and contrasting data. At this step, the focus should be on what is causing the results rather than what action should be taken. In their resource "How to Use Data for Teaching as Inquiry" (2018), scholars at the Education Hub recommend that teachers analyze data by "looking for what seems to 'pop out' or what is surprising or unexpected. Identify patterns, categories and trends, but avoid jumping to conclusions or arriving at certainty which can lead to badly-framed problems and premature solutions. Don't seek to explain or determine problems but continue to mine the data for possibilities" (4). At this stage, visualizing data through charts, graphs, and tables can be a helpful way to get to know the data and begin to identify patterns.

To start exploring data for my data inquiry, I used a line graph, shown in figure 5.2, which allowed me to visualize how the number of hours reported by students in fall 2021 compared to those reported by students in spring 2019. I created the line graph using the Excel Charts tool. The line graph showed that the spring 2019 group had higher highs than the fall 2021 group, indicating that a few students had spent considerably more time on the research project than the others. The fall 2021 group did not have those outlying students. Otherwise, it looked like both groups were pretty comparable, and I suspected that the differences between them were not significant as a result.

BOX 5.4. **Unpaired t Test Results**

P VALUE AND STATISTICAL SIGNIFICANCE:

The two-tailed P value equals 0.4799.
By conventional criteria, this difference is considered to be not statistically significant.

CONFIDENCE INTERVAL:

The mean of Group One minus Group Two equals 2.1025.
95% confidence interval of this difference: from −3.8566 to 8.0616.

INTERMEDIATE VALUES USED IN CALCULATIONS:

$t = 0.7131$
$df = 40$
standard error of difference = 2.948

REVIEW YOUR DATA:

Group	Group One	Group Two
Mean	22.5742	20.4717
SD	12.2237	6.4970
SEM	2.8043	1.3547
N	19	23

To see if this perception was accurate, I further explored the data by running an unpaired t-test using the t-test calculator available from GraphPad on the two groups. I chose the unpaired t-test because it is used to compare two sample means from unrelated groups. This means that there are different people providing scores for each group, and the purpose of this test is to determine if the samples are different from each other. This test indicated that the difference between the groups was not statistically significant, as shown in box 5.4.

Much more detailed information about different methods for exploring data are available in the textbooks and guides typically used in graduate-level research-methods courses, such as the following:

- Creswell, John W., and J. David Creswell. 2017. *Research Design: Qualitative, Quantitative, and Mixed Methods Approaches*. Sage.

- Hoy, Wayne K., and Curt M. Adams. 2015. *Quantitative Research in Education: A Primer.* Sage.
- Martin, William E., and Krista D. Bridgmon. 2012. *Quantitative and Statistical Research Methods: From Hypothesis to Results.* John Wiley & Sons.
- O'Dwyer, Laura M., and James A. Bernauer. 2013. *Quantitative Research for the Qualitative Researcher.* Sage.

For teachers who are more novice than expert when it comes to using data, it can be particularly valuable to work with a partner to explore data. I relied heavily on the advice of statistics experts for several years when I began using data for teaching. Only after I attended the Dartmouth Summer Seminar for Composition Research and completed several trainings on data analysis offered by my institution did I feel confident to begin exploring data on my own.

TRANSFORM DATA INTO INFORMATION

After teachers have explored the data they collected, they create explanations from data (see box 5.5). This is essentially when teachers craft data stories based on the results of their exploration. Teachers should be guided by the four principles for critical data storytelling shown in figure 3.2: using data ethically, engaging data critically, exploring data rhetorically, and reflecting on our use of data. It is particularly important that teachers serve as critical data storytellers, questioning the limitations of what their data inquiry can reveal and to what extent data are useful to them as they interpret the results of data exploration.

Identify Meaningful Patterns

Interpreting data means identifying meaningful patterns. Patterns might include numbers trending upward or downward or correlations between two sets of numbers. This is why data visualization can be so helpful; by making the patterns visible, graphs make them easier to see.

Common graphical techniques include histograms, bar charts, pie charts, scatter plots, and box plots.

However, it is also important to be critical about the patterns we think we see and what they might mean. "How to Use Data for Teaching as Inquiry" (2018) recommends that teachers use the four C's of interpreting data to critically examine patterns in the data (4–5):

- Do the data give a **complete** picture? Often, it is necessary to draw on different types of data—formal and informal, quantitative and

> **BOX 5.5. Questions to consider when transforming data into information.**
>
> **татотранs торм ратаа ілто Іліо мата тіоли**
> TO TRANSFORM DATA INTO INFORMATION
> - Interpret data in the context in which they are to be used.
> - Recognize the limitations of what data can reveal.
>
> **QUESTIONS TO CONSIDER**
> 1. What patterns do the data reveal? What might the patterns mean?
> 2. What data visualizations will make patterns in the data easiest to see and understand?
> 3. How can you test whether the patterns mean what you think? Is statistical analysis needed to assess the patterns?
> 4. What diverse data can you bring together to support your interpretation?
> 5. What are the limitations of the data collected, explored, and interpreted?

qualitative—to get a complete picture. Drawing on different types of data during interpretation can help teachers avoid selecting data as evidence that confirms existing beliefs about teaching and learning rather than using data to uncover and explore issues.

- Are the data **consistent** with other sources of information? It is important to interpret data through the lens of professional judgment. If data seem to contradict what a teacher has observed in the classroom or through their experience, it is worth investigating that discrepancy further. Teachers shouldn't automatically trust data over the evidence of their own experience.
- How do the data **compare** with the standard, your targets, or other institutions? Comparison can help teachers explore data; it doesn't necessarily need to lead to judgments about what is better or worse.
- Might the data be **concealing** something? To avoid missing something in the data, teachers should consider the full set of results and work with disaggregated data when possible to view the achievement of particular groups of students.

After a teacher has identified a meaningful pattern related to the research question, they explain what the pattern could mean. For teaching-related data inquiries, explanations for patterns in the data usually fall into one of five categories: curriculum, instruction, teachers, students, or infrastructure. To avoid jumping to false conclusions, it is best to draft several potential explanations and conclusions for the patterns. For example, if a teacher has identified a pattern of students struggling with a particular core writing concept using assessment data, they might consider multiple explanations:

- Do the current instructional materials scaffold that concept for students? If not, the teacher might craft an explanation for the pattern focused on instruction and/or teachers.
- Is this a core writing concept that students are expected to have learned in prerequisite courses? If so, perhaps the explanation could stem from curriculum and/or students.

Spending time speculating on reasons for the patterns and creating a range of data stories can also be useful in identifying where other information might be needed for the data inquiry.

The results of exploring my students' labor log data revealed a pattern of similarity between two different groups of students. This pattern suggested it might be reasonable to interpret the data to mean that students in fall 2021 did not spend more time on the CURE than the students in spring 2019 did on the traditional research project. This was surprising to me since several fall 2021 students had mentioned to me that they felt they were spending a lot of time on the project. As a result, it was not entirely clear to me how to explain the pattern, and I considered a range of possible explanations for the pattern. Two of the most likely were: Did I and my students perceive that they were spending more time on the CURE even though they were not? And were more or different instructional materials needed to support students' work on the CURE?

Triangulate Sources of Information

To determine which potential explanation is the most likely cause of the pattern in the data, it is helpful to *triangulate* sources of information. Triangulation refers to using multiple methods or sources of data to corroborate or identify weaknesses in an interpretation. For example, a qualitative survey of student perceptions will enhance quantitative measures such as those provided by measuring student activity on a social learning platform. In addition to these, teacher anecdotes or a curriculum analysis can deepen understanding. The idea is to seek multiple and diverse sources of information. In the process, the data inquiry becomes more specific and better able to lead to decision-making that will improve teaching and learning.

To triangulate the results of my data inquiry, I consulted other data I had access to, including students' weekly written reflections and correspondence I had exchanged with them over email about both research projects. These sources of data largely confirmed that students found the workload for the CURE manageable, although I was also able to identify some repeated questions about and issues with the CURE that came up in emails and the weekly reflective writing that I made note of to address in the future. I concluded that adding the CURE had not had the unintended effect of adding to students' workload for the course, which was the original concern that prompted the inquiry, but that additional instructional support could help alleviate some of the common issues students experienced working on the CURE. I did have to consider whether it really was fair to compare the two different classes of students, comprised as they were of entirely different students, and, ultimately, I recognized that this was a limitation of the inquiry.

TRANSFORM INFORMATION INTO DECISION

Transforming information into decision (see box 5.6) is "more about the teaching aspect of data literacy . . . than it is about the data aspect" because in this step teachers draw on their "knowledge of the learning objectives, content, and the curriculum" and their "understanding of pedagogy and pedagogical content knowledge to *determine the next instructional steps*" (Mandinach and Gummer 2016, 54, italics in original). Sometimes a teacher will realize that the data they collected and analyzed did not provide enough information to help them determine the next instructional step. In that case, the teacher may determine that the next step is to gather more data or analyze data differently to provide the information they need to make a decision related to the question/problem they need to address. At other times, a teacher will feel they have enough information to make at least an initial decision and can act on that. For example, if a teacher determines that the current instructional materials used in the course do not adequately scaffold a core writing concept for students, they might decide to create an instructional video for students to watch online and an activity to allow students to discuss or practice applying the concept.

It is important to consider the intended and unintended consequences of the decision as well. For example, if a teacher does add instruction to a class to better scaffold students' learning of a core writing concept, they will likely have to create room in their schedule by removing some other instruction or activity. Recognizing these consequences before committing to an instructional change can help avoid inadvertently creating new issues in the class—such as running out of time during the semester or confusing students by overloading them with information.

> **BOX 5.6. Questions to consider when transforming information into decision.**
>
> **TO TRANSFORM INFORMATION INTO DECISION**
> - Determine next instructional steps.
> - Understand context for the decision.
> - Consider impact and consequences (intended and unintended).
>
> **QUESTIONS TO CONSIDER**
> 1. Do you have enough information based on the data you have collected and analyzed to make a decision about next steps?
> 2. Based on what you know about your students, your discipline, and your programmatic and institutional context, what should happen next for students?
> 3. What instructional adjustments will you need to make as you implement your decision?
> 4. What are the intended and unintended consequences of using the data that you have explored and interpreted on classroom practices and students' learning?

Based on the data inquiry I conducted in my professional writing class, I decided not to change the assignment requirements for the CURE when I taught professional writing again in fall 2022 but to change my approach to teaching the assignment. This was not because I was concerned about the time students were spending on the project outside of class but because I was concerned about their perception that they were spending too much time on the project and by the number of questions and issues that had come up via email about the project. I taught my fall 2022 course in a computer classroom and had students complete more of the project in class, using a flipped classroom model that would allow me to work more directly with students as they completed the project (Gorman 2018).

EVALUATE OUTCOMES

After teachers reach a decision, the final step in the data inquiry cycle is to evaluate the outcomes of that decision (see box 5.7). The data inquiry may or may not have led to instructional changes. In either case, teachers should evaluate the outcomes by considering the extent to which they have addressed the initial issue that started the inquiry cycle and whether they need to go further in addressing it. They should also consider any unintended

> **BOX 5.7. Questions to consider when evaluating outcomes.**
>
> **TO EVALUATE OUTCOMES**
> - Consider need for iterative decision cycles.
> - Re-examine original problem or question.
>
> **QUESTIONS TO CONSIDER**
> 1. How will you evaluate the outcomes of the decisions you've made?
> 2. Do you need to use iterative decision cycles to re-examine the original problem or question?
> 3. How will you track changes in students' performance or in classroom practices?
> 4. How will you determine whether the original problem or question has been adequately addressed?
> 5. How will you recognize unintended consequences resulting from decisions you've made?

consequences that resulted from the changes they made. For this reason, it is not uncommon for one data inquiry to launch another. This kind of iterative inquiry cycle can help to ensure that teachers remain attentive and responsive to changes in their class and among their students.

In fall 2022, I included a CURE again in my professional writing course, only this time I gave the students more time to work on the project during class so I could troubleshoot the issues they experienced more quickly. My perception of the instructional change was that the project went more smoothly and that students did not email me with as many questions about the project. At the end of the semester, I again collected data from the students' labor logs and created a line graph (figure 5.3) to compare the time students reported spending on the CURE during fall 2022 to the results for fall 2021 and spring 2019.

The line graph seemed to show a pattern of students spending a similar amount of time on the CURE during fall 2022 as they had in fall 2021. I did notice that the mean for fall 2022 was lower at 16.83 hours compared to 20.47 hours for fall 2021 and 22.57 hours for spring 2019. However, it was not clear if this difference was really significant or could fall within the margin of error. To see whether the difference was significant, I conducted a one-way analysis of variance (ANOVA) test, which is a statistical test that allowed me

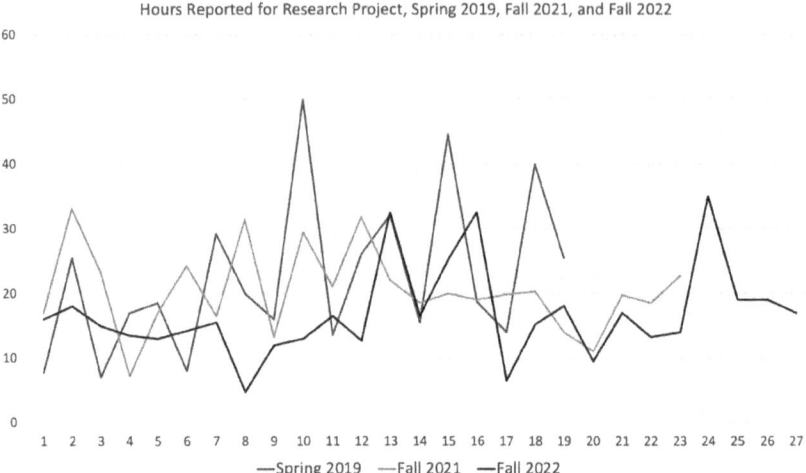

FIGURE 5.3. Line graph comparing the hours students reported spending on a research project in spring 2019, fall 2021, and fall 2022.

to compare the means of three independent groups to see if the differences among them were significant. I used the One-Way ANOVA Calculator available at the website Social Science Statistics to perform this test (https://www.socscistatistics.com/). The ANOVA confirmed that the differences among the groups were not statistically significant. To further evaluate the outcome of the instructional change I had made to the course, I looked at the students' reflective videos and reviewed my email exchanges with them from fall 2022. I noticed that they had emailed me with fewer questions and expressed less anxiety about the project in their reflective videos. Several of them mentioned that they found it helpful to have time in class to work on the project and have their questions answered immediately. As a result, I interpreted the results of this follow-up evaluation to mean that moving more of the project work into class time had smoothed the students' process of completing the project while not significantly reducing the amount of time they spent working on the project outside of class.

Issues to Keep in Mind Throughout a Data Inquiry

As my example of working through the data inquiry cycle to answer a question related to my professional writing course illustrates, this inquiry process is both highly contextual and complex. As a result, the challenges that one teacher experiences during a data inquiry will differ from those another teacher experiences. However, there are several common issues that can undermine data inquiries and of which all teachers should be aware when working with data. It is particularly important for teachers to take steps to avoid the "disease of complexity," secure student data, minimize problems associated with cognitive biases, and focus on evidence rather than action when conducting data inquiries.

AVOID THE DISEASE OF COMPLEXITY

Teachers should beware of the "'disease of complexity' in which complicated methods and presentation are assumed to imply greater scientific rigor or value" (Loeb et al. 2017, 6). To avoid this issue, teachers should aim to use the most accessible data sources and the simplest exploration methods that are both appropriate to their rhetorical situation and will help them address their question(s). In many cases, the simplest option will mean working with student data generated during the ordinary course of instruction and exploring that data using descriptive analysis.

SECURE STUDENT DATA

Teachers have legal and ethical obligations to ensure that student data remains secure. For example, the Family Educational Rights and Privacy Act (FERPA) is a federal law that restricts who has access to student information, allowing only students and educators to view these records. Teachers need to take steps to ensure that students' information is not exposed during a data inquiry or risk potential legal consequences. These steps include checking that any software a teacher uses—especially cloud-based software—meets cybersecurity standards.

Teachers can often find guidance related to protecting students' privacy and securing student data from their Institutional Review Board (IRB). IRBs review research studies to ensure that they comply with applicable regulations, meet commonly accepted ethical standards, follow institutional policies, and adequately protect research participants. Although teachers are not often required to apply for IRB approval to work with student data as part of informal classroom investigations, IRBs can still be a valuable source of information related to protecting students' privacy when teachers use student data. If a teacher has any question about whether they may require IRB approval, they should reach out to the IRB for guidance.

Steps instructors can take to keep students' data secure and honor students' ownership of their data include:

- Asking students for permission to use their data when possible
- Removing identifying information from any student work that will be used for a data inquiry
- Storing and analyzing student data in ways that protect their privacy
- Taking care to avoid impacting students' grades due to the data inquiry
- Helping students to understand exactly which data are being collected and how they will be used
- Informing students of the results of the inquiry when possible so they can benefit from what has been learned—even if only by learning more about how knowledge is constructed in classroom contexts

MINIMIZE COGNITIVE BIASES

Cognitive biases are mental shortcuts that shape individuals' perceptions and interpretations of the world. Although these biases are unavoidable to some extent, they become problematic when working with data because they can limit our awareness of alternative meanings within data. Specific steps teachers can take to limit the negative impact of cognitive biases on our data inquiries include:

- Paying attention to our own cognitive biases
- Examining all available data systematically
- Seeking out disconfirming evidence and taking the time to explore multiple possible interpretations of the evidence
- Remaining open to the implications of the evidence and the possibilities of change
- Collaborating with others who feel comfortable challenging our perspective

FOCUS ON EVIDENCE RATHER THAN ACTION

Teachers usually undertake data inquiries to make decisions about actions they should take, so it is understandable that teachers would be eager to move from evidence to action. However, overemphasizing action can lead to rushing data collection, exploration, and interpretation and weak or compromised decisions. To avoid rushing a data inquiry, work through the steps of the data inquiry cycle systematically and use data to examine and summarize the problem under investigation.

In other cases, teachers can be afraid of taking action even when the result of a data inquiry indicates that change might be needed. It can be tempting to

> **BOX 5.8. Tips for Using Data for Teaching Related Purposes**
>
> · Be open to how data can be used to improve teaching while also recognizing the limitations of data.
> · Seek feedback on your plans for a data inquiry and interpretations of data from stakeholders and partners.
> · Work through the data inquiry cycle systematically and iteratively to address teaching-related questions/problems.
> · Become knowledgeable about the kinds of data and statistical and measurement concepts.
> · Protect students' privacy and respect students' ownership of their data.
> · Be on guard for how cognitive biases can skew the interpretation of data.
> · Use data to examine and summarize the problem under investigation as well as the consequences of making an instructional change.
> · Consider teaching students to examine data about their own learning and use it to set learning goals.

stick with the status quo out of fear of the unintended consequences of making a change or the work involved in making instructional changes. To avoid this tendency, use data to weigh the pros and cons of continuing with current practices versus making a change.

Conclusion

Often, in the day-to-day grind of teaching, my perceptions of how an assignment is going or what students are thinking depend largely on whatever experience I had in the class most recently or by what the most vocal students are saying. Without minimizing the value of these kinds of personal experiences to my teaching, I have also come to appreciate the more distanced view on my teaching practices and students' learning that data can provide. Frequent, informal classroom investigations allow me to check or provide context for my perceptions. I do not have to rely entirely on how things seem to be going in my class or what I suspect is happening but can turn to data to confirm, complicate, or even disprove my perceptions. At the same time, preparing to use data in my classes has helped me become more critical of arguments about the role data should play in teaching and learning—especially when those arguments suggest that algorithmic decision-making might be superior to professional wisdom in higher-education contexts. Moreover, it has helped me to design a better critical data storytelling assignment for my students and to be more prepared to work with them on those assignments and prepare them to navigate datafied information environments.

As writing programs and instructors are increasingly pushed toward becoming more data-driven and evidence-based, it is essential that we are prepared to supply a critical, rhetorical perspective on data and that we feel confident using data to answer teaching-related questions, meet the needs of students who have been shaped by technology, respond to data-based arguments about teaching and learning, and ensure that any technologies included in our course gather and use student data in an ethical way. Although it can be daunting to get started using data, teachers do not need to be experts in data analysis before beginning to use data for teaching-related purposes. I have discussed several ways that instructors can get started using data in this chapter (see box 5.8). Most important is approaching data with the same kind of curious and critical mindset that we expect students to adopt when considering different types of evidence. That is, teachers should be open to how data can be used to improve teaching and learning while also questioning how data used in educational contexts were collected and for what purpose and how the insights provided by data align with what we know from our disciplinary and pedagogical expertise. In this way, teachers can take the lead with data to benefit ourselves and our students.

Conclusion

What Difference Does Data Storytelling Make?

When I began presenting my work on critical data literacy pedagogy at conferences, I was struck by the widespread interest of teachers and scholars in strategies to prepare students to work with data. Often, I would hear from other instructors that I was not alone in having seen students' use of data go awry in their multimodal compositions. I also came to expect one question as inevitable about this work: Do critical data storytelling assignments make any difference to students after the semester is over? On the surface, this question is a straightforward request for information about whether students are able to generalize and adapt their learning about data storytelling to new contexts. Yet it also seems to belie a deeper anxiety about the reach and influence of datafication: can critical data storytelling assignments—or *anything*—make a difference in the face of the continually expanding reach of datafication processes into every aspect of our lives?

Certainly, this question—in both senses—bears serious consideration. It *is* important for teachers to understand what students take away about writing from any given pedagogical approach and whether and how they can adapt their learning in new contexts. Especially when implementing an approach like critical data literacy pedagogy requires changing some familiar teaching practices, we need to know whether those changes are worth the effort.

Additionally, there is value in questioning whether critical data literacy—or any other critical literacy practice—is up to the challenge of helping students navigate datafied information and information environments. Despite the potential that many scholars, policymakers, journalists, and organizations associate with various critical literacies to address a wide range of social problems, (e.g., Grizzle et al. 2021; Hobbs 2017; Stanford History Education Group 2016), the results of critical literacy pedagogy have been mixed. Media studies researcher danah boyd (2018) has famously called into question the assumption that critical media literacy can be a corrective to "fake news." She points out that not all critical media literacy instruction is equally valuable and that developing media-making skills does not, by itself, guarantee that someone will use those skills for productive purposes. The issues boyd raises about media literacy apply equally to data literacy: that is, simply learning more about data and how data stories are produced does not ensure that students will use that information productively—or that they will use it at all. So, in addition to considering whether students can adapt their learning about data in new contexts, it is perhaps even more important to consider whether they can adapt their learning in rhetorically ethical ways and imagine agentive roles for themselves as members of a big data society in doing so.

Although my own work cannot fully answer these important questions, discussions that I have had with students during the year after they completed a data storytelling assignment in my courses offer initial insights into the value students find in these assignments. Throughout *Critical Data Storytelling* I have recounted the stories of students who completed critical data storytelling assignments in my first-year writing, digital writing, and professional writing courses, focusing especially on their experiences while completing the assignment and the artifacts that they produced in response to assignment prompts, and their immediate reflections after the semester ended. In this concluding chapter, I will share what three students told me about how they used data storytelling during the year after they were introduced to data storytelling in one of my courses. These accounts indicate the potentials associated with critical data literacy pedagogy and gesture to questions that remain to be answered through future research.

Katherine: Developing Rhetorical Awareness About Data Storytelling

Katherine was a junior computer science major when she completed a data storytelling assignment in a digital writing course. She had completed an associate degree in math at a community college prior to transferring to the four-year university where I met her, and she worked as a math tutor on campus. She described herself as "pretty comfortable" working with data, as she had considerable experience using data in academic, professional, and personal contexts. Despite her background, Katherine initially struggled with the data storytelling assignment because she believed that "data speaks for itself." As a result, she did not provide enough information in the draft of her data story for her audience to understand the data she provided, particularly in graphs. After receiving peer feedback, Katherine realized that "there is more to it than I thought there would be," further elaborating that, "I kind of just threw a few different graphs together on a slightly bigger rectangle. And then it's like, okay, but that doesn't say anything. Like, I know what it means because I made it, but that doesn't do anything for the audience." Although Katherine described the process of gathering data and creating graphs as "easy," when I spoke with her after the semester ended, she came to appreciate the complexity of communicating what data mean to readers.

Katherine had numerous opportunities to draw on her knowledge of data storytelling during the year following our class. For example, a few months after the semester ended, Katherine completed an internship in computer science for which she researched the impact of cybersecurity measures such as double authentication on vulnerable populations without stable access to technology. She put to work what she had learned about tailoring data stories for audiences as she created a public-facing presentation for her internship, explaining:

> My group did a project on accessibility issues for when you have a lot of cybersecurity measures like, you know, multifactor authentication and things like that. How can that negatively impact certain disenfranchised populations? There are a lot of homeless populations, for example, that have mobile devices, but they may not have actual cell service to get the text message PIN code, for example. I realized that we couldn't just say, "well, this issue affects a lot of people" because it's like, "well how much is a lot? Is that 51%?" It was actually more like 94%, so including the real statistic made it easier for readers to understand how big the problem is.

As Katherine described her experiences in other academic, professional, and personal situations, she frequently drew on specific terms we learned about in class to discuss the use of data. For example, Katherine explained that she was careful to avoid cherry-picking in making her own arguments after learning about it while completing the data storytelling assignment:

> The number one thing that pops up into my head when I'm thinking about any kind of citing sources is the cherry picking and how you can incredibly misrepresent what an article or a study is talking about, if you only are taking like this one line, or a couple of lines, and not providing context. And you can really tell very different stories based off of different pieces that you're pulling out. I remember what we learned about that in class, and I try to be wary, even just in myself in conversation, if you get into a debate with someone and you're making a point.

Terms like "cherry picking" functioned as "metalanguage" to help Katherine discuss data stories. Anne Cloonan (2011) has described the importance of students having language to "name structure and features and frameworks" in multimodal texts since "without a metalanguage, or grammar, for describing multimodal texts, understandings remain tacit rather than explicitly articulated or brought to consciousness" (173). Despite her familiarity with using data in technical contexts, Katherine initially lacked the metalanguage necessary to communicate about and with data in rhetorically effective ways. Working through the process of composing her own data story and gaining language to discuss the use of data in multimodal texts supported her rhetorical and critical awareness of how data stories were invented to serve persuasive ends and development of strategies to shape effective arguments with data.

Katherine's account illustrates how a student can have quite sophisticated technical and statistical knowledge of data yet lack the metalanguage necessary to transform their tacit understanding of how to use data into critical awareness. In this way, it serves as an important reminder that functional data literacy skills are not enough on their own. Especially as generative AI automates some of the basic tasks involved in data analysis—and simultaneously produces more data to contend with—critical and rhetorical data literacy skills are increasingly necessary. As we work to incorporate data storytelling into multimodal composition pedagogy, we will need to identify which data-related terms and concepts are most important to metalanguage and consider how we can better introduce metalanguage to students to facilitate their critical engagement with data. It may be beneficial to adopt a vertical curriculum, which is "an intentionally designed sequence of courses that integrates introductory knowledge into intermediate and advanced levels" (Beardon 2024, 174). This approach offers opportunities for students to develop critical data literacy over time as they repeatedly engage with key terms and concepts, thereby deepening their understanding and enhancing their rhetorical skills. However, it is equally important to consider how to integrate instruction in critical data literacy across the curriculum and to better understand all the different contexts in which data storytelling occurs, including outside of academic spaces.

Olivia: Drawing on Rhetorical Reading Strategies

Olivia, who was introduced in chapter 3, was a junior English education major, who brought few functional data literacy skills with her to class and initially described herself as uncomfortable working with data. She struggled with the data storytelling assignment assigned in her professional writing course, particularly because she underestimated the time and effort involved in collecting and analyzing data. When I spoke with Olivia immediately following the completion of our course, she indicated that although she had enjoyed learning about reading and writing data stories from the assignment, she did not anticipate applying what she had learned in the future. It just did not seem relevant to her remaining coursework in English or future career as an English teacher. When I spoke with Olivia again after six months, she confirmed that she had not used data storytelling again in any of her English courses. Although research projects had been assigned in these courses, she had not felt it was necessary or would be valued by her instructors to evaluate her research sources using rhetorical reading strategies or to incorporate any data in the arguments she developed in these courses.

However, while Olivia did not recognize any opportunities to use data in academic contexts, she was surprised to find that the skills she had developed to read data stories were proving useful in personal and professional contexts. For example, when we met after a year, Olivia brought to her interview a data story that a friend had shared with her, which turned out to be a lengthy online report, comparing experiences of Asian Americans to other racial groups in America. As a second-generation Asian American herself, Olivia took issue with the conclusions reached in the report, suggesting that the writers presented an overly generalized and negative view of Asian Americans' experiences. She described how she had taken bearings through lateral reading to evaluate the report, using questions drawn directly from the rhetorical chart we used in class (which was described in chapter 2). Taking bearings helped her to recognize where the methods used to collect data needed to be more fully detailed: "There were some statistics where I was like, 'You clearly didn't survey me. Which population specifically did you survey? Where? Which states did you gather this from?" She also recognized how the writers presented data in visualizations to support their largely negative view of Asian Americans' experiences: "I started thinking about the colors that they would use because that was a big thing I remembered from the data storytelling assignment. Like 'why blue? Why did you dip it over here? Why red in some areas?' There was this one statistic that they put in that 83% of Americans see China as a threat. And then they use a really red color for the 83%. And it says military/national security threat. When you think of threat, I guess you would associate red to a threat, so they were implying that China was a threat."

Additionally, Olivia had discovered that her original assumption that English teachers do not need to use data was incorrect. In fact, she learned that teachers were expected to track student learning using student data and to use these data in communicating with parents and administrators. Olivia stressed that although she found it helpful to use data to get a high-level view of her students and to communicate with parents, she recognized that the student data provided only a partial view of student learning.

Olivia's experience raises questions about how and when students recognize opportunities to adapt their knowledge of data storytelling in new contexts. Did Olivia really lack opportunities to use her skills in her English classes or did she just not perceive of such opportunities due to her preconceptions about the type of writing necessary for English majors? In recounting the experience of a student who failed to transfer her learning about multimodality from one academic context to another, Kathleen Blake Yancey (2024) contends that the student did not transfer her knowledge despite having the opportunity to do so because she had a personal philosophy of writing "founded on a divide between academic texts and other texts, a divide functioning as a Burkean terministic screen preventing her from seeing similarity across contexts, technologies, and composings" (226). In Olivia's case, her own philosophy of writing seems to have similarly impacted her perceptions of when data storytelling would be valuable. After all, she asserted immediately after finishing the semester that she would not use data storytelling in her other English courses because she did not believe that data storytelling was part of the academic writing necessary for an English major. So she may not have used her rhetorical reading strategies to evaluate sources in other English courses because her theory of writing excluded this possibility.

However, Olivia's theory of writing did not prevent her from recognizing that her skills would be useful in personal and professional contexts, despite her initial assumption that data storytelling would not be relevant to her in these contexts either. Why was Olivia able to recognize opportunities to apply her knowledge of data storytelling in personal and professional contexts? To better support students' transfer of their knowledge about data storytelling to other contexts, we need to know more about the role that a writer's identity plays in their conception of data storytelling and how students link these conceptions to their assumptions about or expectations for specific communities of which they are or hope to be a part. Yancey explains that "writers who claim a stronger writing identity, especially when linked to a clear sense of their future that is typically located in a specific community of practice, are less likely to transfer precisely because they are already committed to a theory of writing, they are less willing to consider revising it" (232). More support and opportunities to cultivate data storytelling skills will not, on their own, help a writer to apply their knowledge in new contexts if their personal philosophy of writing does not account for it. In cultivating critical data literacy pedagogy, we may need to connect academic instruction in data storytelling to personal and professional communities and be more transparent with students about connections among the different contexts in which data storytelling is used.

Shawn: Recognizing the Responsibilities of Data Literacy

Shawn was a freshman with a declared interest in majoring in criminal justice when he completed a data storytelling assignment in first-year writing. He was comfortable working with data and had enjoyed using data in a statistics course he had completed in high school. Shawn also liked working on the data storytelling assignment for class. He saw this as an assignment that was relevant to his future and as a "fun" opportunity to compose a multimodal text. He had not previously learned about information design or used visual editing programs, so he did experience some technical challenges using new techniques and programs. However, by consulting the resources provided in class and asking his classmates for tips when he ran into problems, Shawn created a data story he was proud of and included in his final portfolio for the course.

Shawn found several opportunities to adapt his learning about data storytelling in academic contexts during the year after he completed the assignment. In particular, he recounted how in one of his general education courses, he had been assigned to create a group presentation focused on urban heat deserts. Shawn and his teammates gathered data to share during their presentation, and Shawn volunteered to create the group's slides for the presentation since none of his teammates had prior instruction in multimodal composition. He felt that he had a "leg up" on the assignment given the data storytelling assignment he had completed, and he was encouraged by the instructor feedback the group received, which indicated that the slides and graphs Shawn designed had contributed to a successful and engaging presentation.

Shawn also described himself as newly aware of the role data played in social media. He observed how social media posts were designed to "get people to stop and look so they can track a certain amount of attention and how long people spend reading." He also recognized that his interactions on social media generated data that were then sold to profit social media companies: "And so spending time reading these posts gives them information about you, in terms of what you look at, and then how long you stay on the post or scroll on it. And then when you get to the bottom, there's more to swipe on or more information in the comment section and more graphs and that sort of thing." Shawn's awareness that his online interaction with content was being tracked led him to change the way he behaved. "I'm not scrolling on social media as much anymore," he noted, and he had also largely stopped liking and sharing posts online since he recognized that it was time-consuming to adequately evaluate social media content: "I'm responsible for information that I share, but it takes a long time to check all the sources and see why someone wrote something and what their agenda is."

In Shawn's case, his knowledge of data storytelling gave him an advantage in completing some assignments over his classmates and made him more aware of his agency as a social media user. As Gina Sipley (2024) points out, although individuals' choices to withhold some data by not contributing to online publicity metrics have not tended to be recognized as forms of algorithmic resistance, in the "transactional space" of the Internet, "data is the currency. The ability to withhold some data, to resist engaging in publicity metrics is not universally accessible" (80). In this context, Shawn's decisions about whether and how to participate in social media reflect the kind of agency students can exercise within datafied digital spaces.

While Shawn's story underscores the value of helping students better understand the process of datafication, it also serves as a reminder that data literacy is itself a privilege to which many students and members of society do not have access. Very few students currently receive instruction in critical data literacy except in some advanced disciplinary courses. Despite the advantages associated with critical data literacy, students' access remains very much dependent on whether individual instructors decide to make this a focus of instruction in their courses.

Providing more students with access to critical data literacy will require building what Stuart Selber (2004) refers to as the "composing infrastructure" or the "institutional resources" that support data storytelling and multimodal composing (12). While most universities already provide the "internet backbones, email servers, library databases, wireless networks, spam filters, and more" (12) that are a necessary part of the infrastructure needed to support data analysis and generative AI, today, many universities are also investing in the physical, pedagogical, and organizational spaces within which data-based activities are deeply situated. These spaces often take the form of an interdisciplinary center or lab located within a specific college or university-wide office for teaching and learning and organized around data analysis or visualization, informatics, or, more recently, AI. However, Jeff Naftzinger (2024) has pointed out that simply having access to composing infrastructure is not enough to ensure that instructors make use of these infrastructures for teaching purposes. He argues that to motivate instructors to use the infrastructure, it is necessary to "help them establish generative dispositions by ensuring that they see how [communities of practice] they identify with—locally, in the fields they identify with, or both—can model digital composing and demonstrate its value" (21). The same is true for critical data literacy pedagogy. Instructors need to see how data literacy is practiced in the local context of their program, department, and university and within the field of rhetoric and composition to be encouraged to make use of whatever composing infrastructure is available. As universities and writing programs invest in helping instructors adapt their pedagogy to meet the challenges posed by generative AI and datafied knowledge production more generally, it is important to recognize the role that modeling "generative dispositions" in both local and disciplinary contexts will need to play to ensure that more students have access to critical data literacy.

Conclusion

Critical Data Storytelling does not so much argue for adding data to multimodal composition pedagogy as it does for recognizing the central role that data already play. Datafication has already transformed information and information environments and led to the production of previously unimaginable quantities of data. Data have already become "everyone's responsibility" (Dykes 2020, 6). Software has already made analyzing and visualizing data more accessible than ever before. The rampant spread of mis- and disinformation online has already injected confusion into public discourse and eroded trust in traditional sources of information. Generative AI has already made available new options for producing and interacting with information. Given these changes, the choice facing composition teachers is whether to adapt our pedagogy to help students cultivate the functional, critical, and rhetorical data literacies necessary to evaluate and use data or whether to allow the gap between the information literacies currently emphasized in academic writing instruction and those our students need to navigate contemporary information to continue to widen. The model for critical data literacy pedagogy proposed in this book represents my endorsement of adapting multimodal composition to meet the challenges of this moment.

Incorporating this pedagogy will require an openness to engaging with different ways for students to access and evaluate a wide range of information sources. It might involve working with texts, technologies, and methods that are unfamiliar. It might also de-center classroom authority as instructors learn to work with data and respond to and assess their students' data stories alongside their students. Although this approach involves some risks, I have found that it leads to a multimodal education that benefits students' academic, personal, and professional lives. By providing students with a critical framework for reading and using data in their multimodal compositions, critical data literacy pedagogy gives students the chance to reimagine agentive roles for themselves within big data society as readers and communicators capable of asking and answering genuine questions about and with data.

The model of critical data literacy presented in this book emphasizes the value of a rhetorical perspective on data. Unlike data storytelling approaches that center specific story-telling structures, critical data storytelling considers the entire context in which data stories are invented, arranged, and delivered. This emphasis on rhetorical choice-making is key to moving beyond formalist understandings of data stories. Rather than limiting students' choices to placing content within predetermined story structures or templates, critical data literacy encourages students to recognize the rhetorical dimensions of data stories and data more generally. It encourages them to participate in creating the meaning of data stories as readers of these texts through their analytical and interpretive work and as writers who choose among available options for inventing, arranging, and delivering data stories. My hope is that critical data literacy pedagogy will encourage instructors to incorporate rhetorical reading and critical data communication in their classrooms; to think about what students need to know to navigate online information environments, including the use of generative AI, wisely; and to recognize data storytelling as a vital part of multimodal composition.

Appendix

This study was approved by the Institutional Review Board. All participants' names are pseudonyms.

Data used in this study were collected from two sites and in two distinct phases. The first phase ran from 2016 to 2019. During this phase, I collected and examined classroom data at Marist College (2016–2018) and California State University, Sacramento (2018–2019). The second phase ran from 2020 to 2023. During this phase, I collected surveys, classroom data, and interviews at California State University, Sacramento.

Sites

MARIST COLLEGE

Marist College is a medium, comprehensive private college in Poughkeepsie, New York. In 2018 (the last year I collected data at Marist), the university had a full-time undergraduate population of 5,139 ("Marist University Enrollment [2018–19]" n.d.). Marist is rated a "highly selective" institution. In 2018, the full-time enrolled undergraduate student population at Marist College was 76.7 percent white, 10.3 percent Hispanic/Latino, 4.1 percent

Black or African American, 2.9 percent two or more races, 2.6 percent Asian, 2.5 percent non-resident alien, 0.7 percent race/ethnicity unknown, 0.1 percent Native Hawaiian or other Pacific Islanders, and 0.1 percent American Indian or Alaska Native (Marist Office of Institutional Research and Planning 2021). Fifty-eight percent of full-time enrolled undergraduate students were female, and 42 percent were male (Marist Office of Institutional Research and Planning 2021).

Students are required to complete a one-semester writing course, Writing for College, that meets general education requirements unless they are exempt due to completing an equivalent course in high school or at another institution of higher education. Writing for College courses are required to engage with at least one of the following themes: cultural diversity, nature and the environment, civic engagement, and/or quantitative reasoning (Marist University 2024).

Students majoring in English at Marist choose among three concentrations: literature, theatre, and writing (they may choose more than one concentration). The department also offers a minor in professional writing. One of the foundational courses for the professional writing minor is Introduction to Professional Writing. Elective courses for English majors in any concentration or professional writing minors include Technical Writing and Writing in the Digital Age and special-topics courses like Environmental Writing.

CALIFORNIA STATE UNIVERSITY, SACRAMENTO

California State University, Sacramento (Sacramento State University), is a regional, state-funded, four-year university in northern California. In fall 2023, it had a full- and part-time population of 27,640 undergraduates ("Sacramento State Fact Book" 2024). Designated an Asian American and Native American Pacific Islander Serving Institution (AANAPISI) and Hispanic-Serving Institution (HSI), this university has a highly diverse student body. In fall 2023, the student body was 38 percent Hispanic/Latino, 22 percent white, 20 percent Asian American, 6 percent African American, 6 percent other/multiracial, 3 percent international, 3 percent unknown, 1 percent Pacific Islander, and 1 percent American Indian. Fifty-six percent of students were female, and 44 percent were male; with 67 students identifying as nonbinary ("Sacramento State Fact Book").

At Sacramento State, the English Department's Writing Program houses directed self-placement (DSP), the first-year writing graduation requirement—which satisfies a written communication general education requirement—

the Composition II graduation requirement, and the Graduation Writing Assessment Requirement (GWAR). In addition to first-year writing and Composition II, students are required to complete an upper-level writing-intensive course. The English Department offers several writing-intensive courses, including Professional Writing and Digital Writing and Rhetoric, that students from across the university can complete to fulfill their writing-intensive requirement. English majors may also complete these courses to fulfill major elective requirements.

Participants

PHASE 1

During the first phase of my research, I collected classroom data, including assignment descriptions, my teaching log, and student artifacts. After the semester was over and grades were submitted, I requested that students who completed critical data storytelling assignments in my writing courses share their assignments with me for research purposes. I collected seventy-four artifacts that included students' brainstorming work, drafts, revised drafts, and reflective assignments. Table A.1 shows how many students participate from seven courses during phase 1.

TABLE A.1. Courses included in Phase 1

Course title	Semester taught	Site	# of students enrolled	# of students who participated
Writing for College	Spring 2016	Marist College	19	13
Technical Writing	Spring 2016	Marist College	13	10
Introduction to Professional Writing	Fall 2016	Marist College	17	12
Writing in the Digital Age	Fall 2016	Marist College	18	11
Environmental Writing	Fall 2017	Marist College	9	5
Topics in Composition: Multimedia Writing	Fall 2018	California State University, Sacramento	30	18
Professional Writing	Spring 2019	California State University, Sacramento	30	20

PHASE 2

During the second phase of data collection, I collected surveys, classroom data (including assignment descriptions, my teaching log, and student artifacts), and interviews from students in six writing courses. I approached students to participate in the study after the semester was over and grades had been submitted.

I asked for students' permission to use introductory surveys they had completed for class, 154 students in total. Since the students had already completed the surveys as part of their regular coursework, the participation rate was high, with 129 consenting to have their surveys included, a participation rate of 84 percent. Table A.2 shows how many students participated in the survey from each of the six courses.

TABLE A.2. Courses included in Phase 2

Course title	Semester taught	# of students enrolled	# of students who participated
Accelerated Academic Literacies	Fall 2021	24	19
Accelerated Academic Literacies	Fall 2021	25	21
Professional Writing	Fall 2020	27	17
Professional Writing	Fall 2021	27	25
Digital Writing and Rhetoric	Summer 2022	26	24
Digital Writing and Rhetoric	Summer 2023	25	23

The introductory survey that students completed includes ten questions and focused on students' demographics, including math classes they had already completed and other experiences they may have had working with data, and their perceptions of their own data literacy. Table A.3 shows the breakdown of survey participant characteristics. The majority of students who participated in this study were upper-level students who identifed as female. This reflects the fact that the upper-level courses included in the study have larger enrollment numbers than the first-year writing courses do. The gender and racial and ethnic diversity of participants in the study does not entirely mirror the diversity of the university but does indicate a high level of diversity among participants.

TABLE A.3. Survey participant characteristics

Participant characteristics	Survey participants (N = 129)
Classification	27% (35) freshman 4% (5) sophomore 19% (24) junior 49% (63) senior 1% (2) other
Gender	62% (80) female 31% (40) male 3% (4) transgender and nonbinary 4% (5) prefer not to answer
Racial/ethnic identity	32% (41) Hispanic/Latino 19% (25) white 15.5% (20) Asian 13% (17) Black or African American 5% (6) Native Hawaiian or other Pacific Islander 3% (4) Hispanic/Latino, white 2% (3) Black or African American, white 1.5% (2) Asian, white 3% (4) other racial/ethnic identity 6% (7) prefer not to answer
Major	44.5% (57) English 12% (15) psychology 9% (12) business 7% (9) engineering 4% (5) communications 3% (4) communication sciences and disorders 3% (4) computer science 2% (3) political science 1.5% (2) child and adolescent development 1.5% (2) sociology 1.5% (2) American Sign Language/deaf study 1.5% (2) art 1.5% (2) undeclared 8% (10) other (biology, mathematics, health science, kinesiology, biomedical science, graphic design, public health, construction management)

continued on next page

TABLE A.3. —*continued*

Participant characteristics	Survey participants (N = 129)
Math courses completed in high school or college Percentages exceed 100% because most students reported completing more than 1 math course	88% (114) algebra 77% (99) geometry 71% (92) statistics 60% (78) advanced algebra 43% (55) precalculus 35% (45) trigonometry 33% (43) calculus 8% (10) finite mathematics

I also asked students to share the texts they had created for their data storytelling assignment during the semester (including pre-writing, early and revised drafts, and reflective writing) and to complete a separate interest form if they were willing to participate in three interviews (conducted one month, six months, and twelve months after completing the semester). Sixty-three respondents submitted their assignment artifacts to the study, and thirty-nine completed the interest form. I analyzed the sixty-three artifacts, but I only conducted interviews with fifteen of the students due to time and resource limitations and/or the students' failure to reply to scheduling emails. The interviews were scheduled in the month following the completion of the semester and then again six months and one year after the completion of the semester. During the interviews, I asked students about their perceptions of and experiences with data storytelling, and I asked them to read and evaluate a sample data story. Table A.4 shows the list of interview participants.

TABLE A.4. Interview participants

Pseud-onym	Classification	Major	Course in which they completed a data storytelling assignment	Comfort level working with data
Faith	Freshman	Communications	Accelerated Academic Literacies	Strongly uncomfortable
Grace	Freshman	Business	Accelerated Academic Literacies	Not sure/unfamiliar
Ajay	Freshman	Political science	Accelerated Academic Literacies	Somewhat comfortable
Shawn	Freshman	Criminal justice	Accelerated Academic Literacies	Comfortable
Mateo	Sophomore	Business administration	Accelerated Academic Literacies	Somewhat uncomfortable
Ahri	Senior	English	Digital Writing and Rhetoric	Comfortable
Katherine	Junior	Computer science	Digital Writing and Rhetoric	Somewhat comfortable
Jordan	Senior	English	Digital Writing and Rhetoric	Uncomfortable
Diandra	Senior	English education	Digital Writing and Rhetoric	Somewhat uncomfortable
Gabriel	Junior	English education	Digital Writing and Rhetoric	Somewhat comfortable
Charlotte	Senior	Psychology	Professional Writing	Comfortable
Haley	Senior	Childhood and adolescent education	Professional Writing	Uncomfortable
Luke	Senior	English	Professional Writing	Somewhat comfortable
Olivia	Junior	English education	Professional Writing	Comfortable
Ryo	Senior	Civil engineering	Professional Writing	Very comfortable

Methods

In order to understand whether and how a multiliteracies approach to critical data storytelling in multimodal composition pedagogy can foster students' data and multimodality literacy skills, I wanted to study a wide range of learners in a variety of writing classes. I was pleased that students with varying degrees of comfort and experience working with data, from a range of majors, and who earned widely different grades on the data storytelling assignment were willing to contribute their surveys and assignment texts to the study and agreed to participate in interviews.

This study was exploratory. Classroom data gathered during phases 1 and 2 were examined retrospectively after the conclusion of the semester, and I categorized the data stories students composed by genre and purpose and analyzed them for their use of strategies to communicate multimodally and represent data. I also coded students' reflective writing for repeated phrases and themes. I referred to the assignment descriptions and pre-writing drafts to provide context.

The survey introduced during phase 2 was designed to collect demographic data and data on students' previous experiences with and perceptions of working with data. These surveys, which were completed by all the students in a course as part of regular instruction, helped me to tailor instruction in data storytelling for different classes based on the general comfort level of the students in the class and their previous experiences. Although I used the surveys during the semester to inform my teaching, I did not analyze the surveys for the study until after the completion of the semester, and then I included only surveys by consenting students in the analysis. During analysis, I first examined the responses to closed-ended survey questions, looking at frequency counts for the various multiple-choice questions and cross-tabulating responses for certain questions to see if students from different groups had different responses. In analyzing students' responses to open-ended survey questions, I first read through all responses, looking for repeated phrases and themes. I then reviewed the data again, this time developing categories for how students described experiences impacting their comfort and interest in working with data.

The interviews conducted during phase 2 were designed with general questions about the data storytelling assignment, which would then lead to more open-ended discussions based on the participants' responses. I interviewed the participants three separate times over the course of a year so I could see how their responses might change over time, which involved asking similar questions about data storytelling at different times. I also asked students to read a sample data story for meaning and to determine whether it was a credible source of information during each interview so I could see what rhetorical reading strategies they used to read and evaluate a data story.

I audio-recorded the interviews and took field notes during and after interviews. I examined the transcripts and field notes for repeated phrases and themes, and these transcripts and notes informed my questions in the next set of interviews. While transcribing the interviews, I kept analytical memos to identify trends and a preliminary list of codes. I subsequently coded all the transcripts using the program MAXQDA, which enabled me to see if specific codes were appearing across different participants and to quickly recall passages that referenced a particular theme. As is common with an inductive coding approach, I ended up adding additional codes during the coding process, ranging from basic demographic data (e.g., major) to self-perception (e.g., motivation, engagement, interest) to information about how students applied what they learned through the assignment (e.g., in courses, for internships or jobs, in reading news stories).

I triangulated the data used in this study by continually analyzing survey responses, classroom data, and interview transcripts. I compared student comments about reading and writing data stories to the texts they composed and the reading strategies they used to examine sample texts during the interviews, and I compared their data stories to the assignment descriptions to which they were responding.

Glossary

artificial intelligence (AI). Technology that enables computers to simulate human intelligence and perform tasks that typically require human intelligence.
AI algorithms. A set of rules or procedures that generative AI models use to process data, learn patterns, and create new content.
AI literacy. The knowledge and skills necessary to understand, use, and evaluate AI technologies critically.
AI models. AI software programs that have been trained on datasets to perform specific tasks without additional human intervention.
algorithms. A step-by-step set of instructions or rules designed to solve a problem or perform a task.
chatbot. A computer program that simulates conversation with a human user.
cognitive biases. Mental shortcuts that shape individuals' perceptions and interpretation of the world.
construct. Those ideas, attributes, or concepts that will be measured during a data inquiry.
datafication. The process of converting real-world data into a digital format, making it accessible for analysis and AI applications.
data inquiry. A multi-part process involving the use of data analysis to identify and study student learning needs.
data literacy. The ability to ask and answer real-world questions using large and small data sets through an ethical inquiry process.

dataveillance. The use of data to monitor individuals and groups for the purpose of guiding behavior.

data violence. Harm resulting from the implicit and explicit choices in data systems, whether or not that harm is intentional.

data visualization. The representation of data using visual tools like graphs, charts, and maps, among others.

deep learning (DL). A type of machine learning that uses neural networks to teach computers to learn from data.

DFW rate. A rate that refers to the percentage of grades of D or F or of students withdrawing from the course entirely.

filter bubble. A phenomenon caused by algorithms that personalize an Internet user's online experience in which an individual only encounters information and opinions online that reflect their own beliefs.

foundational datasets. Large and diverse collections of data used to train AI models, providing a broad base of knowledge and patterns.

generative AI. The ability of an AI model to generate new text, images, and other content based on the data it has been trained on.

Institutional Review Board (IRB). A group formally designated by an institution to review research studies to ensure that they comply with applicable regulations, meet commonly accepted ethical standards, follow institutional policies, and adequately protect research participants.

large language model (LLM). Advanced neural network architectures trained on vast amounts of text data, enabling them to understand and generate humanlike language.

learning analytics. An umbrella term for tools and techniques used to measure, collect, analyze and report data about learners and learning contexts.

learning analytics dashboard (LAD). A single digital display that aggregates, analyzes, and visualizes educational data.

learning management system (LMS). Software that facilitates creating, delivering, and reporting on online courses and programs.

machine learning (ML). A branch of AI and computer science that focuses on a computer using algorithms to identify patterns in datasets and to then make predictions on new, similar data without additional human intervention.

measure. The relevant constructs that represent the features a researcher wants to study through a data inquiry.

misinfodemic. An overabundance of mis- and disinformation related to a particular medical topic or disease.

natural language processing (NLP). A field of AI focusing on enabling machines to understand, interpret, and generate human language, bridging the gap between humans and computers.

neural networks. Computational models inspired by the human brain, capable of complex pattern recognition and processing information.

post-truth. A situation in which objective facts are less influential in shaping public opinion than are emotions and personal beliefs.

predictive AI. Technology that uses machine learning to identify patterns in datasets and make predictions about future events.

prompt. The process of entering instructions and/or keywords to direct AI software to generate an output, such as text or an image.

proxy data. Data that relate to, but are not a direct measure of, a construct.

structured data. Data such as numbers and values that are organized and formatted in a standard way that makes them easy to read and use by humans and computers.

training. Feeding data into AI software so that it begins the machine learning process.

triangulation. The use of multiple methods or data sources to corroborate or identify weaknesses in an interpretation.

unstructured data. Information such as text, images, and audio and video files that is not organized or stored in a predefined format.

References

Abelson, Robert P. 1995. *Statistics as Principled Argument*. Lawrence Erlbaum Associates.
Adler-Kassner, Linda. 2017. "2017 CCCC Chair's Address." *College Composition and Communication* 69 (2): 317–340.
Adsanatham, Chanon. 2012. "Integrating Assessment and Instruction: Using Student-Generated Grading Criteria to Evaluate Multimodal Digital Projects." *Computers and Composition* 29 (2): 152–174.
Agostinho, Daniela. 2019. "The Optical Unconscious of Big Data: Datafication of Vision and Care for Unknown Futures." *Big Data & Society* 6 (1): 1–10. https://doi.org/10.1177/2053951719826859.
Aguilar, Gabriel Lorenzo. 2024. "Rhetorically Training Students to Generate with AI: Social Justice Applications for AI as Audience." *Computers and Composition* (71). https://doi.org/10.1016/j.compcom.2024.102828.
Aizenberg, Evgeni, and Jeroen Van Den Hoven. 2020. "Designing for Human Rights in AI." *Big Data & Society* 7 (2): 1–14. https://doi.org/10.1177/2053951720949566.
American Association of Colleges and Universities. 2022. "High Impact Practices." AAC&U. https://www.aacu.org/trending-topics/high-impact.
Anderson, Chris. 2008. "The End of Theory: The Data Deluge Makes the Scientific Method Obsolete." *Wired* 16 (7): 108.
Anderson, Daniel. 2008. "The Low Bridge to High Benefits: Entry-Level Multimedia, Literacies, and Motivation." *Computers and Composition* 25 (1): 40–60.
Andrews, R. J. 2019. *Info We Trust, How to Create Value with Data Graphics*. John Wiley & Sons.

Anson, Chris M. 2008. "The Intelligent Design of Writing Programs: Reliance on Belief or a Future of Evidence." *Writing Program Administration* 32 (1–2): 11–37.

Aull, Laura. 2015. *First-Year University Writing: A Corpus-Based Study with Implications for Pedagogy*. Palgrave Macmillan.

Aull, Laura. 2021. "Big Data as Mirror: Writing Analytics and Assessing Assignment Genres." In *Composition and Big Data*, edited by Amanda Licastro and Benjamin Miller, 85–100. University of Pittsburgh Press.

Bakke, Abigail. 2020. "Everyday Googling: Results of an Observational Study and Applications for Teaching Algorithmic Literacy." *Computers and Composition* 57 (1). https://doi.org/10.1016/j.compcom.2020.102577.

Ball, Cheryl E., Tarez Samra Graban, and Michelle Sidler. 2021. "The Boutique is Open: Data for Writing Studies." In *Composition and Big Data*, edited by Amanda Licastro and Benjamin Miller, 196–211. University of Pittsburgh Press.

Bay, Jennifer, and Rachel Atherton. 2021. "Rhetorics of Data in Nonprofit Settings: How Community Engagement Pedagogies Can Enact Social Justice." *Computers and Composition* 61 (1): 1–16. https://doi.org/10.1016/j.compcom.2021.102656.

Beardon, Logan. 2024. "Rhetoric in Its Fullness: Metalanguage and Multimodal Transfer." In *Multimodal Composing and Writing Transfer*, edited by Kara Poe Alexander, Matthew Davis, Lilian W. Mina, and Ryan P. Shepherd, 170–189. Utah State University Press.

Beck, Estee N. 2016. "Writing Educator Responsibilities for Discussing the History and Practice of Surveillance and Privacy in Writing Classrooms." *Kairos: A Journal of Rhetoric, Technology, and Pedagogy* 20 (2). https://kairos.technorhetoric.net/20.2/topoi/beck-et-al/beck.html.

Beck, Estee, and Les Hutchinson Campos, eds. 2021. *Privacy Matters: Conversations About Surveillance Within and Beyond the Classroom*. Utah State University Press.

Beck, Estee, M. Ellen Goin, Andrew Ho, Alexis Parks, and Stephen Rowe. 2021. "Critical Digital Literacy as Method for Teaching Tactics of Response to Online Surveillance and Privacy Erosion." *Computers and Composition* 61 (2): 1–19. https://doi.org/10.1016/j.compcom.2021.102654.

Beck, Jori S., and Diana Nunnaley. 2021. "A Continuum of Data Literacy for Teaching." *Studies in Educational Evaluation* 69: 1–8. https://doi.org/10.1016/j.stueduc.2020.100871.

Beveridge, Aaron. 2015. "Looking in the Dustbin: Data Janitorial Work, Statistical Reasoning, and Information Rhetorics." *Computers and Composition Online*. http://cconlinejournal.org/fall15/beveridge/.

Beveridge, Aaron. 2017. "Writing Through Big Data: New Challenges and Possibilities for Data-Driven Arguments." *Composition Forum* 37. https://files.eric.ed.gov/fulltext/EJ1162166.pdf.

Blevins, Brenta. 2013. "Visualizing Data through Infographics." *Digital Rhetoric Collaborative*, November 14, 2013. https://www.digitalrhetoriccollaborative.org/2013/11/14/visualizing-data-through-infographics.

Bonde Thylstrup, Nanna, Mikkel Flyverbom, and Rasmus Helles. 2019. "Datafied Knowledge Production: Introduction to the Special Theme." *Big Data & Society* 6 (2): 1–5. https://doi.org/10.1177/2053951719875985.

Borton, Sonya C., and Brian Huot. 2007. "Responding and Assessing." In *Multimodal Composing: Resources for Teachers*, edited by Cynthia L. Selfe, 99–111. Hampton Press.

boyd, danah. 2018. "You Think You Want Media Literacy . . . Do You?" *Apophenia*, March 9, 2018, posted by zephoria, https://www.zephoria.org/thoughts/archives/2018/03/09/you-think-you-want-media-literacy-do-you.html.

boyd, danah, and Kate Crawford. 2012. "Critical Questions for Big Data: Provocations for a Cultural, Technological, and Scholarly Phenomenon." *Information, Communication & Society* 15 (5): 662–679.

Brown, Malcolm, Joanne Dehoney, and Nancy Millichap. 2015. "The Next Generation Digital Learning Environment." *ELI Paper* 5 (1): 1–13. https://library.educause.edu/~/media/files/library/2015/4/eli3035-pdf.

Brown, Michael. 2020. "Seeing Students at Scale: How Faculty in Large Lecture Courses Act upon Learning Analytics Dashboard Data." *Teaching in Higher Education* 25 (4): 384–400.

Byrd, Antonio, Leonardo Flores, David Green, Holly Hassel, Sarah Z. Johnson, Matthew Kirschenbaum, A. Lockett, Elizabeth Matthews Losh, and Anna Mills. 2023. *MLA-CCCC Joint Task Force on Writing and AI Working Paper: Overview of the Issues, Statement of Principles, and Recommendations*. MLA-CCCC Joint Task Force on Writing and AI, July 2023. https://hcommons.org/app/uploads/sites/1003160/2023/07/MLA-CCCC-Joint-Task-Force-on-Writing-and-AI-Working-Paper-1.pdf.

Carillo, Ellen C. 2018. *Teaching Readers in Post-Truth America*. Utah State University Press.

Carter, Marcus, and Ben Egliston. 2023. "What are the Risks of Virtual Reality Data? Learning Analytics, Algorithmic Bias and a Fantasy of Perfect Data." *New Media & Society* 25 (3): 485–504.

Cavanaugh, Andrew J., and Liyan Song. 2014. "Audio Feedback Versus Written Feedback: Instructors' and Students' Perspectives." *MERLOT Journal of Online Learning and Teaching* 10 (1): 122–138.

Chen, Chen. 2021. "How Can We Better Support Teaching Multimodal Composition? A National Survey of Institutional Professional Development Efforts." *WPA: Writing Program Administration-Journal of the Council of Writing Program Administrators* 45 (1): 70–89.

Chou, Wen-Ying Sylvia, Anna Gaysnysky, and Robin C. Vanderpool. 2021. "The COVID-19 Misinfodemic: Moving Beyond Fact-Checking." *Health Education & Behavior* 48 (1): 9–13. https://doi.org/10.1177/1090198120980675.

Chun, Randall. 2017. "The Dangers of Fake News Spread to Data Visualization." MediaShift, February 23, 2017. http://mediashift.org/2017/02/the-dangers-of-fake-news-spread-to-data-visualization.

Cloonan, Anne. 2011. "Creating Multimodal Metalanguage with Teachers." *English Teaching: Practice and Critique* 10 (4): 23–40.

Cohn, Janae. 2021. *Skim, Dive, Surface: Teaching Digital Reading*. West Virginia University Press.

Colenso, Francesca. 2024. "Seeing is Believing: How AI Can Help Visualize Data to Drive Impact and Insight." TechRadar. June 20, 2024. https://www.techradar.com

/pro/seeing-is-believing-how-ai-can-help-visualize-data-to-drive-impact-and-insight.

Coughlin, Sean. 2017. "What Does Post-Truth Mean for a Philosopher?" BBC, January 12, 2017, http://www.bbc.com/news/education-38557838.

Craig, Jacob W. 2017. "Navigating a Varied Landscape: Literacy and the Credibility of Networked Information." *Literacy, Democracy, and Fake News*, special issue of *Literacy in Composition Studies* 5 (2): 24–42. http://dx.doi.org/10.21623%2F1.5.2.3.

Crow, Angela. 2013. "Managing Datacloud Decisions and 'Big Data:' Understanding Privacy Choices in Terms of Surveillance Assemblages." In *Digital Writing Assessment and Evaluation*, edited by Heidi McKee and Dánielle Nicole DeVoss. Computers and Composition Digital Press.

Cunningham, Kelly J. 2019. "Student Perceptions and Use of Technology-Mediated Text and Screencast Feedback in ESL Writing." *Computers and Composition* 52: 222–241.

Dahlman, Jill. 2021. "Making Do: Working with Missing and Broken Data." In *Composition and Big Data*, edited by Amanda Licastro and Benjamin Miller, 279–290. University of Pittsburgh Press.

Danner, Patrick. 2020a. "Story/telling with Data as Distributed Activity." *Technical Communication Quarterly* 29 (2): 174–187.

Danner, Patrick. 2020b. "Storytelling With and Around Data." *Kairos* 25 (1). https://praxis.technorhetoric.net.

The Data Literacy Project. 2022. *Data Literacy: The Upskilling Evolution*. https://thedataliteracyproject.org/wp-content/uploads/2022/11/Data-Literacy-The-Upskilling-Evolution-Report-1.pdf.

Devito, Michael A., Jeremy Birnholtz, Jeffry T. Hancock, Megan French, and Sunny Liu. 2018. "How People Form Folk Theories of Social Media Feeds and What It Means for How We Study Self-Presentation." In *Proceedings of the 2018 CHI Conference on Human Factors in Computing Systems, 21–26 April 2018*, 1–12. Association for Computing Machinery.

D'Ignazio, Catherine, and Rahul Bhargava. 2016. "DataBasic: Design Principles, Tools and Activities for Data Literacy Learners." *The Journal of Community Informatics* 12 (3): 83–107.

DiSalvo, Carl. 2012. "Spectacles and Tropes: Speculative Design and Contemporary Food Cultures." *The Fibreculture Journal: Digital Media + Networks + Transdisciplinary Critique* 20: 109–121. https://twenty.fibreculturejournal.org/2012/06/19/fcj-142-spectacles-and-tropes-speculative-design-and-contemporary-food-cultures/.

Dixon, Stacy Jo. 2022. "Number of Global Social Network Users from 2018 to 2027." Statista, September 16, 2022. https://www.statista.com/statistics/278414/number-of-worldwide-social-network-users/.

Dixon, Zachary, and Joe Moxley. 2013. "Everything is Illuminated: What Big Data Can Tell Us About Teacher Commentary." *Assessing Writing* 18 (4): 241–256.

Donahue, Christiane. 2010. "First Annual Summer Seminar for Composition Research: 'Got Data—Now What?'" *International Writing Centers Association*, September 30, 2010. https://writingcenters.wordpress.com/2010/09/30/first-annual-summer-seminar-for-composition-research/.

Drucker, Johanna. 2011. "Humanities Approaches to Graphical Display." *Digital Humanities Quarterly* 5 (1). http://www.digitalhumanities.org/dhq/vol/5/1/000091/000091.html.

Duarte, Nancy. 2013. *Resonate: Present Visual Stories that Transform Audiences*. John Wiley & Sons.

Duarte, Nancy. 2019. *Data Story: Explain Data and Inspire Action through Story*. Idea Press.

Duffy, John. 2019. *Provocations of Virtue: Rhetoric, Ethics, and the Teaching of Writing*. Utah State University Press.

Duin, Ann Hill, and Jason Tham. 2020. "The Current State of Analytics: Implications for Learning Management System (LMS) Use in Writing Pedagogy." *Computers and Composition* 55. https://doi.org/10.1016/j.compcom.2020.102544.

Dwivedi, Dwijendra Nath, and Ghanashyama Mahanty. 2024. "Guardians of the Algorithm: Human Oversight in the Ethical Evolution of AI and Data Analysis." In *The Ethical Frontier of AI and Data Analysis*, edited by Rajeev Kumar, Ankush Joshi, Hari Om Sharan, Sheng-Lung Peng, and Chetan R. Dudhagara, 196–210. IGI Global.

Dykes, Brent. 2020. *Effective Data Storytelling: How to Drive Change with Data, Narrative, and Visuals*. John Wiley & Sons.

Emig, Janet. 1971. *The Composing Processes of Twelfth Graders*. NCTE.

Eslami, Motahhare, Aimee Rickman, Kristen Vaccaro, Amirhossein Aleyasen, Andy Vuong, Karrie Karahalios, Kevin Hamilton, and Christian Sandvig. 2015. "'I Always Assumed That I Wasn't Really That Close to [Her]': Reasoning About Invisible Algorithms in News Feeds." In *CHI '15: Proceedings of the 33rd Annual ACM Conference on Human Factors in Computing Systems*, 153–162. Association of Computing Machinery. https://doi.org/10.1145/2702123.2702556.

Faigley, Lester L. 2006. "Rhetorics Fast and Slow." In *Rhetorical Agendas: Political, Ethical, Spiritual*, edited by Patricia Bizzell, 3–9. Lawrence Erlbaum Associates.

Fanning, Shannon N. 2020. "Following the Narrative: Using Data Visualization in the Composition Classroom." *Kairos* 25 (1). https://praxis.technorhetoric.net/.

Farina, Andrew G. 2022. "The Impending Data Literacy Crisis Among Military Leaders." *The Cyber Defense Review* 7 (4): 91–98.

Farmer, Donald. 2024. "Generative AI Capabilities Increase Data Analytics Value." TechTarget, March 22, 2024. https://www.techtarget.com/searchbusinessanalytics/tip/Generative-AI-capabilities-increase-data-analytics-value.

Few, Stephen. 2007. "Save the Pies for Dessert." *Visual Business Intelligence Newsletter*, August 2007, 1–14.

Firat, Mehmet. 2023. "Integrating AI Applications into Learning Management Systems to Enhance e-Learning." *Instructional Technology and Lifelong Learning* 4 (1): 1–14.

Fisher, James. 2023. "Is AI Literacy the New Data Literacy?" *Qlik*, October 30, 2023. https://www.qlik.com/blog/is-ai-literacy-the-new-data-literacy.

Flaherty, Colleen. 2018. "DFW Fail." Inside Higher Ed, May 30, 2018. https://www.insidehighered.com/news/2018/05/31/savannah-state-professors-object-new-unwritten-policy-linking-dfw-grades-teaching.

Floridi, Luciano. 2015. "How AI is Reshaping Human Reality." YouTube. Uploaded by Thinking Digital Conference, July 28, 2015. https://www.youtube.com/watch?v=htSvT_v8okY.

Flower, Linda, and John R. Hayes. 1980. "The Cognition of Discovery: Defining a Rhetorical Problem." *College Composition and Communication* 31 (1): 21–32.

Franconeri, Steven L., Lace M. Padilla, Priti Shah, Jeffrey M. Zacks, and Jessica Hullmann. 2021. "The Science of Visual Data Communication: What Works." *Psychological Science in the Public Interest* 22 (3): 110–161.

Frank, Mark, Johanna Walker, Judie Attard, and Alan Tygel. 2016. "Data Literacy: What Is It and How Can We Make It Happen? Editorial." *The Journal of Community Informatics* 12 (3): 4–8.

Gallagher, John R. 2020. "The Ethics of Writing for Algorithmic Audiences." *Computers and Composition* 57 (4). https://doi.org/10.1016/j.compcom.2020.102583.

Gallagher, John R. 2023. "Lessons Learned from Machine Learning Researchers About the Terms 'Artificial Intelligence' and 'Machine Learning.'" *Composition Studies* 51 (1): 149–154.

Gershon, Nahum, and Ward Page. 2001. "What Storytelling Can Do for Information Visualization." *Communications of the ACM* 44 (8): 31–37.

Gillespie, Tarleton. 2014. "The Relevance of Algorithms." In *Media Technologies: Essays on Communication, Materiality, and Society*, edited by Tarleton Gillespie, Pablo J. Boczkowski, and Kirsten A. Foot, 167–193. MIT Press. https://doi.org/10.7551/mitpress/9780262525374.003.0009.

Gitelman, Lisa, ed. 2013. *Raw Data is an Oxymoron*. MIT Press.

Gorman, Michael. 2018. "Project Based Learning and the Flipped Classroom ... A Great Combination." *Tech and Learning*, February 20, 2018. https://www.techlearning.com/tl-advisor-blog/project-based-learning-flipped-classroom-great-combination.

Graham, S. Scott. 2023. "Post-Process but Not Post-Writing: Large Language Models and a Future for Composition Pedagogy." *Composition Studies* 51 (1): 162–168.

Greenwood, April, Benjamin Lauren, Jessica Knott, and Dànielle Nicole DeVoss. 2019. "Dissensus, Resistance, and Ideology: Design Thinking as a Rhetorical Methodology." *Journal of Business and Technical Communication* 33 (4): 400–424.

Griffith, Eric. 2018. "90 Percent of the Big Data We Generate Is an Unstructured Mess." *PC Mag*, November 15, 2018. https://www.pcmag.com/news/90-percent-of-the-big-data-we-generate-is-an-unstructured-mess.

Grizzle, Alton, Carolyn Wilson, and Dorothy Gordon, eds. 2021. *Media and Information Literate Citizens: Think Critically, Click Wisely!* UNESCO. https://unesdoc.unesco.org/ark:/48223/pf0000377068.

Gummer, Edith S., and Ellen B. Mandinach. 2015. "Building a Conceptual Framework for Data Literacy." *Teachers College Record* 117: 1–22. https://doi.org/10.1177/016146811511700401.

Haas, Christina, and Linda Flower. 1988. "Rhetorical Reading Strategies and the Construction of Meaning." *College Composition and Communication* 39 (2): 167–183.

Harbert, Tam. 2021. "Tapping the Power of Unstructured Data." MIT Sloan, February 1, 2021. https://mitsloan.mit.edu/ideas-made-to-matter/tapping-power-unstructured-data.

Haswell, Richard H. 2005. "NCTE/CCCC's Recent War on Scholarship." *Written Communication* 22 (2): 198–223.

Head, Alison J., Barbara Fister, and Margy MacMillan. 2020. "Information Literacy in the Age of Algorithms: Student Experiences with News and Information, and the Need for Change." Project Information Literacy, January 15, 2020. https://projectinfolit.org/pubs/algorithm-study/pil_algorithm-study_2020-01-15.pdf.

Hennig, Christian. 2002. "Confronting Data Analysis with Constructivist Philosophy." In *Classification, Clustering, and Data Analysis: Recent Advances and Applications*, edited by Krzysztof Jajuga, Andrzej Sokołowski, and Hans-Hermann Bock, 235–243. Springer Berlin Heidelberg.

Hoag, Trevor, and Nicole Emmelhainz. 2021. "Learning to Read Again: Introducing Undergraduates to Critical Distant Reading, Machine Analysis, and Data in Humanities Writing." In *Composition and Big Data*, edited by Amanda Licastro and Benjamin Miller, 22–34. University of Pittsburgh Press.

Hobbs, Renee. 2017. "Teach the Conspiracies." *Knowledge Quest* 46 (1): 16–24.

Hoetker, James, and Barbara Hoetker Ash. 1984. "An Experiment with the Wording of Essay Topics." *College Composition and Communication* 35 (4): 423–425.

Hoetker, James, and Gordon Brossell. 1986. "A Procedure for Writing Content-Fair Essay Examination Topics for Large-Scale Writing Assessments." *College Composition and Communication* 37 (3): 328–335.

Hoetker, James, and Gordon Brossell. 1989. "The Effects of Systematic Variations in Essay Topics on the Writing Performance of College Freshmen." *College Composition and Communication* 40 (4): 414–421.

Hoffman, Anna Lauren. 2018. "Data Violence and How Bad Engineering Choices Can Damage Society." Medium, April 30, 2018. https://medium.com/s/story/data-violence-and-how-bad-engineering-choicescan-damage-society-39e44150e1d4.

Honebein, Peter C. 1996. "Seven Goals for the Design of Constructivist Learning Environments." In *Constructivist Learning Environments: Case Studies in Instructional Design*, edited by Brent Gayle Wilson, 11–24. Educational Technology Publications.

"How to Use Data for Teaching as Inquiry." 2018. The Education Hub, June 2018. https://theeducationhub.org.nz/wp-content/uploads/2018/06/How-to-use-data-for-teaching-as-inquiry.pdf.

Huh, Kil, Amber Ivey, and Dan Kitson. 2018. "Using Data to Improve Policy Decisions: Insights to Help Governments Address Complex Problems." PEW, August 14, 2018. https://www.pewtrusts.org/en/about/news-room/opinion/2018/08/13/using-data-to-improve-policy-decisions.

Huot Brian. 2002. "Toward a New Discourse of Assessment for the College Writing Classroom." *College English* 65 (2): 163–180.

Ice, Phil, Karen Swan, Sebastian Diaz, Lori Kupczynski, and Allison Swan-Dagen. 2010. "An Analysis of Students' Perceptions of the Value and Efficacy of Instructors' Auditory and Text-Based Feedback Modalities Across Multiple Conceptual

Levels." *Journal of Educational Computing Research* 43 (1): 113–134. https://doi.org/10.2190/EC.43.1.g.

Inoue, Asao. 2005. "Community-Based Assessment Pedagogy." *Assessing Writing* 9: 208–238.

Jamieson, Sandra, and Rebecca Moore Howard. 2013. "Sentence-Mining: Uncovering the Amount of Reading and Reading Comprehension in College Writers' Researched Writing." In *The New Digital Scholar: Exploring and Enriching the Research and Writing Practices of NextGen Students*, edited by Randall McClure and James P. Purdy, 111–133. American Society for Information Science and Technology.

Johnson, Gavin P. 2021. "Grades as a Technology of Surveillance." In *Privacy Matters: Conversations about Surveillance within and beyond the Classroom*, edited by Estee Beck and Les Hutchinson Campos, 53–72. Utah State University Press.

Johnson, Gavin P. 2023. "Don't Act Like You Forgot: Approaching Another Literacy 'Crisis' by (Re)Considering What We Know about Teaching Writing with and Through Technologies." *Composition Studies* 51 (1): 169–175.

Jones, Kyle M. L. 2019. "Learning Analytics and Higher Education: A Proposed Model for Establishing Informed Consent Mechanisms to Promote Student Privacy and Autonomy." *International Journal of Educational Technology in Higher Education* 16 (1): 1–22.

Joswiak, Regan, and Mike Duncan. 2020. "Inform or Persuade? An Analysis of Technical Communication Textbooks." *Technical Communication* 67 (2): 29–41.

Kennedy, Helen, and Rosemary Lucy Hill. 2018. "The Feeling of Numbers: Emotions in Everyday Engagements with Data and Their Visualisation." *Sociology* 52 (4): 830–848.

Kesari, Gane. 2024. "The Enduring Power of Data Storytelling in the Generative AI Era." *MIT Sloan Management Review*, Jan. 17, 2024. https://sloanreview.mit.edu/article/the-enduring-power-of-data-storytelling-in-the-generative-ai-era/.

Khadka, Santosh, and J. C. Lee, eds. 2019a. *Bridging the Multimodal Gap: From Theory to Practice*. Utah State University Press.

Khadka, Santosh, and J. C. Lee. 2019b. "Introduction: Extending the Conversation: Theories, Pedagogies, and Practices of Multimodality." In *Bridging the Multimodal Gap: From Theory to Practice*, edited by Santosh Khadka and J. C. Lee, 3–16. Utah State University Press.

Kington, Raynard S., Stacey Arnesen, Wen-Ying Sylvia Chou, Susan J. Curry, David Lazer, and Antonia M. Villarruel. 2021. "Identifying Credible Sources of Health Information in Social Media: Principles and Attributes." NAM Perspectives, July 16, 2021. https://doi.org/10.31478/202107a.

Kitchin, Rob, and Tracey P. Lauriault. 2014. "Towards Critical Data Studies: Charting and Unpacking Data Assemblages and Their Work." The Programmable City Working Paper 2, July 29, 2014. http://ssrn.com/abstract=2474112.

Kitchin, Rob, and Tracey P. Lauriault. 2015. "Small Data in the Era of Big Data." *GeoJournal* 80: 463–475.

Knaflic, Cole Nussbaumer. 2015. *Storytelling with Data: A Data Visualization Guide for Business Professionals*. John Wiley & Sons.

Knox, Liam. 2023. "Can Turnitin Cure Higher Ed's AI Fever?" Inside Higher Ed, April 3, 2023. https://www.insidehighered.com/news/2023/04/03/turnitins-solution-ai-cheating-raises-faculty-concerns.

Kulak, Andrew. 2021. "Ethics in Big Data Composition Research: Cybersecurity and Algorithmic Accountability as Best Practices." In *Composition and Big Data*, edited by Amanda Licastro and Benjamin Miller, 230–244. University of Pittsburgh Press.

Laflen, Angela. 2020. "Preparing Students to Read and Compose Data Stories in the Fake News Era." In *Teaching Critical Reading and Writing in the Era of Fake News*, edited by Ellen Carillo and Alice Horning, 193–210. Peter Lang.

Laflen, Angela. 2021. "Quantitative Literacy in the Composition Classroom: Using Infographics' Assignments to Teach Ethical and Effective Data Use." In *Literacy and Pedagogy in an Age of Misinformation and Disinformation*, edited by Tara Lockhart, Brenda Glascott, Chris Warnick, Juli Parrish, and Justin Lewis, 34–58. Parlor Press.

Laflen, Angela. 2022. "Learning to 'Speak Data:' Data Literacy and Multimodal Composition Pedagogy." In *Multimodal Composition: Faculty Development Programs and Institutional Change*, edited by Shyam Pandey and Santosh Khadka, 127–143. Routledge.

Laflen, Angela, and Michelle Smith. 2017. "Responding to Student Writing Online: Tracking Student Interactions with Instructor Feedback in a Learning Management System." *Assessing Writing* 31: 39–52.

Lang, Susan, and Craig Baehr. 2012. "Data Mining: A Hybrid Methodology for Complex and Dynamic Research." *College Composition and Communication* 64 (1):172–194.

Lange, Alex C., Antonio Duran, and Romeo Jackson. 2019. "The State of LGBT and Queer Research in Higher Education Revisited: Current Academic Houses and Future Possibilities." *Journal of College Student Development* 60 (5): 511–526. https://doi.org/10.1353/csd.2019.0047.

Langreo, Lauraine. 2023. "AI Is Making Data Literacy a 'Survival Skill' That Schools Must Teach, Experts Argue." Education Week, Nov. 16, 2023. https://www.edweek.org/technology/ai-is-making-data-literacy-a-survival-skill-that-schools-must-teach-experts-argue/2023/11.

Laquintano, Timothy, and Annette Vee. 2017. "How Automated Writing Systems Affect the Circulation of Political Information Online." *Literacy, Democracy, and Fake News*, special issue of *Literacy in Composition Studies* 5 (2): 43–62. http://dx.doi.org/10.21623%2F1.5.2.4.

Lavazza, Andrea, and Mirko Farino. 2023. "Infosphere, Datafication, and Decision-Making Processes in the AI Era." *Topoi* 42: 843–856.

Leake, Eric. 2021. "The Multiple Lives of News Stories: Civic Literacies and Rhetorical Transformations." In *Literacy and Pedagogy in an Age of Misinformation and Disinformation*, edited by Tara Lockhart, Brenda Glascott, Chris Warnick, Juli Parrish, and Justin Lewis, 71–84. Parlor Press.

Licastro, Amanda, and Benjamin Miller, eds. 2021. *Composition and Big Data*. University of Pittsburgh Press.

Lockhart, Tara, Brenda Glascott, Chris Warnick, Juli Parrish, and Justin Lewis, eds. 2021. *Literacy and Pedagogy in an Age of Misinformation and Disinformation*. Parlor Press.

Lockhart, Tara, and Jennifer Hofmann. 2021. "Civic Literacies, Despair, and Hope: Our Current Information Moment Unfolding." In *Literacy and Pedagogy in an Age of Misinformation and Disinformation*, edited by Tara Lockhart, Brenda Glascott, Chris Warnick, Juli Parrish, and Justin Lewis, 59–70. Parlor Press.

Loeb, Susanna, Susan Dynarski, Daniel McFarland, Pamela Morris, Sean Reardon, and Sarah Reber. 2017. *Descriptive Analysis in Education: A Guide for Researchers* [NCEE 2017–4023]. US Department of Education, Institute of Education Sciences, National Center for Education Evaluation and Regional Assistance.

Long, Phil, and George Siemens. 2011. "Penetrating the Fog: Analytics in Learning and Education." *EDUCAUSE Review* 46 (5): 31–40.

Macfadyen, Leah P., and Shane Dawson. 2010. "Mining LMS Data to Develop an 'Early Warning System' for Educators: A Proof of Concept." *Computers & Education* 54 (2): 588–599.

Mandinach, Ellen B., and Edith S. Gummer. 2016. *Data Literacy for Educators: Making It Count in Teacher Preparation and Practice*. Teachers College Press.

Manovich, Lev. 2012. "Trending: The Promises and the Challenges of Big Social Data." In *Debates in the Digital Humanities*, edited by Matthew K. Gold, 460–475. University of Minnesota Press.

Marche, Stephen. 2022. "The College Essay is Dead" *The Atlantic*, December 6, 2022. https://www.theatlantic.com/technology/archive/2022/12/chatgpt-ai-writing-college-student-essays/672371/.

Marist University. 2024. "Academic Core Overview." https://www.marist.edu/academics/core.

"Marist University Enrollment (2018–19)." n.d. New York State Education Department, https://data.nysed.gov/highered-enrollment.php?year=2019&instid=800000034131.

Marist Office of Institutional Research and Planning. 2021. "Student Body Demographics." Factbook 2021. https://www.marist.edu/documents/86200/94377/Full-Time%20Undergraduate%20Student%20Body%20Demographics.pdf/ac2e0dec-ce98-68a8-65d2-e35cc2f34cfd?t=1671651084381.

Markham, Annette N. 2019. "Critical Pedagogy as a Response to Datafication." *Qualitative Inquiry* 25 (8): 754–760.

Markham, Annette N. 2020. "Taking Data Literacy to the Streets: Critical Pedagogy in the Public Sphere." *Qualitative Inquiry* 26 (2): 227–237.

Mathivanan, Pavithra, and Akshaya Devi. 2021. "5 Most Common Data Visualization Types and When to Use Them." *Happy Fox Blog*, April 6, 2021. https://blog.happyfox.com/types-of-data-visualization-and-when-to-use-them/.

Mayer-Schönberger, Viktor, and Kenneth Cukier. 2013. *Big Data: A Revolution that Will Transform How We Live, Work, and Think*. Houghton Mifflin Harcourt.

McAfee, Andrew, and Erik Brynjolfsson. 2012. "Big Data: The Management Revolution." *Harvard Business Review* 90 (10): 60–68.

McCandless, David. 2012. *Information is Beautiful*. Collins.

McComiskey, Bruce. 2017. *Post-Truth Rhetoric and Composition*. Utah State University Press. https://doi.org/10.2307/j.ctt1w76tbg.

Mearian, Lucas. 2023. "Schools Look to Ban ChatGPT, Students Use It Anyway." Computerworld, April 25, 2023. https://www.computerworld.com/article/1623825/schools-look-to-ban-chatgpt-students-use-it-anyway.html.

Miller, Benjamin, and Amanda Licastro. 2021. "Introduction: Reasons to Engage Composition through Big Data." In *Composition and Big Data*, edited by Amanda Licastro and Benjamin Miller, 3–21. University of Pittsburgh Press.

Miller, Richard E. 2016. "On Digital Reading." *Pedagogy: Critical Approaches to Teaching Literature, Language, Composition, and Culture* 16 (1): 153–164.

Miller, Thomas P., and Adele Leon. 2017. "Introduction to Special Issue on Literacy, Democracy, and Fake News: Making It Right in the Era of Fast and Slow Literacies." *Literacy, Democracy, and Fake News*, special edition of *Literacy in Composition Studies* 5 (2): 10–23. http://dx.doi.org/10.21623%2F1.5.2.2.

Modern Language Association. 2018. "Checklist: Evaluating Sources." The MLA Style Center Teaching Resources, March 9, 2018. https://style.mla.org/app/uploads/sites/3/2018/09/Checklist-for-Evaluating-Sources.pdf.

Monea, Bethany. 2020. "Screen Reading: A Gallery of (Re)Imagined Interaces." *Kairos* 24 (2). https://kairos.technorhetoric.net/24.2/disputatio/monea/index.html.

Moran, Charles, and Anne Herrington. 2003. "Evaluating Academic Hypertexts." In *Teaching Writing with Computers: An Introduction*, edited by Pamela Takayoshi and Brian Huot, 247–257. Houghton Mifflin.

Morris, Janine. 2015. "A Genre-Based Approach to Digital Reading." *Pedagogy: Critical Approaches to Teaching Literature, Language, Composition, and Culture* 16 (1): 125–136. https://doi.org/10.1215/15314200-3158685.

Moxley, Joseph. 2008. "Datagogies, Writing Spaces, and the Age of Peer Production." *Computers and Composition* 25 (2): 182–202.

Moxley, Joseph. 2013. "Big Data, Learning Analytics, and Social Assessment." *Journal of Writing Assessment* 6 (1): 1–10.

Murray, Elizabeth A., Hailey A. Sheets, and Nicole A. Williams. 2009. "The New Work of Assessment: Evaluating Multimodal Compositions." *Computers and Composition Online*, September 8, 2009. http://cconlinejournal.org/murray_etal/index.html.

Nærland, Torgeir Uberg, and Martin Engebretsen. 2023. "Towards a Critical Understanding of Data Visualisation in Democracy: A Deliberative Systems Approach." *Information, Communication & Society* 26 (3): 637–655.

Naftzinger, Jeff. 2024. "If You Build It, Will They Use It: Composing Infrastructures, Communities of Pracice, and Instructor Dispositions." In *Multimodal Composing and Writing Transfer*, In *Multimodal Composing and Writing Transfer*, edited by Kara Poe Alexander, Matthew Davis, Lilian W. Mina, and Ryan P. Shepherd, 209–225. Utah State University Press.

Naisbitt, John. 1982. *Megatrends: Ten New Directions Transforming Our Lives*. Warner.

Nemorin, Selena. 2017. "Post-Panoptic Pedagogies: The Changing Nature of School Surveillance in the Digital Age." *Surveillance and Society* 15 (2): 239–253.

Noble, Safiya Umoja. 2018. *Algorithms of Oppression*. New York University Press.

Norgaard, Rolf, and Caroline Sinkinson. 2016. "Writing Information Literacy: A Retrospective and a Look Ahead." In *Information Literacy: Research and Collaboration*

Across Disciplines, edited by Barbara J. D'Angelo, Sandra Jamieson, Barry Maid, and Janice R. Walker, 15–36, WAC Clearinghouse.

Nouri, Ali, Beatriz Cabrero-Daniel, Fredrik Torner, Hakan Sivencrona, and Christian Berger. 2024. "Welcome Your New AI Teammate: On Safety Analysis by Leashing Large Language Models." In *Proceedings of the IEEE/ACM 3rd International Conference on AI Engineering-Software Engineering for AI*, 172–177. Association of Computing Machinery. https://doi.org/10.1145/3644815.3644953.

Noyes, Katherine. 2015. "Companies Must Teach Employees How to Swim in New Oceans of Data." Computer World, May 1, 2015. https://www.computerworld.com/article/2917915/companies-must-teach-employees-how-to-swim-in-new-oceans-of-data.html.

Odukha, Oleksandr. 2023. "How Will Urban Infrastructure Change with Autonomous Driving?" Intellias, August 21, 2023. https://intellias.com/how-will-urban-infrastructure-change-with-autonomous-driving/.

O'Neill, Cathy. 2017. *Weapons of Math Destruction: How Big Data Increases Inequality and Threatens Democracy*. Crown.

Orlando, John. 2016. "A Comparison of Text, Voice, and Screencasting Feedback to Online Students." *American Journal of Distance Education* 30 (3): 156–166. https://doi.org/10.1080/08923647.2016.1187472.

Otto, Laura. 2021. "Mapping the Harm of COVID-19 Misinformation on Social Media." UWM Report, Dec. 30, 2021. https://uwm.edu/news/mapping-the-harm-of-covid-19-misinformation-on-social-media/.

Overstreet, Matthew. 2021. "Networked Reading: How Digital Reading Experts Use Their Tools." *College English* 83 (5): 357–378.

Oxford English Dictionary. 2023. "Post-truth, Adj., Sense 2." https://doi.org/10.1093/OED/7768605775.

Palmquist, Mike. 2019. "Directions in Writing Analytics: Some Suggestions." *The Journal of Writing Analytics* 3: 1–12.

"Pandemic Exposes Data Literacy Crisis." 2021. Business Wire, October 20, 2021. https://www.businesswire.com/news/home/20211020005223/en/Pandemic-Exposes-Data-Literacy-Crisis.

Pandey, Anshul Vikram, Anjali Manivannan, Oded Nov, Margaret Satterthwaite, and Enrico Bertini. 2014. "The Persuasive Power of Data Visualization." *IEEE Transactions on Visualization and Computer Graphics* 20 (12): 2211–2220.

Pennell, Michael C. 2014. "(Re)Placing the Literacy Narrative: Composing in Google Maps." *Literacy in Composition Studies* 2 (2): 44–65.

Perl, Sondra. 1979. "The Composing Processes of Unskilled College Writers." *Research in the Teaching of English* 13 (4): 317–336.

Persico, Donatella, and Francesca Pozzi. 2015. "Informing Learning Design with Learning Analytics to Improve Teacher Inquiry." *British Journal of Educational Technology* 46 (2): 230–248.

Pew Research Center. 2020. "Explore the Data." *Pew Research Center's American News Pathways Data Tool*. https://www.pewresearch.org/pathways-2020/covidcover2/main_source_of_election_news/us_adults.

Phelps, Johanna. 2021. "Ethics, the IRBs, and Big Data Research: Toward Disciplinary Datasets in Composition." In *Composition and Big Data*, edited by Amanda Licastro and Benjamin Miller, 212–229. University of Pittsburgh Press.

Pigg, Stacey, Missy Hannah, and Melissa Stone. 2018. "Teaching Information Design that Emphasizes Data: Revisiting Professional Writing Outcomes and Assignments." In *SIGDOC '18: Proceedings of the 36th ACM International Conference on the Design of Communication*. Association of Computing Machinery. https://doi.org/10.1145/3233756.3233957.

Polizzi, Gianfrano. 2021. "Digital and Data Literacy: Comparing Children's Understanding of Data and Online Privacy with Experts' and Advocates' Data Literacy Practices." Media Hopper Create. Uploaded by Claire Sowton, January 22, 2021. https://media.ed.ac.uk/media/1_qb6pyfjq.

Poovey, Mary. 1998. *A History of the Modern Fact: Problems of Knowledge in the Sciences of Wealth and Society.* University of Chicago Press.

Porter, Theodore M. (1986) 2020. *The Rise of Statistical Thinking, 1820–1900.* Princeton University Press.

Price Waterhouse Coopers and Business-Higher Education Forum. 2017. "Investing in America's Data Science and Analytics Talent: A Case for Action." Business-Higher Education Forum, April 2017. https://www.bhef.com/sites/default/files/bhef_2017_investing_in_dsa.pdf.

Quadri, Adedayo, and Nurbiha Shukor. 2021. "The Benefits of Learning Analytics to Higher Education Institutions: A Scoping Review." *International Journal of Emerging Technologies in Learning (iJET)* 16 (23): 4–15.

Rasheed, Zeeshan, Muhammad Waseem, Aakash Ahmad, Kai-Kristian Kemell, Wang Xiaofeng, Anh Nguyen Duc, and Pekka Abrahamsson. 2024. "Can Large Language Models Serve as Data Analysts? A Multi-Agent Assisted Approach for Qualitative Data Analysis." arXiv, February 2, 2024. https://doi.org/10.48550/arXiv.2402.01386.

Reardon, Kristina. 2021. "News as Text: A Pedagogy for Connecting News Reading and Newswriting." In *Teaching Critical Reading and Writing in the Era of Fake News*, edited by Ellen C. Carillo and Alice S. Horning, 161–176. Peter Lang.

Reilly, Colleen A. 2021. "Reading Risk: Preparing Students to Develop Critical Digital Literacies and Advocate for Privacy in Digital Spaces." *Computers and Composition* 61 (1). https://doi.org/10.1016/j.compcom.2021.102652.

Reilly, Colleen A., and Anthony Atkins. 2013. "Rewarding Risk: Designing Aspirational Assessment Processes for Digital Writing Projects." In *Digital Writing Assessment and Evaluation*, edited by Heidi A. McKee and Dànielle Nicole DeVoss. Computers and Composition Digital Press/Utah State University Press.

Rodrigue, Tanya K. 2017. "Digital Reading: Genre Awareness as a Tool for Reading Comprehension." *Pedagogy: Critical Approaches to Teaching Literature, Language, Composition, and Culture* 17 (2): 235–257. https://doi.org/10.1215/15314200-3770133.

Rutz, Carol, and Nathan D. Grawe. 2009. "Pairing WAC and Quantitative Reasoning through Portfolio Assessment and Faculty Development." *Writing Across the Curriculum and Assessment*, special issue of *Across the Disciplines: A Journal of Language, Learn-*

ing, and Academic Writing 6: 1–13. https://wac.colostate.edu/docs/atd/assessment/rutz_grawe.pdf.

"Sacramento State Fact Book." 2024. Sacramento State University Communications. https://www.csus.edu/experience/fact-book/_internal/_documents/fact-book24-web.pdf.

Schwartz, Sarah. 2023. "Students' Data Literacy Is Slipping, Even as Jobs Demand the Skill." Education Week, February 14, 2023. https://www.edweek.org/teaching-learning/students-data-literacy-is-slipping-even-as-jobs-demand-the-skill/2023/02.

Segel, Edward, and Heer, Jeffrey. 2010. "Narrative Visualization: Telling Stories with Data." *Visualization and Computer Graphics, IEEE* 16 (6): 1139–1148.

Selber, Stuart. 2004. *Multiliteracies for a Digital Age*. Southern Illinois University Press.

Shipka, Jody. 2009. "Negotiating Rhetorical, Material, Methodological, and Technological Difference: Evaluating Multimodal Designs." *College Composition and Communication* 61 (1): W343–W366.

Shipka, Jody. 2011. *Toward a Composition Made Whole*. University of Pittsburgh Press.

Simpson, Jill. 2020. "Visualizing Data: A Lived Experience." In *Data Visualization in Society*, edited by Martin Engebretsen and Helen Kennedy, 157–168. Amsterdam University Press.

Singer, Sarah Ann. 2019. "Embracing Wildcard Sources: Information Literacy in the Age of Internet Health." *College English* 82 (2): 152–172.

Sipley, Gina. 2024. *Just Here for the Comments: Lurking as Digital Literacy Practice*. Bristol University Press.

Snaith, Ben. 2023. "What Do We Mean by 'Without Data, There is No AI'?" Open Data Institute, December 1, 2023. https://theodi.cdn.ngo/media/documents/20231221_-_Data-centric_AI_Short_Paper_-_What_do_we_mean_by_without_data_there_3AEHdDW.pdf.

Sorapure, Madeleine. 2006. "Between Modes: Assessing Student New Media Compositions." *Kairos* 10 (2): 1–15. https://kairos.technorhetoric.net/10.2/coverweb/sorapure/between_modes.pdf.

Sorapure, Madeleine. 2010. "Information Visualization, Web 2.0, and the Teaching of Writing." *Computers and Composition* 27 (1): 59–70.

Sorapure, Madeleine, and Austin Fauni. 2020. "Teaching Dear Data." *Kairos* 25 (1). https://Kairos.technorhetoric.net/25.1/praxis/sorapure-fauni/index.html.

Stanford History Education Group. 2016. *Evaluating Information: The Cornerstone of Civic Online Reasoning*, November 22, 2016. https://purl.stanford.edu/fv751yt5934.

Stanton, Courtney. 2023. "A Dis-Facilitated Call for More Writing Studies in the New AI Landscape; or, Finding Our Place Among the Chatbots." *Composition Studies* 51 (1): 182–186.

Steen, Lynn, ed. 2004. *Achieving Quantitative Literacy*. Mathematical Association of America.

Stephens-Davidowitz, Seth. 2023. "Interview with Meghan McCarty Carino." *Marketplace*, Minnesota Public Radio, April 24, 2023. https://www.marketplace.org/shows/marketplace-tech/tmi-the-problem-with-too-much-data/.

Taylor, James Stacey. 2024. "Why I Ban AI Use for Writing Assignments." Inside Higher Ed, July 12, 2024. https://www.timeshighereducation.com/campus/why-i-ban-ai-use-writing-assignments.
Taylor, Petroc. 2025. "Big Data—Statistics and Facts." Statista, March 31, 2025. https://www.statista.com/topics/1464/big-data/.
Teston, Christa, Brittany Previte, and Yanar Hashlamon. 2019. "The Grind of Multimodal Work in Professional Writing Pedagogies." *Computers and Composition* 52: 195–209.
Tossell, Mark. 2021. "Are You Drowning in Data, or Swimming in Insights?" LinkedIn, April 15, 2021. https://www.linkedin.com/pulse/you-drowning-data-swimming-insights-mark-tossell/.
Tufte, Edward R. 1983. *The Visual Display of Quantitative Information*. Graphics Press.
Tufte, Edward R. 1990. *Envisioning Information*. Graphics Press.
Turner, Will, and John West. 2013. "Assessment for Digital First Language Speakers: Online Video Assessment and Feedback in Higher Education." *International Journal of Teaching and Learning in Higher Education* 25 (3): 288–296.
Tygel, Alan Freihof, and Rosana Kirsch. 2016. "Contributions of Paulo Freire for a Critical Data Literacy: A Popular Education Approach." *The Journal of Community Informatics* 12 (3): 108–121.
US Department of Education. 2021. "Data Literacy." U.S. Department of Education STEM Resources, October 15, 2021. https://www.ed.gov/sites/default/files/documents/stem/20211015-data-literacy.pdf.
van Dijck, José. 2014. "Datafication, Dataism and Dataveillance: Big Data Between Scientific Paradigm and Ideology." *Surveillance & Society* 12 (2): 197–208. https://doi.org/10.24908/ss.v12i2.4776.
Verma, Pranshu. 2023. "The Rise of AI Fake news is Creating a 'Misinformation Superspreader.'" *The Washington Post*, December 17, 2023. https://www.washingtonpost.com/technology/2023/12/17/ai-fake-news-misinformation/.
Warnock, Scott. 2008. "Responding to Student Writing with Audio-Visual Feedback." In *Writing and the iGeneration: Composition in the Computer-Mediated Classroom*, edited by Terry Carter and Maria A. Clayton, 201–227. Fountainhead Press.
Webber, Karen L., and Henry Y. Zheng, eds. 2020. *Big Data on Campus: Data Analytics and Decision Making in Higher Education*. Johns Hopkins University Press.
Weise, Karen, and Cade Metz. 2023. "When A.I. Chatbots Hallucinate." *New York Times*, May 1, 2023. https://www.nytimes.com/2023/05/01/business/ai-chatbots-hallucination.html.
White, Ed. 1994. *Teaching and Assessing Writing*, 2nd ed. Jossey-Bass.
WHO, UN, UNICEF, UNDP, UNESCO, UNAIDS, ITU, UN Global Pulse, IFRC. 2021. "Managing the COVID-19 Infodemic: Promoting Healthy Behaviours and Mitigating the Harm from Misinformation and Disinformation." World Health Organization, November 10, 2021. https://www.who.int/news/item/23-09-2020-managing-the-covid-19-infodemic-promoting-healthy-behaviours-and-mitigating-the-harm-from-misinformation-and-disinformation.

Williams, Bronwyn T. 2007. "Why Johnny Can Never, Ever Read: The Perpetual Literacy Crisis and Student Identity." *Journal of Adolescent & Adult Literacy* 51 (2): 178–182.

Williamson, Ben, Sian Bayne, and Suellen Shay. 2020. "The Datafication of Teaching in Higher Education: Critical Issues and Perspectives." *Teaching in Higher Education* 25 (4): 351–365.

Wineburg, Sam, and Sarah McGrew. 2019. "Lateral Reading and the Nature of Expertise: Reading Less and Learning More When Evaluating Digital Information." *Teachers College Record* 121 (11): 1–40.

Wolfe, Joanna. 2009. "How Technical Communication Textbooks Fail Engineering Students." *Technical Communication Quarterly* 18 (4): 351–375.

Wolfe, Joanna. 2010. "Rhetorical Numbers: A Case for Quantitative Writing in the Composition Classroom." *College Composition and Communication* 61 (3): 452–475.

Wolfe, Joanna. 2015. "Teaching Students to Focus on the Data in Data Visualization." *Journal of Business and Technical Communication* 29 (3): 344–359.

Wolff, Annika, Daniel Gooch, Jose J. Cavero Montaner, Umar Rashid, and Gerd Kortuem. 2016. "Creating an Understanding of Data Literacy for a Data-Driven Society." *The Journal of Community Informatics* 12 (3): 9–26.

Wood, Shane. 2019. "Multimodal Pedagogy and Multimodal Assessment: Toward a Reconceptualization of Traditional Frameworks." In *Bridging the Multimodal Gap: From Theory to Practice*, edited by Santosh Khadhka and J. C. Lee, 244–262. University Press of Utah.

Womack, Ryan. 2014. "Data Visualization and Information Literacy." *IASSIST Quarterly* 38 (1): 12–17. https://doi.org/10.7282/T3X92CZF.

"WPA Outcomes Statement for First-Year Composition (3.0)." 2014. Council of Writing Program Administrators. http://wpacouncil.org/aws/CWPA/pt/sd/news_article/243055/_PARENT/layout_details/false.

Wysocki, Rick, Jon Udelson, C. Ray, J. Newman, Laura Sceniak Matravers, Ashanka Kumari, and D. DeVoss. 2019. "On Multimodality: A Manifesto." In *Bridging the Multimodal Gap: From Theory to Practice*, edited by Santosh Khadka and J. C. Lee, 17–29. Utah State University Press.

Yancey, Kathleen Blake. 1998. *Reflection in the Writing Classroom*. Utah State University Press.

Yancey, Kathleen Blake. 2024. "Afterword: Transfer Happens; Transfer Doesn't Happen." In *Multimodal Composing and Writing Transfer*, edited by Kara Poe Alexander, Matthew Davis, Lilian W. Mina, and Ryan P. Shepherd, 226–233. Utah State University Press.

Zambrano, Raul Niño, and Yuri Engelhardt. 2008. "Diagrams for the Masses: Raising Public Awareness-From Neurath to Gapminder and Google Earth." In *Diagrammatic Representation and Inference 5th International Conference, Herrsching, Germany, September 19–21*, edited by Gem Stapleton and John Howse, 282–292. Springer Berlin Heidelberg.

Zoetewey, Meredith W., and Julie Staggers. 2003. "Beyond Current-Traditional Design: Assessing Rhetoric in New Media." *Issues in Writing* 13 (2): 133–157.

Index

Page numbers followed by b indicate boxes, page numbers followed by f indicate figures, page numbers followed by n indicate notes, and page numbers followed by t indicate tables.

abductive reasoning, 38
Academia ERP by Serosoft, 163t
academic enterprise dashboards, 163t
Accelerated Academic Literacies course, 192t, 195t
acceptance of data, 50, 51
ad blockers, 39
Adams, Curt M., 168
adaptability of contexts, 179
Adobe Express/Spark, 92t
Adobe Illustrator, 93t
Adsanatham, Chanon, 114, 116, 123, 124
agency of social media users, 41, 186
AI (artificial intelligence), 17; data literacy, 8–9, 12; data storytelling, 40–41; design tools, 92; digital literacy, 36; disinformation/misinformation, 187–88; emergence, 15; large language models (LLMs), 10, 11; learning management systems (LMS), 26–27, 31, 33–34; oversight, 28–30, 83; privacy policy analysis bots, 93; teaching practices, 153; traditional academic information skills, 7, 16, 37–38, 54–55
algorithms: abductive reasoning, 38; bias, 7, 57, 151; composing, 153; data analysis, 48; datafication, 11, 27; decision-making, 29,

177–78; digital trails, 7, 24–25, 30, 35, 57; fairness, 91; learning management systems (LMSs), 25, 31, 33–34; online interaction, 186; platforms, 39
analysis of data. *See* data collection/data analysis
Analytics for Learning (Blackboard), 31, 32f
Anderson, Chris, 27
Anderson, Daniel, 15, 90–92
animation, 92t
annotation reading strategy, 58, 65
annual reports, 92t
ANOVA (one-way analysis of variance), 173, 174
Anson, Chris, 150, 151
AntConc, 93t
Anyword, 93t
Apple iMovie, 93t
ArcGIS StoryMaps, 93t
Aristotle, 41, 85
arrangement of data stories, 8, 85
artificial intelligence. *See* AI (artificial intelligence)
Asian American and Native American Pacific Islander Serving Institutions (AANAPISIs), 5, 190

assessments. *See* instructive assessment; multimodal projects; peer review assignments. *See* critical data storytelling assignments; data visualization
Atkins, Anthony T., 121
Attard, Judie, 11, 82
attendance data, 26, 163t
audience, 41, 45t, 64t, 66, 68t, 71, 72, 73, 111, 126f, 127, 130f, 155
Aull, Laura, 148
automated writing assistants, 146
automation, data analysis, 28–30, 182

Baehr, Craig, 147, 148, 150
Ball, Cheryl E., 138
bar chart races, 67, 68t–69t, 70f, 71, 72
bar charts, 91, 92t, 94–97, 99f, 108, 133, 168
Bayne, Sian, 33
Beck, Jori S., 155
behavior, datafication, 27, 33–35, 47–48
Bernauer, James A., 168
best practices, 147, 154
Beveridge, Aaron, 39, 40, 55–56, 104
bias in algorithms, 7, 28, 56, 57, 151, 176, 177b
big data, 6, 19, 39, 40, 80–83, 88
BingAI, 93t
bio-data surveys, 5
Blackboard, 26, 29–31, 32f, 163t
Borton, Sonya C., 121–22, 124
botnet networks, 57
box plots, 168
boyd, danah, 104, 180
Bridgmon, Krista D., 168
Brynjolfsson, Bryn, 80
business intelligence software, 93t

Cairo, Alberto, 104
California State University, Sacramento, 189–90, 191t
Caliskan, Alyin, 104
Campbell, Joseph, 41
Canva, 4, 93t, 105, 117, 118b, 119f, 138, 142
Canvas Gradebook, 43–45, 46f, 47
Canvas, 26, 96, 101, 130, 139, 143, 163t
capta, 19
Carillo, Ellen C., 53
Carter, Marcus, 29–30
Center for American Progress, 13
charts, 56, 92t, 133, 166
chatbots, 8, 9, 55, 93t
ChatGPT, 9, 38, 55, 93t
checklists, data evaluation, 54–55
Chen, Chen, 36

cherry-picking, 49–50, 103, 181–82
chosen stories, data sets, 41, 44t, 62, 63t, 65
Chun, Randall, 13, 55
citations, 9, 37, 55, 91f, 126f, 138, 143, 182
citizen types, 13, 14f
civic engagement, 190
civic online reasoning, 12–13
classification, research participants, 193t, 195t
classroom strategies. *See* teaching practices
Claude, 55, 93t
cleaning data, 28, 164, 165t
click-and-go literacies, 51
Cloonan, Anne, 182
cloud-based software, 175, 176
coding, data collection, 28, 197
cognition, 47–48, 56
cognitive biases, 176, 177b
Cohn, Jenae, 61, 138
collaborative peer reviews, 119, 125, 155
collected data. *See* data collection/data analysis
College Composition and Communication, 104, 150
College English, 150
college majors, 193t, 194t, 195t
column charts, 72, 73, 74f, 92t
communication tools, 155, 163t
communicator data literate citizen type, 13, 14f
completeness of data, 168–69
complexity of data storytelling assignments, 78, 86–87, 90
composing infrastructure, 186–87
Composition and Big Data, 19
Composition Forum, 152
Composition II graduation requirement, 191
composition process, 3, 39, 44t, 45, 55, 62f, 64
computational thinking, 25, 29, 34
computer systems, 38
Computers and Composition, 152
Computers and Writing Online, 104
constructivist approach to data, 18–20
constructs, 61, 159–61, 169b
contemporary literacy, 4
content creation, 8–9, 10f
contextualization, rhetorical reading, 61
continuity of inquiry cycles, 155
contract grading, 135–37, 145
cookies, 39
copyright issues, 91f, 134, 135
core writing concepts, 171
Council of Writing Program Administrators' (CWPA), 35–36
course assessments, 26

course-based undergraduate research experience (CURE), 159, 170–73, 174*f*
coursework assignments, research participation, 191*t*, 192*t*, 196, 197
COVID-19 misinfodemic, 21, 50, 51, 52, 67, 69–75
Craig, Jacob W., 55, 57
Crawford, Kate, 104
credibility of sources, 50, 55, 57, 59, 63–66, 72–76, 126*f*, 138
Creswell, J. David, 167
Creswell, John W., 167
critical awareness, 110*f*, 111, 112
critical communicators, 39, 43, 44*t*–45*t*, 78, 89*t*, 90, 91*f*, 147–48, 153–54
critical data literacy pedagogy, 86; assessments, 137; context adaptability, 179; generative AI, 8–9; informed critique, 18*t*; literacy skills, 3, 6, 17, 18*t*; multimodal composition pedagogy, 7–9, 14–16, 20; parameters, 26; rhetoric and composition scholarship, 20, 21, 25, 35–36, 76; student access, 43, 186–88; teaching practices, 44*t*–45*t*, 66, 178, 188; vertical curriculum, 182. *See also* multimodal composition pedagogy
critical data storytelling assignments: audience, 42, 45*t*, 64*t*; chosen stories, 65; citations, 55, 143; classroom context, 178; complexity, 86–87; composing infrastructure, 186–87; composition process, 44*t*, 62*f*; deadlines, 148; ethical issues, 9, 12, 17, 18*t*, 20, 155, 175–76; evaluation criteria, 115, 127, 134–37, 139; evidence-based data, 127, 130*f*, 137–39; generative AI, 40–41; instructive assessment, 22, 116–21, 122–27, 136*b*; knowledge transfer, 184–85; metalanguage, 182; multiliteracies approach, 43; narrative structure, 84–85; peer review, 96–97, 105–7, 124, 125, 133, 138, 181; personal contexts, 183–84; persuasiveness, 43, 51, 56; project goals, 78, 90, 92*t*, 104–5, 114, 128, 140–41; reflection assignment, 106, 107*f*, 108, 168; rhetorical awareness, 3, 7, 13, 121, 180–83; self-assessments, 126*f*, 130, 142; small data, 78, 89*t*, 98–100, 101, 102*f*; student participants, 195*t*; taking bearings, 44*t*, 63*t*, 76; trial and error, 113, 118*b*, 119–21. *See also* data visualization
critical reading strategies, 44*t*, 47, 58, 63*t*
Cukier, Kenneth, 4, 17, 27, 29
cultural diversity, 190
CURE (course-based undergraduate research experience), 159, 170–73, 174*f*

Current Biology, 104
curriculum, 23, 90, 149, 169, 177*b*
cybersecurity standards, 175, 176

D2L, 26, 163*t*
DALL-E, 8, 9, 92*t*
Danner, Patrick, 65, 85, 94
Dartmouth Summer Seminar for Composition Research, 152, 168
data collection/data analysis: algorithms, 4, 27, 34, 48; cherry-picking, 49–50, 103, 181–82; coding, 28, 197; cognitive biases, 176, 177*b*; constructivist approach, 18–20; critical awareness, 110*f*, 111–12; critical communicators model, 78, 89*t*, 90, 98; decision-making, 29, 138; divide, 25; effective use of, 9, 13; ethical issues, 43, 44*t*, 63–64, 87*f*, 91*f*, 175, 178; evaluation criteria, 17, 27, 62*f*, 130*f*, 139–40; exploration, 165–68; generative AI, 10*f*, 12, 83; knowledge transfer, 184; learning analytics, 28–29; limitations, 154–55, 169*b*; patterns, 148–49, 168–70; politicization, 70*f*, 71–72; rhetorical context, 69*t*, 71–75, 86, 88; social media role, 186; software, 187; sources of data, 162, 163*t*, 164–65; strengths and weaknesses, 94–97, 170–71; unexpected data, 166; usefulness, 11, 188
data communication strategies, 41, 83
data infrastructure, 151, 186–87
data inquiries: constructs, 159, 160*t*, 161; cycles, 156, 157*f*; collection, 162–65; decision-making, 29, 173*b*; disease of complexity, 175; instructional changes, 171, 172; outcomes, 172–74; patterns, 169; proxy data, 160–61; research questions, 154; teaching practices, 176, 177*b*; triangulation, 170–71; t-test calculator, 167*b*; unexpected data, 166
data literacy crisis, 21, 37–39, 80, 83
data literacy for teachers (DLFT), 7–8, 22, 154–56
Data Literacy Project, 83
Data Literacy: The Upskilling Evolution, 83
data literacy: 13, 14*f*; collaboration, 155; cultivating, 82; generative AI, 11, 83; multimodal composition pedagogy, 4–6, 12, 22, 23, 40, 111–12, 139, 149; practices, 116–17; rhetorical reading, 13, 18*t*, 43; strategies of hypermediacy, 59–60; strategies of immediacy, 58, 59; transparency, 8
data manipulation, 10*f*, 50, 64, 68*t*, 71–75, 130*f*, 139–40
data privacy, 17, 175–76, 177*b*

data sets, 10f, 62, 63t, 65, 81
data sources. *See* information sources
data stories: arrangement, 85; audience, 45t, 64t; composition process, 44t, 55, 62f; contextualization, 61; credibility, 55, 59, 63–64; decision-making, 29, 83; disinformation/misinformation, 7, 14; instructive assessment, 21–22, 114; persuasiveness, 43, 51, 56; post-truth era, 52–53; reading strategies, 50; reflection assignment, 78, 96–97; rhetorical context, 47; rhetorical reading, 13, 20–21, 60, 66, 67, 136b; self-assessments, 126f, 128f, 129f; strategies of hypermediacy, 59–60; strategies of immediacy, 58, 59; student reflection, 46f; taking bearings, 44t, 63t, 76; teaching strategies, 66; visualization, 94; wildcard, 54, 55, 57
Data Story: Explain Data and Inspire Action Through Story, 84, 85
data storytelling. *See* critical data storytelling assignments; data visualization
data violence, 30
data visualization: charts, 67, 68t, 69t, 70f, 71–73, 74f, 92t, 94–97, 99f, 166; chatbots, 93t; cognitive shortcuts, 56; copyright issues, 134–35; credibility, 55, 59, 63–64; critical communicators model, 78, 89t, 90, 91f; datafication, 30–31; first drafts, 95–96, 110f, 111, 128, 141–42; flawed, 78, 92t, 107f; framework design, 41, 79–80, 85, 188; graphs, 73, 74f, 75–78, 91, 94, 96, 97, 99f, 166, 168; infographics, 78, 104–6, 107f, 108, 117, 118b, 119f, 127; information literacy skills, 48; labeling, 65; low-bridge technologies, 86–87, 89t, 90, 91f; maps, 92t, 97, 99f; mockups, 105, 129–30, 132f, 133, 138, 141, 142; narrative, 40–41; page design, 78, 92t, 103; patterns, 27, 44t, 63t, 65–66, 169b, 170; persuasiveness, 44t, 56; revisions, 78, 105–6, 107f, 108, 121, 134–35; risk failure, 113, 119f, 121; rough cuts, 142; scripts, 128, 141; slide shows, 127; software tools, 86–87, 93t, 94, 187; speculative design, 45, 48; static/interactive, 78, 103, 128, 133, 141; symbolic representation of numbers, 62, 64–65; tables, 92t, 166; technological tools, 16, 44t–45t, 46, 47; textbooks, 37; thumbnails, 128, 131f, 133; time series analysis, 89t, 92t; timelines, 92t, 128, 141; video essays, 127; wireframes, 129–30, 138, 142; word clouds, 92t. *See also* critical data storytelling assignments
Data Visualization in Society, 98
Data.gov, 92t

data-based arguments, 40, 86, 116, 117
data-driven inquiry process: critical data literacy pedagogy, 44f; data literacy, 83; lateral reading, 63t; networked writing, 86; research projects, 152; rhetoric and composition studies, 60–61, 149–51; statistical knowledge, 62–63, 64; writing programs, 147, 178. *See also* critical data storytelling assignments
datafication: behavior, 33–35, 47–48; digital trails, 30, 39; digitization, 17; everyday life, 4, 10–12, 26, 27; information environments, 4, 20, 25, 187; multimodal composition pedagogy, 187; student engagement, 42
datafied information environments, 12, 28–30, 39, 89t
datagogies, 149
dataveillance, 151, 152
Dear Data Two, 98
Dear Data, 92t, 98
A Decade in Internet Time: Symposium on the Dynamics of the Internet and Society, 104
decision-making: algorithms, 34, 177–78; automation, 29–30; big data, 80–83, 138, 156, 157f, 170
deep learning (DL) architectures, 10f
deepfakes, 7
demographics of research participants, 163, 189–90, 192t, 193t
descriptive statistics tables, 92t
design issues, multimodal projects, 79–80, 90, 117, 119f, 122
design software, 93t
DFW rates, 147, 148, 151–52
DHQ: Digital Humanities Quarterly, 98
digital humanities methods, 86
digital information sources, 17, 50–51, 55, 57, 58t
digital interface, 45–48
digital literacy, 16–17, 57, 67, 138
digital surveillance, 151–52
digital trails, 24–26, 30, 35, 38–39, 81
Digital Writing and Rhetoric course, 192t, 195t
digital-based reading strategies, 57–58
digitization of information, 17, 26, 45
direct self-placement (DSP), 190–91
disciplinary teaching practices, 154, 187
Disconnect, 93t
discrepancies in data, 169
discussion forums, 26, 163t
disease of complexity, 175

disinformation/misinformation, 13–14, 21,
    25, 50, 52, 53*f*, 57–59, 66, 75–76, 83, 103, 106*f*,
    107, 187–88
diversity, research participants, 192
DLFT (data literacy for teachers), 22, 154–56
document sharing, 26
drafting process, 62*f*, 64, 194
drowning metaphor, 82
Drucker, Johanna, 18, 19, 94, 98
dual axis line graphs, 108
Duarte, Nancy, 84, 85
DuckDuckGo, 39
Duran, Antonio, 154
Dykes, Brent, 12, 82, 85
dynamic feedback models, 116

Edmodo, 163*t*
Education Hub, 166
education requirements, 190–91
Education Week, 83
educational contexts, 16
effectiveness of data stories, 9, 12, 13, 17, 18*t*,
    104, 114, 147–48, 180
Egliston, Ben, 29–30
Eli Review, 125
email systems, 163*t*
Emig, Janet, 150
Emmelhainz, Nicole, 42
empirical research, 150, 151
Engage eReader, 163*t*
engagement. *See* student engagement
English instructors, 184, 190
Envisioning Information, 40
eReaders, 163*t*
ethical research standards, 175, 176
ethical use of data, 17, 18*t*, 19, 20, 43, 44*t*, 50,
    63–64, 69–72, 72–75, 78, 86, 87*f*, 88–90, 91*f*,
    92*t*, 103–8, 155, 168, 178
evaluation criteria: checklists, 54–55; data
    sources, 110*f*, 111, 126*f*, 130*f*, 139–40; data
    storytelling, 7, 21, 62*f*, 67; design issues,
    122; digital content, 55, 57, 58*t*; instruc-
    tive evaluation, 114; outcomes, 156, 157*f*;
    peer review; rhetorical reading, 123; self-
    assessment, 125, 126*f*; social media, 186;
    student-generated, 115–16, 119, 124, 126*f*, 134,
    137; testing, 127, 130*f*, 139–40, 143. *See also*
    instructive assessment; peer review
everyday life, datafication, 10–12, 27
evidence-based data, 110*f*, 111, 127, 139–43, 147,
    149–50, 176–78
Excel tools, 17, 93*t*, 94, 95, 164, 165*t*, 166
Exigence, rhetorical reading, 66, 68*t*, 71, 72, 73

expert readers, 60, 61
exploration of data, 162, 165–68
external sources of information, 66
extraction of data, 11, 27, 28, 63

Facebook, 53*f*, 81
fact sheets, 92*t*
fact-checking, 38, 59, 60, 63
Faigley, Lester L., 51
fake news, 7, 57, 94, 180
Family Educational Rights and Privacy Act
    (FERPA), 175
Fanning, Shannon N., 40
Farino, Mirko, 34
Fauni, Austin, 86, 98
feedback, 144–48, 150–51, 177*b*
FERPA (Family Educational Rights and Pri-
    vacy Act), 175
fiction writing, 84–85
film data visualization, 92*t*
filter bubble, 24
first drafts, 95–96, 110*f*, 111, 128–30, 141–42
Fisher, James, 11
Fister, Barbara, 25
Flower, Linda, 61, 75–76, 150
fluttering, 59
Follett, 163*t*
formal data, 169
formal narrative structure approach, 84, 85
foundational datasets, 10*f*
framework design, 7–9, 79–80, 159*b*
Franconeri, Steven L., 56
Frank, Mark, 11, 82
frequency data visualization, 92*t*
Freytag's Pyramid, 41, 85
functional data literacy, 16, 17, 18*t*, 23, 43, 76,
    110*f*, 111, 137, 182, 188

Gagich, Melanie, 138
game theory, 104
Gapminder, 93*t*
gaps in information literacy skills, 15
gender of research participants, 193*t*
general education curriculum, 23, 190–91
generative AI. *See* AI (artificial intelligence)
genre conventions, 58*t*, 78, 91*f*, 92*t*, 103, 116
genre of text, 68*t*, 71, 72, 73
global development statistics tool, 93*t*
goals, data storytelling assignments, 44*t*–45*t*,
    63*t*, 65–66, 114, 116
Google applications, 92*t*, 93*t*, 94, 95, 134, 140,
    162, 163*t*
government data sources, 51, 73, 74*f*, 75, 92*t*

gradebook tool, 148
grading criteria, 22, 113, 115, 135, 136b, 137, 151, 152, 163t
graduate students, 152
Graduation Writing Assessment Requirement (GWAR), 191
Graham, S. Scott, 38
Grammarly, 93t
Graphesis: Visual Forms of Knowledge Production, 94
GraphPad, 167
graphs, 17, 109, 121, 129, 166; bar, 91, 108; creating, 117, 118b; critical data storytelling, 77–78, 168; frequency, 92t; infographics, 73, 74f, 75; line, 108; networks, 92t; pitch presentations, 132f, 133f
Grawe, Nathan D., 14, 15
Grayling, A.C., 52–53
Griffith, Eric, 81
Gummer, Edith S., 154–56, 157f

Haas, Christina, 61, 75–76
Harvard Business Review, 80
Hashlamon, Yanar, 116
Haswell, Richard, 150
Hayes, John, 150
Head, Alison J., 24–25, 38–39
Hennig, Christian, 18
Hero's Journey, 41
higher education: algorithmic decision-making, 177–78; big data, 81; data infrastructure, 186–87; learning management systems (LMS), 20, 26, 28–29, 31, 33–34; static approach to information, 35–39
Hill, Rosemary Lucy, 48
Hispanic-Serving Institutions (HSIs), 5, 190
histograms, 168
Hoag, Trevor, 42
Hoffman, Anna Lauren, 30
How Charts Lie: Getting Smarter about Visual Information, 104
Hoy, Wayne K., 168
Huh, Kil, 80
human activity, datafication, 4, 26, 27, 33–35
humanistic engagement, 18–19
Huot, Brian, 114–16, 121–22, 124
hypermediacy, strategies of, 57, 59–61

identification of data sources, 159, 160t, 161, 162b
identify problems/frame questions, 156, 157f
Imagen, 8
immediacy, strategies of, 57, 58, 59

inaccuracies in data, 103, 110f, 111
indexability, 17
infographics. *See* data visualization
informal data, 169
informatics, 187
information environments, 4, 15–16, 20, 26, 80, 187
information literacy skills, 4–8, 15–16, 25, 48
information sources: AI design tools, 92t; citations, 55, 182; cleaning, 28, 164, 165t; credibility, 50, 66, 72, 73, 75, 76, 126, 138; data stories, 64t; datafication, 4, 27, 187; evaluation criteria, 17, 55, 110f, 111, 126f, 130f, 139–40; external, 66; government agencies, 72–75, 92t; graphs, 117, 118b, 119f; identification, 161, 162b; interaction, 188; online, 6, 7, 15; personal data, 92t; print-reading practices, 15, 54; scholarly, 127; social media, 68t, 69t, 71, 72, 73, 75; static approach, 35–39; transforming data, 156, 157f, 169b; triangulation, 170–71; wildcard, 54, 55, 66, 127
information visualization, 86, 139
infrastructure patterns, 169
Inoue, Asao, 123
in-progress data stories, 5
inquiry cycles, 155, 156, 157f
Instagram, 39, 81
institutional research dashboards, 163t
institutional resources, 186–87
Institutional Review Board (IRB), 5n1, 113, 156, 175, 189
instruction patterns, 169
instructional changes, 171, 172b, 173, 174, 177b
instructional software programs, 163t
instructive assessment, 145; data literacy, 54, 111–12; data storytelling, 116–21, 127, 136b; design issues, 122; feedback, 163t; grading schemes, 22, 113, 155, 136–37; intentions and goals, 124–25; mockups, 129–30, 132f; multimodal projects, 21, 121–22; peer review, 119, 125; rhetorical reading, 123; risk failure, 119f, 121; self-assessments, 125–26. *See also* evaluation criteria; peer review; teaching practices
interactive genres, 92t, 188
interdisciplinary centers, 187
International Conference on Writing Analytics, 152
Internet, 11, 44t, 63t, 67, 82
interview research method, 5–6, 116–17, 163t, 192, 194, 195t, 196, 197
introductory surveys, 113, 116–17, 192

IRB (Institutional Review Board), 5n1, 113, 156, 175, 189
iterative decision cycles, 173b
Ivey, Amber, 80

Jackson, Romeo, 154
Jasper, 93t
Journal of Business and Technical Communication, 94
Journal of Writing Analytics, 152

K–12 education, 26, 154
Kairos, 45, 152
Kennedy, Helen, 48
Kesari, Gane, 41
Khadka, Santosh, 36
Kitchin, Rob, 18–19, 154
Kitson, Dan, 80
Knaflic, Cole Nussbaumer, 85
knowledge transfer, 184–85
knowledge-making practices, 20, 25, 26
Kriebel, Andy, 98

labeling data visualization, 65
labor logs for research assignments, 161, 162, 164t, 166f, 170, 173, 174f
labor-based contract grading, 116, 135–37
Laflen, Angela, 94, 104, 139
Lang, Susan, 147, 148, 150
Lange, Alex C., 154
Langreo, Lauraine, 83
Laquintano, Timothy, 57
large language models (LLMs), 10f, 11
lateral reading, 43, 44t, 58t, 60, 63t, 66, 67, 73, 76, 183
Lauriault, Tracey P., 18–19, 154
Lavazza, Andrea, 34
Lawrence, Peter, 104
learning analytics, 11, 28–29
learning analytics dashboards (LADs), 31
learning management systems (LMS), 20, 25–27, 31, 33–34, 125, 144–48, 159–61, 163t
learning objectives, 171, 177–78
learning theory, 18–20
Lee, J.C., 36
Leon, Adele, 51, 57
Licastro, Amanda, 19
limitations of data, 41, 154, 155, 169b
line charts, 92t
line graphs, 94, 96, 108, 166f
linguistic diversity, 16
lists, 92t
local government, 80–81

low-bridge technologies, 15, 86–87, 89t, 90, 91f, 92
Lupi, Giorgia, 98

machine learning processes, 10f
MacMillan, Margy, 25
maker data literate citizen type, 13, 14f
mandated rubrics, 135, 136b, 137
Mandinach, Ellen B., 154–56, 157f
Manovich, Lev, 25, 81–82
manual collection of online data, 78, 89t, 98
maps, 92t, 97, 99f
Marche, Stephen, 38
Marist College, 189–90, 191t
Markel, Mike, 95
Markham, Annette N., 34–35
Martin, William E., 168
mathematics instruction. *See* statistical literacy
MAXQDA, 197
Mayer-Schönberger, Viktor, 4, 17, 27, 29
McAfee, Andrew, 80
McComiskey, Bruce, 51
McCorkle, Ben, 57
McGraw Hill, 163t
McGrew, Sarah, 59, 60, 61
meaningful data patterns, 168, 169b, 170
measurement concepts, 177b
measuring constructs, 160–61
media literacy, 180
media viewers, 163t
Megatrends: Ten New Directions Transforming Our Lives, 82
metalanguage, 182
metrics, 104
MidJourney, 9, 92t
Miller, Benjamin, 19
Miller, Thomas P., 51, 57
Minard, Charles Joseph, 40
mindful reading, 58t
misinfodemic, 21, 50, 51, 52, 67, 69–75
misinformation. *See* disinformation/misinformation
misleading data, 103
mixed methods of research, 167
MLA-CCCC Joint Task Force on Writing and AI Working Paper: Overview of the Issues, Statement of the Principles, and Recommendations, 154
mockups, 78, 92t, 105, 129–30, 132f, 133, 138, 142
model training, 10f
modeling critical reading strategy, 58

Modern Language Association (MLA) and Conference on College Composition and Communication (CCCC) Joint Task Force on Writing and AI, 36
Monea, Bethany, 45–46, 47
Morris, Janine, 57
motion charts, 92*t*
MoveOn.org, 12–13
MovieMaker Online, 93*t*
Moxley, Joe, 149
MS Word, 105, 142
multilingualism, 116
multiliteracies approach, 16–18, 43
multimodal composition pedagogy: adapting, 188; assessment frameworks, 7–9, 21, 113, 115, 121; best practices, 147; data literacy, 12, 14, 16, 20, 54, 111–12, 137, 139; datafication, 187–88; DFW rates, 148; evaluation criteria, 54–55, importance of, 36; infrastructure, 186–87; labor-based grading contracts, 116; professional development, 112, 139; risk and failure, 116; traditional approach, 54–55. *See also* critical data literacy pedagogy
Multimodal Composition: Faculty Development Programs and Institutional Change, 139
multimodal projects: assessments, 115–16, 126*f*, 130*f*, 134, 139, 143; citations, 37, 55, 91*f*, 138; contract grading, 145; design issues, 117, 119*f*; instructive assessment, 112–14, 121–22, 136, 145–46; low-bridge technologies, 15, 86–87, 89*t*, 90, 91*f*, 92; self-assessment, 116; social media, 49; STEM-related majors, 5; tracking, 173*b*. *See also* critical data storytelling assignments; data visualization
Murray, Elizabeth A., 115, 137

Naftzinger, Jeff, 187
Naisbitt, John, 82
narrative structure, 40–42, 84–85
National Council for Teachers of English, 150
natural language processing (NLP), 9, 10*f*, 17, 27
nature and the environment, 190
Nature, 104
Nemorin, Selena, 151
networked information ecosystems, 51, 86
neural networks, 10*f*
New London Group, 16
news filter bubble, 24
news-as-text pedagogy, 7
Noble, Safiya Umoja, 11
Norgard, Rolf, 37

Numbers spreadsheet program, 93*t*, 94
numbers, symbolic representation, 62, 64–65
Nunnaley, Diana, 155

O'Dwyer, Laura M., 168
O'Neil, Cathy, 104
observations, constructive approach, 18, 163*t*
Observe, Collect, Draw! A Visual Journal, 98
one-way analysis of variance (ANOVA), 173, 174
online information sources: algorithms, 34, 186; big data, 81; civic online reasoning, 7, 12; content, 23–24, 66; data collection, 78, 89*t*, 98; data stories, 8, 62; digital trails, 24, 30, 35; discussion boards, 81; disinformation/misinformation, 15, 66, 103, 106*f*, 107, 187–88; instructor feedback, 144–45; metrics, 186; surveillance, 17; tracking, 186; usefulness, 6, 7, 11–13; writing projects, 97–102
Open Data Institute, 9
Oracle CloudWorld Tour, 82
outcome evaluation, 156, 157*f*, 172–74
oversight, AI (artificial intelligence), 28–30, 38, 40–41, 83
Overstreet, Matthew, 59, 75–76
ownership of student, 177*b*

page design principles, 78, 91*f*, 92*t*, 103, 129
Panopticlick, 93*t*
partisanship. *See* politicization of data stories
patterns, data visualization, 44*t*, 63*t*, 64*t*, 65–66, 168, 169*b*, 170–71
Pearson, 163*t*
pedagogical knowledge, 154
pedagogy. *See* multimodal composition pedagogy
peer review: data storytelling projects, 96–97, 124, 130, 137–38, 140, 142–43; infographics, 78, 92*t*, 106, 107*f*; instructive assessments, 119, 125; student-generated evaluation criteria, 106, 163*t*
PeopleSoft Campus Solutions, 163*t*
Perl, Sondra, 150
perpetual literacy crisis, 84
Persico, Donatella, 146
personal data, 88, 92*t*, 98–102, 183–84
persuasiveness of data stories, 43, 44*t*, 51, 56, 63*t*
Perusall, 163*t*
Pew Research Center, 52, 80, 92*t*
pie charts, 91, 92*t*, 94, 96, 97, 99*f*, 110*f*, 111, 168
Piktochart, 4, 93*t*, 131*f*, 133, 138
PIL (Project Information Literacy), 15, 24–25

pitch presentations, 127, 132*f*, 133*f*
pivot tables, 92*t*
plagiarism, 91*f*
podcasts, 127
Poetics, 85
Polisis, 93*t*
politicization of data stories, 51, 70*f*, 71, 72
Posavec, Stefanie, 98
posters, 92*t*
post-truth era, 8, 21, 50, 52, 53, 76
PowerPoint, 105, 140, 142
Pozzi, Francesca, 146
Previte, Brittany, 116
pre-writing process, 62*f*, 64, 194
Pribot, 93*t*
principles of data storytelling assignments, 86, 87*f*, 88, 168
print-based reading strategies, 15, 25, 36, 57–58
privacy issues, 91*f*, 151, 152, 177*b*
process-based labor, 115
professional communication courses, 78, 86
professional development, 112
project goals, 78, 92*t*, 93–101, 104–5, 128, 133*f*, 138, 140–41, 143
Project Information Literacy (PIL), 15, 24–25
prompts, 9, 10*f*, 151
proxy data, 151–52, 159–61
pseudonyms of research participants, 5*n1*
public sector, 80–81
public service announcements, 92*t*
publicity metrics, 186
publishers, 163*t*
purpose of text, 41, 65–66, 68*t*, 71, 72, 73

Qlik, 11
Quadri, Adedayo, 29
qualitative data, 167, 169
Qualtrics, 93*t*
Quantitative and Statistical Research Methods: From Hypothesis to Results, 168
quantitative methods of data analysis, 4, 14, 23, 29, 104, 139, 149–50, 167, 169, 190
Quantitative Research for the Qualitative Researcher, 168
Quantitative Research in Education: A Primer, 168
questioners of data, 16, 18*t*

racial/ethnic identity, 193*t*
raw data, 50, 56, 68*t*, 69, 71–75
reader data literate citizen type, 13, 14*f*
reading practices. *See* rhetorical reading
realist view of data, 18–19

reflection assignments, 46*f*, 47, 78, 86, 87*f*, 88, 92*t*, 96–97, 101, 102*f*, 106, 107*f*, 108, 125–26, 168, 174–75, 194
Reilly, Colleen A., 121
rejection of data, 50–51
remote sensing techniques, 11
replicable/aggregable/data-supported (RAD) studies, 150
research assignments, 113, 161, 162, 164*t*, 166*f*, 170, 173, 174*f*, 192, 194, 196
Research Design: Qualitative, Quantitative, and Mixed Methods Approaches, 167
Research in the Teaching of English, 150
research methods, 5–6, 189, 191*t*, 192, 196, 197
research participants: college majors, 193*t*, 194*t*, 195*t*; coursework assignments, 191*t*, 192*t*, 196, 197; demographics, 189–91, 192*t*, 193*t*; ethical treatment, 19; interviews, 5–6, 113, 116–17, 194, 195*t*; pseudonyms, 5*n1*; reading practices scholarship, 59–61; student recruitment, 192
research projects, 152; decision-making, 156, 157*f*; ethical standards, 175, 176; frameworks, 156, 157*f*, 158, 159*b*; rhetoric composition studies, 150–51; traditional, 7, 15
Resonate, 85
response modalities. *See* instructive assessment; multimodal projects; peer review
response tools. *See* learning management systems (LMS)
revisions, data storytelling assignments, 62*f*, 64, 78, 92*t*, 102–6, 107*f*, 108, 121, 127, 134–36, 142–43
rhetoric and composition: AI (artificial intelligence), 35, 36, 187; big data, 6; classroom technologies, 151, 152; critical engagement, 85–86; data literacy, 25, 111–12, 156; data storytelling, 20, 21, 76, 78, 84, 85, 86, 87*f*, 88, 90; data-driven inquiry processes, 60–61; instructor feedback, 150–51; multimodal instruction, 35–36; narrative structure, 41–42; quantitative methods, 149–50
rhetorical arguments, 110*f*, 111, 112–16, 121, 135, 180–83
rhetorical frameworks, 4, 7–8
rhetorical reading: audience, 68*t*, 71–73, 111, 126*f*, 127, 130; contextualization, 61; critical data literacy pedagogy, 6, 13, 16, 17, 18*t*, 44*t*, 137, 188; DFW rates, 148; digital information, 50–51; fact-checking, 38, 59; lateral reading, 60; multimodal evaluation, 116; politicization, 70*f*, 71, 72, 75; print-based, 57–58; purpose of text, 65–66; skills

development, 39, 43; slow thinking, 51; strategies of hypermediacy, 57; strategies of immediacy, 57–58; taking bearings, 66–67, 73; teaching practices, 61–62, 75–76, 147–48, 153–54, 156. *See also* critical data storytelling assignments; data visualization
risk failure, 113, 116, 119f, 121
rough cuts, 142
rubrics. *See* grading criteria
Rutz, Carol, 14, 15
Rytr, 93t

Salinas, Carlos, 139
satellite imagery, 11
SC Training, 163t
scaffolding, 6, 171
scatter plots, 31, 32, 168
scholarly sources of information, 127
Schoology, 163t
scientist (data literate citizen type), 13, 14f
scripts, 128, 141
search engines, 15–17
securing student data, 175–76
Selber, Stuart, 16–17, 18t, 95, 186–87
self-assessments, 116, 125–26, 128f, 129f, 130, 137, 142–43
self-awareness, 97–102
self-reports, 163t
semi-structured data, 81
Shaffer, Jeffrey, 98
Shay, Suellen, 33
Sheets, Hailey A., 115
Shipka, Jody, 112–13, 116
Shukor, Nurbiha, 29
Simpson, Jill, 98
Singer, Sarah Ann, 54, 55, 66
Sinkinson, Caroline, 37
Sipley, Gina, 186
site statistics tool, 145, 148
skills development, 39
Skim, Dive, and Surface: Teaching Digital Reading, 61
slideshow data visualization, 92t, 127
slow reading, 58t
slow thinking, 51
small data assignments, 78, 88, 89t, 97–101, 102f
Snaith, Ben, 9
social learning platforms, 163t
social media: credibility, 57; data, role of, 186; datafication, 11; disinformation/misinformation, 103, 106f; evaluation, 186; information environments, 15–16; multimodal texts, 49; post, 92t; rhetorical reading, 68t, 69t, 71–75; student engagement, 23–24; unstructured data, 81–82
Social Science Statistics, 174
software for data storytelling, 42, 86–87, 162, 163t, 164, 165t, 187
Sorapure, Madeleine, 42, 86, 98, 139
source checklists, 54–55
specialized algorithms, 4
speculative design assessment, 26, 43–47, 48, 92t
spreadsheet software, 93t, 94
Stable Diffusion, 92t
Staggers, Julie, 112
Stanford History Education Group (SHEG), 12, 59
Stanton, Courtney, 38
static approach to information, 35–39
static infographics, 78, 92t, 103, 128, 133, 141, 142
statistical literacy, 11–15, 23, 50, 59, 62–64, 78–79, 87, 104, 111, 177b, 181, 194t
statistical variances, 173, 174
Steen, Lynn Arthur, 14
STEM-related majors, 5
Stephens-Davidowitz, Seth, 82
storyboards, 128, 138, 141
StoryMapJS, 93t
Storytelling with Data: A Data Visualization Guide for Business Professionals, 85
strategies of hypermediacy, 57, 59–60
strategies of immediacy, 57, 58, 59
strengths and weaknesses, data interpretation, 94–97, 170–71
structured data, 81
student access, 186–87
student engagement: abductive reasoning, 38; ability to learn, 155; adaptability, 181, 183, 185; artifacts, 113, 192–96; civic online reasoning, 12–13; classroom technologies, 153b; critical data storytelling, 5–6; critical reading strategies, 44t, 47, 63t; data, 49–50, 168; data inquiries, 175–76; data literacy, 17, 21, 23, 43, 54, 62, 65, 117, 118b, 120; digital trails, 26, 30, 31, 32f, 35, 39, 45; labor logs, 161, 162, 164t, 166f, 170, 173, 174f; learning analytics, 28–29; patterns, 169; privacy issues, 91f, 151, 177b; reflection assignments, 46f, 78, 86, 87f, 88, 174; revisions, 135–36; rhetorical reading, 20, 59, 61, 85–86; scores, 159–61; self-assessments, 78; self-awareness, 97–102; social media, 23–24; time management, 119f, 121, 148; usage of

data, 16, 18*t*, 86, 87*f*, 88; working memory capacity, 66; writing skills, 77–78, 90, 116, 144–47, 150–51, 163*t*
student-generated evaluation criteria, 106, 115–16, 123–24, 126*f*, 130*f*, 134–37
surveillance data, 151, 152
Survey Monkey, 93*t*
survey research data, 5, 93*t*, 113, 163*t*, 192, 193*t*, 196, 197
sustainable data infrastructures, 151
symbolic representation of numbers, 56, 62, 64–65

Tableau, 93*t*
tables, 92*t*, 166
taking bearings, 44*t*, 58*t*, 60, 63*t*, 66–67, 73, 76, 183
Teaching Critical Reading and Writing in the Era of Fake News, 94
teaching practices: assignments, 90, 173–74, 178, 192; critical reading, 44*t*–45*t*, 47; data-veillance, 151, 152; data literacy, 5, 22, 54, 188; disease of complexity, 175; evidence-based, 149–50, 176–77; functional data literacy, 76; graduate students, 152; hypermediacy, 60–61; information literacy, 4–8; instructional changes, 172*b*; learning goals, 65–66, 171; multimodal assessments, 121; professional development, 112; problems/questions, 158–59; replicable/aggregable/data-support (RAD), 150; rhetorical reading, 61–62, 75–76, 147–48, 153–54; teaching logs, 192; technological tools, 146, 151, 152, 153*b*; writing prompts, 151. *See also* instructive assessment; writing instructors
technical communication writing, 4, 86, 94, 95, 97, 99*f*, 111–12, 191
technological tools, 8, 16, 44*t*–45*t*, 46–47, 57, 86–87, 89*t*, 90, 91*f*, 146
testing data patterns, 169*b*, 170
Teston, Christa, 116, 124
Text Analysis and Visualization Portal (TAPoR), 93*t*
text analysis software, 93*t*
text editors, 117, 118*b*, 119*f*
textbooks, 37
three-act structure, 41, 85
thumbnails, 128, 131*f*, 133, 138, 141
Thunderbeam-Lightbeam for Chrome, 93*t*
TikTok, 81
time measurement. *See* student engagement
time series analysis, 89*t*, 92*t*
timeline-based texts, 92*t*, 128, 141–42

Topics in Composition: Multimedia Writing course, 191*t*
Tossell, Mark, 82
tracking tools, 93*t*, 173*b*, 186
Trackography, 93*t*
traditional academic research skills, 7, 15, 16, 37–38, 54–55, 57
traditional assessment frameworks, 115, 146
transform data into decision-making, 29, 156, 157*f*, 168, 171–72
transparency, 8
trial and error, 113, 118*b*, 119–21
triangulation patterns, 170–71
t-test calculator, 167*b*
Tufte, Edward, 40, 104
tutorial videos, 119
Twitter, 67, 69, 72
Tygel, Alan, 11, 82

underlying assumptions, 43, 44*t*, 47, 89*f*
university dashboards, 163*t*
Unizin consortium, 163*t*
unpaired t-test results, 167
unpreparedness, teaching strategies, 25, 83
unstructured data, 81–82
usability test report, 92*t*
usage of data, 157*f*
usefulness of data, 6, 7, 11–13, 188
user interface, 7, 9, 57

validity of data, 54, 69, 91*f*, 160*t*
van Dijck, José, 27
variances, 173–74
Vee, Annette, 57
vertical curriculum, 59, 182
video data visualization, 92*t*, 93*t*, 127
Vimeo Create, 93*t*
virtual private networks (VPNs), 39
Visme, 93*t*
visual arguments. *See* data visualization
Visual Display of Quantitative Information, The, 104
vocabulary, 44*t*, 47, 63*t*, 64*t*, 65–66
Voyant, 93*t*

Walker, Johanna, 11, 82
Weapons of Math Destruction, 104
Web 2.0, 27
web mapping platforms, 93*t*
Webber, Karen L., 81
websites, 92*t*, 112, 127, 132*f*, 133*f*
West, Jevin, 104
white papers, 3, 92*t*

White, Ed, 123
wildcard sources of information, 54, 55, 57, 66, 127
Williams, Bronwyn T., 84
Williams, Nicole A., 115
Williamson, Ben, 33
Windows Video Editor, 93t
Wineburg, Sam, 59–61
Wired, 27
wireframes, 129–30, 138, 142
Wisenet, 163t
Wolfe, Joanna, 37, 40, 55, 95, 104, 139
Wolff, Annika, 13, 14f, 54, 62f, 63, 66, 83, 155
Wood, Shane, 115–16, 121, 136
word clouds, 92t
working memory capacity, 56, 66
Writer/Designer: A Guide to Making Multimodal Projects, 138
writing and rhetoric scholarship. *See* rhetoric and composition
writing courses: digital surveillance, 151–52; digital writing, 49–50, 78, 89t, 98–101, 102f, 112, 180–81; first-year, 5, 26, 109, 127, 185–87, 190–92; goals, 128, 133f, 138, 140–41, 143; peer review, 119, 124–25, 130, 138; professional writing, 4, 77, 111–12, 159, 170–73, 174f, 183–85, 195t; self-assessments, 126f, 137, 142, 143; teaching-related problems/questions, 158–59; undergraduate level, 3–4; writer guidelines, 44t, 62, 63t, 65
writing instructors: data literacy skills, 16, 77–78, 111–12, 151, 153b, 187; data visualization, 40–42; DFW rates, 148; direct self-placement (DSP), 190–91; generative AI, 9, 153; learning management systems (LMS), 31, 33–34, 144–47; multimodal pedagogy, 35–38, 115; online spaces, 97–102; rhetorical reading, 9, 10f, 14, 17–18, 183, 188; teaching strategies, 66, 149–50, 154, 163t, 175–77. *See also* instructive assessment; teaching practices
writing process, 35, 115–16, 121, 145, 149–50
Writing Spaces, 138–39
WTF Visualizations, 104

Yancey, Kathleen Blake, 125–26, 184–85
YouChat, 93t
YouGov, 92t
YouTube, 39, 78, 81, 93t, 106f

Zheng, Henry, 81
Zoetewey, Meredith, 112

About the Author

Angela Laflen is an associate professor of English at California State University, Sacramento. She teaches undergraduate and graduate courses in composition and professional writing. Her scholarship has been published in *Computers and Composition, Kairos, Assessing Writing, The Journal of Response to Writing, Pedagogy,* and *Writing Spaces,* among others, and in several edited collections.

www.ingramcontent.com/pod-product-compliance
Lightning Source LLC
Chambersburg PA
CBHW052136070526
44585CB00017B/1850